The Financial Times Guide to Business Travel

FINANCIAL TIMES
Prentice Hall

In an increasingly competitive world, it is quality
of thinking that gives an edge – an idea that opens new
doors, a technique that solves a problem, or an insight
that simply helps make sense of it all.

We work with leading authors in the fields of
management and finance to bring cutting-edge thinking
and best learning practice to a global market.

Under a range of leading imprints, including
Financial Times Prentice Hall, we create world-class
print publications and electronic products giving
readers knowledge and understanding which can then
be applied, whether studying or at work.

To find out more about our business and professional
products, you can visit us at www.business-minds.com

For other Pearson Education publications, visit
www.pearsoned-ema.com

Pearson
Education

The Financial Times
Guide to Business Travel

Edited by Stuart Crainer & Des Dearlove

FINANCIAL TIMES
Prentice Hall

An imprint of **Pearson Education**
London / New York / San Francisco / Toronto / Sydney / Tokyo / Singapore
Hong Kong / Cape Town / Madrid / Paris / Milan / Munich / Amsterdam

PEARSON EDUCATION LIMITED

Head Office:
Edinburgh Gate, Harlow, Essex CM20 2JE
Tel: +44 (0)1279 623623 Fax: +44 (0)1279 431059

London Office:
128 Long Acre, London WC2E 9AN
Tel: +44 (0)207 447 2000 Fax: +44 (0)207 240 5771
Website: www.business-minds.com

First published in Great Britain 2001

ISBN 0 273 65439 X

British Library Cataloguing in Publication Data
A CIP catalogue record for this book can be obtained from the British Library.

This publication is designed to provide accurate and authoritative information in regard to the subject matter covered. It is sold with the understanding that neither the authors nor the publisher is engaged in rendering legal, investing, medical, or any other professional service. If legal advice or other expert assistance is required, the service of a competent professional person should be sought.

The publisher and contributors make no representation, express or implied, with regard to the accuracy of the information contained in this book and cannot accept any responsibility or liability for any errors or omissions that it may contain.

10 9 8 7 6 5 4 3 2 1

Designed by Design Deluxe, Bath
Typeset by Northern Phototypesetting Co, Ltd., Bolton
Printed and bound in Great Britain by Biddles Ltd, Guildford & King's Lynn

The publishers' policy is to use paper manufactured from sustainable forests.

Contents

Do you remember your first business trip? It is a landmark, a statement of your rising place in the corporate firmament. The world opens up, bright new horizons adorned by hotels with overflowing mini-bars, meetings on the 87th floor, offices with glorious urban panoramas, and the extended leg room of business class.

Yet, after the bright new beginning, business travel can quickly become hard work, jet-setting drudgery. This is a pity. True, constant travelling is demanding and exhausting. But it can also be enriching and endlessly stimulating.

The question for globe-trotting businesspeople and domestic business travellers alike is how they can maximize the value of business travel for themselves and their organizations. If business travel is a given, what can be done to keep down the costs – human and financial? What can business travellers do to make the experience less exhausting, ease some of the frustration, and generally improve its effectiveness?

The Financial Times Guide to Business Travel aims to help make life easier, richer and more enlightening for business travellers everywhere. The main focus is on international business travellers, for whom air travel is the most frequent mode of transport, and navigating cultural nuances is the most acute business challenge they now face. Yet much of the advice applies equally to those whose business trips are predominantly domestic. It is a collection of tips, tricks of the trade, and anecdotes from those who fill the corporate skies and clog the transport arteries of the world.

The Financial Times Guide to Business Travel is not the final word. The world of business travel is all embracing, too big to be confined to a single volume. (For this reason the *Guide* does not include recommendations of hotels or restaurants – there are many other books that do so.) Rather the *Guide* is a compendium of practical insights and experiences, more of a smorgasbord than a club sandwich.

The best advice is that routinely, and often insincerely, tendered in hotel receptions and restaurants worldwide: enjoy. We mean it.

Stuart Crainer & Des Dearlove
Editors
June 2001

Contributors

No book is a genuinely solo undertaking. This is more of a team effort than most. We are grateful to the following, who contributed research, editing and writing to the *Guide*:

George Bickerstaffe   Author of the annual guide to business schools, *Which MBA?*, and a contributing editor to *FT Dynamo*.

Stephen Coomber   Writer and chief researcher at Suntop Media; co-author of *Architects of the Business Revolution*.

Steve Fitzgerald   Organization development consultant; co-author of *Appreciative Inquiry – The New Frontier.*

Gerry Griffin   Author of *The Power Game* and *.Con*. Communications director of joose.tv.

Kathryn Hall   Writer/columnist and founder of her own California-based book publicity agency that specializes in promoting transformational business books. Her articles have appeared in *Training* and *Development Journal*, *Journal for Quality and Participation* and the *San Francisco Business Times*.

Mark Hillsdon   Based in Manchester, UK, Mark contributes to lifestyle and travel magazines worldwide including *Business Traveller*, *Maxim* and others.

Stuart Crainer & Des Dearlove   Stuart and Des are the founders of the business content company, Suntop Media. Their books include *Generation Entrepreneur*, *Firestarters!* and *Gravy Training*. They contribute articles to magazines and newspapers worldwide, including the *Industry Standard*, *Business 2.0* and *The Times*.

Despite the stellar support of the above, all errors, omissions and crass oversights are the sole responsibility of the editors. If you wish to comment on the *Guide* or have ideas and experiences that you think should be included in the second edition, please contact Stuart Crainer and Des Dearlove: <u>editors@suntopmedia.com.</u>

Why we are still on the road

'Business class is not just something in an airline.'

HENRY MINTZBERG, CANADIAN MANAGEMENT THINKER

Chapter 1 | From the Silk Road to road warriors

oday's international business travellers are a breed apart. They leap whole continents in a single bound, and bestride the world's time zones. Red eyed yet self-assured, they march purposefully across airports around the globe, cutting through the throng of meandering tourists with laser-like precision. To these corporate elite, national borders are nothing more than lines on a map – to be effortlessly crossed and re-crossed as they hurtle from one high-powered meeting to the next.

For the corporate chieftains of the 21st century, distance is no object. They are armed to the gunnels with the latest in technological gadgetry. No matter how far from their corporate homes, they are connected to the commercial pulse. The modern-day road warrior or corporate eagle can set up office in a hotel room anywhere in the world within minutes. Wherever they hang their laptop is their home. Even in the most far-flung corners of the globe, they remain in touch, resolutely communicating – day and night. These citizens of the global village are the business jet-set. Self-reliance is their credo.

That at least is the popular image of the modern business traveller. The reality, however, is very different. For all the advances in transportation and communications technology, business travel remains a challenging and sometimes unpleasant activity.

Often, it is anything but glamorous. Many business travellers complain that they spend their lives in an exhausting, soulless and often thankless orbit. Some spend more time in the air than at their desks and are more able to open a mini-bar than their garage doors. Even in business class, travelling can be stressful and demanding unless certain rules are obeyed. The first and most simple of these is that if you look like your passport photo, you are too ill to travel. For the vast majority of executives who flit endlessly around the globe as part of their jobs, the reality of lugging suitcases across airports, train stations and in and out of taxis is all too stark. Yet it remains a fact of corporate life.

Today's business travellers follow in a long tradition. From the earliest times trade has relied on the willingness of individuals to suffer personal privation and hardship to transport themselves and their merchandise to their customers. One of the most celebrated Western business travellers was Marco Polo, who chronicled his travels in China, accompanying his father and uncle on a protracted business trip in the 13th century. (Some modern scholars believe that the medieval Venetian himself may not have been as well travelled as he claimed, perhaps reaching only as far as Persia.) But long before Marco Polo wrote of his adventures, merchants were conducting business in strange and exotic lands. (There was no business class and many of their accounts suggest they didn't like travel much either.)

Business travel is as old as business itself. Records show that as far back as the seventh century AD, the Silk Road – not one road, in fact, but many – was peopled by itinerant businesspeople plying their trade in everything from silk and spices to Buddhist scriptures. The city of Changan, the starting point of the great Silk Road, which stood where Xian is today, grew fat on the exploits of these early mercantile travellers. The 754 AD census of the city indicates more than 5000 foreigners based in the city, from as far afield as India, Japan and Malaysia. The route was a conduit for rare plants, medicines and textiles which were traded in the city's bazaars. In those days, the representatives of the emperor took their pick of the goods before trade could commence. The emperors have gone, but the need to understand local traditions and comply with the relevant authorities remains integral to the business traveller's licence to operate. Today, navigating cultural nuances and national laws still requires a deep knowledge.

In most parts of the world business travel is safer than it used to be, but it remains a minefield (sometimes literally) for the uninitiated. In centuries past, the intrepid trader risked life and liberty whenever they left the safety of their home to pursue their business interests. Today, airport delays are an inconvenience, but hold little of the terror of highway robbery, or attacks from pirates. Air turbulence is infinitely preferable to the life-threatening discomfort of storms at sea. The modern business traveller has a reasonable expectation of returning to their loved ones.

There are other compensations of modern business travel, too. Today, the homes of executives throughout the world enjoy a constantly replenished supply of shampoos that can't be opened, unused shower caps and thick white bathrobes with the word Hilton or Sheraton on their fronts.

Safer but not totally safe

Modern business travel is sophisticated and high-tech, but it is not without its perils. At the time of writing, the UK's Foreign & Commonwealth Office was warning against travelling to the following places unless on essential business: Albania (certain regions), Algeria, Angola, Central African Republic, Republic of the Congo, Côte d'Ivoire, East Timor, El Salvador, Haiti, earthquake-hit areas of India, Liberia, Sierra Leone, and the Kosovo region of Yugoslavia. Today's tropical paradise can easily become tomorrow's war zone.

In transit: Tom Knighton

Nationality: American

Job: Executive vice president of The Forum Corporation and leader of Forum's global Customer Experience business

Favourite hotel: The Bostonian

Favourite place: Sydney

Favourite airport: Denver

Frequency: Over 100 times a year

Essentials: Workout gear

In-flight worker: Yes, mostly writing and thinking assignments.

Tale: I was in the club of a prominent airline and went to the bar to request a Coke. Since I was thirsty, I asked for a tall glass. The bartender told me he was not allowed to give me a tall glass, because the smaller glasses were designated for Coke. I looked at the cabinets behind the bar and pointed to the glass I wanted. He continued to refuse my request. Finally he said, 'I can't give you a large glass of Coke, but I can give you two small glasses'! Rules … rules … rules.

Best experience: My best experience was on Singapore Airlines. I was put on Singapore because I had missed an earlier flight. When I sat down in my business-class seat, the gentleman sitting next to me asked if I flew to the Orient often. I said, 'Only every couple of years.' He asked if I had ever flown Singapore. I said no. He commented, 'You're going to have a great experience!' And Singapore did not disappoint. Now that's a customer experience worth coming back for.

Chapter 2 | Face time

In the early 1990s, there was a flood of enthusiasm for the virtues of virtual working. We would all be connected. We would work at home. In the new working utopia, business trips – and even offices – would disappear into history. Video conferencing and a raft of other technological marvels would liberate the business traveller. No more commuting drudgery. No more red eyes.

But the celebration was premature. For all the talk of virtual working, face-to-face contact with clients, customers and colleagues remains the preferred way of doing business. Face time rules. To date, the office cubicle and water fountain have proved stubbornly resistant to the march of technology. Business travel, too, remains an obstinate feature of modern corporate life.

The question is why? At a fundamental level, the answer appears to be rooted in the way that human beings relate to one another. 'Human beings have substantial social needs,' explains Cary Cooper, professor of organizational psychology and health at the University of Manchester Institute of Science and Technology (UMIST) in the UK. 'Most of us still want face-to-face contact.'

Just as importantly, eyeball-to-eyeball contact is route one to trust. This is one explanation for why business travel continues to be a significant fixture in many of our lives. Among the most frenetic frequent fliers are management consultants. They routinely cross entire continents for a face-to-face meeting, only to dash to the airport for a return flight the minute it is over. These are rational people, so why do they continue with their mad existence? For a profession built on analysis, it seems illogical. Face-to-face meetings when one of the parties is exhausted and jetlagged seem unlikely to benefit anyone. But most consultants act as if e-mail and satellite links have never been invented. Consultants cite the importance of personal contact. For the masters of logic, only the face-to-face experience will do.

Business relationships are based on communication. So why have all the new communication mediums failed to make a dent in travel schedules? The answer seems to lie with a simple statistic. More than 80 per cent of human communication is non-verbal (some studies put it as high as 93 per cent). In other words, e-mail, telephone, video conferencing and all the other communications marvels do not have the bandwidth to carry more than 20 per cent of the face-to-face experience. F2F (face-to-face) equals H2H (human-to-human).

Facial expressions, body language, eye contact – these are key conduits. Without them you can't get past first base. It's tough to bond over the internet. Ergo: unless your client is in the next office, to do business you have to travel.

'A lot of people rely on their personalities to persuade others,' says Professor Cooper. 'That doesn't come out in e-mails, and even video conferencing is stultifying. They may also want to influence people outside of the meeting. A lot of lobbying and politicking goes on before and after meetings. That's why eyeball-to-eyeball is so important. We still don't fully trust the technology even though it's been around for a while. We prefer to talk behind closed doors.'

We also read body language to pick up the atmosphere or 'vibes', he says. 'We walk into a meeting and pick up the feel of what the other people are thinking. We watch how Y reacts to what X is saying. You can't do that by video conference.'

Adds Professor Cooper: 'Most of us don't have the self-confidence to believe we can build the sorts of relationships we need with clients and suppliers down the wire. Business travel won't decrease for that reason. It's a shame because at the moment we're burning out an awful lot of people.'

He's right. Every year, a lot of people get very bent out of shape by work-related travel. Worse than that – much worse – business travellers suffer from a host of related misfortunes. Their home lives are dislocated, and they miss out on seeing their children, partners and friends, sometimes to the detriment of their relationships; they get run-down and may suffer health problems. They waste inordinate amounts of time in airports and other terminuses, waiting for travel connections; eat large quantities of airline food (less healthy than the average meal at McDonald's, according to one report); and endure the dehumanizing effects of spending too much time in hotels.

On the other hand, they get to meet a huge number of people and develop relationships that are important to them as business people and as human beings. Travel allows people to connect. It can be a richly rewarding personal experience. Travel not only broadens the expense account. Business trips offer new and exciting vistas. Surveys consistently show that young people entering the workforce regard travel as a perk. A recent survey of 350 Oxford University students in their final year of study, for example, sought to understand what motivates young people to join estab-lished firms. The survey found that foreign travel was among the factors most valued by the students, surpassed only by achieving the right balance between work and leisure – and pay.

More experienced business travellers, too, see business travel as an opportunity for a personal experience. Many try, where possible, to combine the company's work with a little R&R. Research by market research company OAG and the Travel Industry Association of America (TIA), for example, indicates that two out of ten American business travellers combined business and vacation on their last business trip. (Interestingly, women and less frequent travellers are more likely to combine business and a vacation on the same trip – 25 and 23 per cent respectively.)

Over time, though, the pleasure of travel can easily be lost. For many frequent business travellers the joy of seeing new places is inversely related to the amount of travelling they have to do. For those who rack up thousands upon thousands of miles every year, the novelty tends to wear very thin.

But, whether you regard it as a welcome break from the office treadmill or just another day on the corporate carousel, business travel is unlikely to disappear any time soon.

In transit: Warren Bennis

Nationality: American

Job: Leadership guru

Best hotel: I have two: Villa San Michele in Florence and Sharrow Bay Hotel in the UK's Lake District.

Favourite country to visit on business: UK

Favourite airport: Are you kidding?

Frequency: About 40 times a year

Always takes: Wife, laptop, palm pilot and lots of magazines and books.

Chapter 3 | The travellers

The paradox of the wired world is that businesspeople actually spend more time than ever shuttling to and from meetings. Look no further than Silicon Valley. In the cradle of the technological revolution it is estimated that $3.5 billion is frittered away annually because of clogged highways and gridlocks. With the latest communication tools and gadgetry at their fingertips, the men and women of Silicon Valley still feel compelled to get into their cars and travel. In California's technological dreamland, the roads to the airports are lined with good inventions.

Ironically, too, the very people who espouse the digital revolution are often the same people whose lifestyles are an admission that new technology cannot replace face-to-face contact. One bestselling author – an internationally renowned e-guru – calculates that he spends 75 per cent of his time 'on the road'. Bits and bytes only get you so far. (The uncrowned queen of the road warriors is another digital guru Esther Dyson – see box on p.13.)

The globetrotting guru is not alone. The move to cyber commerce has been accompanied by a cloud of dust in the real world. Road warriors abound. In their book *A Future Perfect,* John Micklethwait and Adrian Wooldridge, two senior *Economist* journalists, put the number of men and women criss-crossing time zones at 20 million worldwide and predict that the number will double by the year 2010.

What does the average business traveller look like and how often does he or she pack a suitcase? Figures for international travel are patchy. But research by OAG and the Travel Industry Association of America (TIA) shows that:

- The typical US business traveller spent at least one night away from home on their most recent business trip (84 per cent), with nearly three-quarters (74 per cent) staying at a hotel or motel.
- The average business trip included 3.3 nights away in 1998. Frequent business travellers spend fewer nights away than their less road-weary counterparts – an average of 3.1 nights per trip versus 3.4.

- Almost half of US business travellers (47 per cent) said that a meeting, trade show or convention was the reason for their latest trip. Frequent business travellers are much more likely to have made their last trip for consulting, sales or company operations.

- Almost a third (32 per cent) of US business travellers participate in at least one frequent flyer programme, and 16 per cent in a frequent lodger programme.

Between 1994 and 1998 the number of US business travellers went up 14 per cent to 43.9 million.[1] In the USA, one in five adults (22 per cent) took at least one business trip in 1999.

According to the National Business Travel Association (NBTA), in the USA, business travellers represent 62 per cent of airline revenues, but they are a much smaller percentage of travellers than leisure travellers. Corporations spend more than $175 billion for travel annually. This now involves about 44 million employees and 243 million business trips per year. And the trend remains upward. American Express predicts that the number of international business trips will increase by almost a third in the next few years.

Despite the onset of new technology, the demographic profile of business travellers has remained largely unchanged over the past decade. There are slight increases in age, moderate increases in income, and some shift in occupation, but the world of the road warrior is still dominated by men (60 per cent). The average age is now 42, a time in their lives when many people have children at home; the average household income in 1998 was $76,100. (These figures are not representative of international business travellers, however; only 3 per cent of those in the survey stepped off US soil.) What has changed in the demographic make-up of US business travellers is that more older people are travelling for business (the average age is up from 40 at the beginning of the 1990s to 42 at the end of the decade). This manifests in a rise in the number of business travellers in the 45-to-54-year-old bracket, and a fall in the number of 25-to-34-year-olds.

Those who travel for business are more likely to work in the health, legal and educational services than in the past – between 1991 and 1998 the proportion of business travellers in these sectors rose from 19 per cent to 25 per cent. By far the largest proportion of business travellers work in professional and managerial roles. This reached 55 per cent, an all-time high, in 1994, but has fallen back to 47 per cent.

The average European Union business traveller was profiled in a recent study by the London-based OAG Worldwide as a 42-year-old college graduate, a married father who is a professional or manager, with an annual income of at least $75,000. The survey indicated that in the period of two years there has been a 30 per cent increase in the average number of nights spent in hotels. The number of nights away in a 12-month period rose to 48, from 45 in 1998 and 37 in 1997. And, OAG says, one in ten business travellers spend 100 nights or more away from home.

Overall, Europeans take most international short-haul flights. Those on the American continent take most domestic flights. And those in the Asia/Pacific region lead in international long-haul flights. North America is the most popular business destination.

In transit: Ahmet Aykac

Nationality: Turkish

Job: Dean of Theseus, an international business school in southern France.

Best hotel: In Europe it is the Istanbul Bosphorus Swissotel; in Asia it is the Oriental in Bangkok; but I don't like the hotels in the USA.

Favourite country to visit on business: Holland

Favourite airport: Zurich – it is central, has all the connections, is efficient and most, important of all, of human proportions.

Frequency: I make about 35 trips a year.

Always takes: My mobile phone, something to read, and clean underwear.

Queen of the road warriors

If there was an award for the most prolific business traveller, high-tech high priestess Esther Dyson would be a strong candidate. She is a phenomenon of the digital age – an information guru, internet pioneer, venture capitalist, sage to governments and leaders. Her opinions are much sought after. She has advised, among others, Bill Clinton and Bill Gates, as well as governments from around the world. Small wonder that *Fortune* magazine named her as one of the 50 most powerful women in US business.

The restless Dyson rarely stays on the same continent for more than a few days at a time. She logs a quarter-million frequent-flier miles a year from her home in New York. She estimates that she's on the road two-thirds to three-quarters of the time, and averages a flight every other day.

How does she deal with jetlag? 'I ignore it,' she says. 'I suffer more from lack of sleep than from the timing of it.'

Dyson has always been a restless soul. Her career journey started early. Precociously bright, she attended Harvard at the age of 16. After a spell in journalism, she founded her own company, Edventure Holdings, and started to disseminate her views about how the net would change the world.

She prefers to deliver the message in person. She has racked up over 6 million air miles (enough, you'd think, to buy an aircraft of her own). An exceptional individual, her stamina is legendary, enabling her to cope with a gruelling global travel schedule that would guarantee most hardened business travellers a spell in a sanatorium.

Dyson, it seems, has settled into her own circadian rhythm, often rising at 4.30 am to fit into a day more than many people would contemplate fitting into a week. She spends sufficient time in Moscow and Silicon Valley to warrant being a member of a health club and retaining a locker for her possessions in both places. Wherever Dyson lays her locker key is her home.

Links: www.edventure.com

Notes

1 *Survey of Business Travelers*, 1999 ed, sponsored by OAG and conducted by the Travel Industry Association of America (TIA).

Chapter 4 | The costs

All of this frenetic movement costs money, a great deal of money. Consider this: travel is now the third-largest expense in most corporations after payroll and information systems.

And business travel isn't getting any cheaper. The National Business Travel Association (NBTA) calculates that business airfares have increased 8 per cent annually for the past several years, with an average flight costing just under $1000. According to American Express's *Business Travel Monitor*, between May 1999 and May 2000, the average business class one-way fare rose 4 per cent from $2640 to $2760.

The *2000 Survey & Analysis of Business Travel Policies & Costs*, a biennial study (produced by Runzheimer), now in its tenth edition, indicates a mixed bag for business travellers. It found that the average number of travel days for frequent travellers decreased in 2000 to 45 days per year from 48 days in 1998. But the percentage of travellers in the survey who travel internationally reached an all-time high – 89 per cent – a full seven percentage points increase since 1998.

Advance purchase coach (economy) was the most popular airfare in 2000, comprising 31 per cent of coach airfares purchased. The average domestic trip cost was $970 for three days, $3455 for an international trip of seven days, and $1650 for an overall trip cost average. Forty-five per cent of respondent organizations had on-site travel departments.

Technology is also playing a growing role in business travel. When planning business trips, 15 per cent of flights, 15 per cent of hotel reservations and 10 per cent of car rentals are now made over the internet, according to OAG. And one-quarter of all air tickets now are paperless and issued electronically.

Companies, too, are intent on using new technology to streamline the way that travel is organized internally. To save on costs, organizations are turning to technology to coordinate and track travel and automate operations. Bruce Berkley, finance manager at the Woodcliff, NJ-based industrial equipment company Ingersoll-Rand, estimates that use of new technology will save his company as much as $2 million a year in areas such as employee reimbursements and supplier contract negotiations.

Attacking the processing of expense reports can reap similar rewards. One calculation is that it costs $50 to process a single expense report. Automation can reduce this to less than $5. If a company is handling even 20,000 such reports a year – a relatively modest amount – savings can quickly approach $1 million.

How a company is organized can directly relate to its travel costs. When IBM reorganized its European operations it produced some unforeseen results. The company restructured itself around businesses rather than around countries. This led to an increase in travel between European countries. Travel budgets mushroomed – by 20 per cent a year over the following three years. Soon, IBM's travel expenditure in the UK alone amounted to around $48 million. In the rest of Europe the company estimated that its budget was $300 million. Not surprisingly, IBM then sought to make sense of where the money was going. Here, it ran into trouble. Actually tracing the source and destination of nearly $350 million was much easier said than done.

The company dealt with 40 to 50 different travel agents throughout Europe. Even its own highly technical systems could not establish how much had been spent with particular airlines or hotels. The only possible way to retrieve the figures was to go through the records of each agent. Enough was enough. To cut through the complexity, IBM Europe decided to work through a single travel agent; it has also appointed single agents for North America and Asia.

This appears to be a simple solution to a thorny operational problem. The reality is more complex. In fact, IBM attempted to sort the problem out on a number of occasions but faced internal opposition. Country units were understandably unwilling to desert their local agents with whom they had long-established amicable relationships. It took a multinational team 18 months to coordinate the selection of an agency. IBM can now show individual airlines what would happen if it moved its business elsewhere. This highly persuasive statistic was previously buried in the corporate mire.

There is nothing unusual in the situation IBM found itself in. Companies typically spend 20 to 25 per cent of sales with third-party suppliers for goods and services not directly related to the end product or services of the business. Travel budgets form a significant part of this.

Corporate travel managers face a dilemma. They must maintain and improve the quality of a vital service while keeping expenses down in the face of rising costs. The corporate emphasis is on containing costs; the executive emphasis is on travelling comfortably and safely. The two are not necessarily happy bedfellows. In many companies, balance is elusive. Centralized travel policies may make sense from a cost perspective, but they are not necessarily good news for business travellers. The lowest fare may involve numerous connections and a great deal of hanging around.

In transit: Peter Fisk

Nationality: British

Job: Leader of marketing and innovation consulting with PA Consulting Group, and currently setting up a new venture business which seeks to make the working life of the global business professional more stimulating, more effective and more fun.

Best hotel: The Mercer on Madison Avenue is great for short business trips to New York. It's certainly not corporate, never appears busy, has a great free breakfast in the art deco dining room, the bedrooms are an immediate jetlag antidote, and it's also handy for a sneak round the shops after your meetings.

Favourite country to visit on business: West Coast USA. Driving out of San Francisco airport and down the main highway towards San José gives you an immediate reminder of the opportunities of business, the buzz of entrepreneurship, the richness of technology. Driving past the likes of Apple, Sun, HP and all the others is exhilarating.

Favourite airport: Airports are always stressful. Queues, tickets, seats, upgrades, luggage, ticking time ... Zurich's Kloten airport has a calm, business-like precision which addresses these very fears. None of the retail squeeze, or the bewildering signage. Switzerland at its modern, designed best.

Frequency: It all depends on the projects I'm working on. It could be back and forwards long-haul flights every week, or nothing for ages. Hardest work are the day-trip flights to Europe, which mean a 6 am start from Heathrow, four or five hours at the meeting, then a rush back to the airport, and late back home. Don't do too many of these in a week!

Always takes: My Compaq handheld computer, which contains everything I used to take my laptop for, but fits in the pocket and only takes seconds to fire up. Other essentials would include my passport and a credit card, my running gear if it's more than a day trip, mobile phone unless it's the USA, and a photo of my wife and baby daughter.

Pluses: Travel is an opportunity, an adventure and personal stimulus. When I used to develop products for British Airways it was always frustrating that so few people thought of it like this. I always have my best ideas when travelling – often as a result of what I observe (so get an IXUS camera to carry with you). And go for a run wherever you go – that way you can see the sights in 30 minutes. Best tip is have some fun with the work.

Tips: Always check out the flight options yourself (for example through one of the online itinerary guides) before asking your travel office to book the trip, get a handluggage-size trolley bag, get to the airport lounge as quickly as possible, and before you go print out a destination guide for where you are going from Expedia.

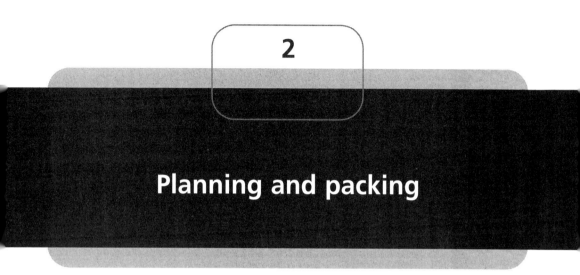

2

Planning and packing

'People don't plan to fail. They fail to plan.'

MARK McCORMACK, SPECTACULARLY ITINERANT SPORTS AGENT

Chapter 5 | Planning: back to basics

Of course, planning isn't everything. Any businessman or woman is fully clued up on the lengthy litany of well-planned disasters that have befallen businesses with regularity throughout history. Strategies can be carefully analyzed and measured, looked at from every angle, and still backfire badly. But, while there is a yawning chasm between planning and execution, good planning can make a great deal of difference to your business trips.

The first steps of planning are simplistic, but they are still worth going through. The questions may be basic, but if you get the answers wrong it could cost you and your company dear. So, the first big question:

Is your trip necessary?

Of course, you wouldn't take a business trip that isn't strictly necessary. Not you. You are blissfully and admirably unmotivated by other temptations such as:

- the acquisition of extra frequent flyer miles to secure free flights for the family vacation
- the attractions of a visit to a city renowned for its beauty/restaurants/museums/golf courses/whatever turns you on
- the pleasure of being in another country away from your colleagues/family/or both.

Business travel must be entered into for business purposes. Are the costs of you going on a trip covered by extra revenues?

Do you understand all the internal rules and regulations?

Companies tend not to make things easy. They do not want to encourage their employees to decamp en masse on business class trips to Paris in spring. There are rules, which are neatly encapsulated in a travel policy. This will lay out what expenses are covered and not covered on business trips.

Essential Links

www.visa.com/pd/atm/main.html
ATM locator for Visa users

http://mastercard.com/atm/
ATM locator for Mastercard users

All business travellers are not created equal – even if they work for the same organization. The business traveller cannot assume the right to travel business class. Rules on this are often vague. One person may get away with it while another in a similar job may not be prepared to take the risk. Often it is worth asking – though some companies have strict policies that forbid executives from travelling business class.

Similarly, it is worth establishing where you stand on additional expenses. These include: hotels (subject to similar vagaries as flights), car rentals, meals, phone calls, laundry, mini-bars and more.

Who pays expenses?

It is always worth making a personal connection with the person in charge of paying expenses. Anyone who holds the reins of power over corporate travel is an important person. They have control over your flights, hotels, car rentals and other sundry items. It is useful to know how they like things to be done. How do they expect information to be presented? Would they like a consignment of duty free? Creepy, we know, but potentially useful.

How do people travel?

Organizations differ in their rules and attitudes towards travel. This is reflected in the travel culture that exists and takes in a multitude of issues, including the amount of free time you can reasonably allot yourself before and after meetings without causing raised eyebrows, and how long you have to recover after the trip. In some companies, for example, a dim view is taken of anyone dallying to take in the sights. Similarly, at more hard-driving organizations, if you arrive back at dawn, you are still expected to arrive at the office at 8 am. Others have a less strict approach. It is worth talking to colleagues to see what their business travel experiences have been and how people behave and are expected to behave.

Will you have enough credit?

So, you've justified your trip and covered various internal bases. The trouble is that your credit card is at its limit and your bank account is creaking. And now you're expected to cover your cash expenses on a business trip.

Some companies provide a company credit card. Others do not. Your credit card – and it is wise to have more than one in case of difficulties – has to be able to cover the worst of disasters. What if you have to buy a new ticket home or go on to another destination?

Do you have the essentials?

You may not have travelled anywhere since backpacking ten years ago. Or you may never have travelled anywhere on business. The sooner you begin to think about what you need to take and how you are going to carry it, the better. What kind of luggage do you need? What kind of clothes? Do you have a passport or appropriate visas?

Savvy traveller: Neville Thrower

Nationality: British

Job: International business projects director CGNU

Essentials No. 1: Mobile phone, as there is no need for change when passing through airports. You can use a credit card, I hear you say, but do you know of a machine that will give you a receipt even when asked?

Essentials No. 2: A good credit card is essential too, so that it is possible to change flights and pay more if circumstances justify it. I recall having to pay a supplement of £4000-plus on one occasion.

Essentials No. 3: My other joy is a KLM Royal Wing Card – it gets me into any business lounge worldwide without even having to be travelling on KLM and regardless of ticket status (i.e. even if I am on a package deal holiday!). This is one of the few cards that permits this.

Chapter 6 | Planning your itinerary

Time management is a much-admired science, but one that is often poorly applied. It is the key to planning an effective travel itinerary. Most business trips are organized for a specific purpose – a scheduled meeting with a client or prospective client, a conference or trade show, or some other fixed event – though it makes sense to try to squeeze in some other contacts. But while it is sensible to combine the main event with speculative meetings – seeing old or new business contacts or acquaintances – don't overload your itinerary. It is tempting to think that you can pack in more than you can.

If you don't go to the USA frequently, for example, you may be tempted to think that while you're in Boston for a conference, you could easily drop in on a client in New York. It's possible, of course. A domestic flight will get you there in a few hours from hotel lobby to hotel lobby, but do you really have the time? It's tempting to arrange to hook up with old friends – just a four-hour drive away in New Hampshire – but is it wise? The key to planning an itinerary is to prioritize appointments and ring-fence the one or two that matter. There's no point catching up with old business contacts if you pitch up to the meeting with the new client late, unprepared and hung over.

Less is more. Better to find that the meeting ends early and you have a few hours to while away in cafés, bars or seeing sights, than that you are boxed in by your own over-zealous schedule. Ensure there is plenty of slack to deal with unforeseen events. What if the meeting over-runs? What if you have to make an unscheduled visit to a doctor, or track down your luggage that's gone astray? These things do happen. Leave yourself some downtime. When you're arranging to meet that former colleague for dinner – or breakfast – while you're in town, remember, too, that when the appointed hour arrives you may be in – or dreaming of – your bed.

The other side of this is that spending your entire trip shuffling between meetings and your hotel is to miss out on the cultural experience. All work and no play sucks. Unless you are a frequent visitor, this may be the best chance you get to see the city or area you are going to. Take that opportunity. Go and look at the art galleries, museums and historical monuments that are there. Go to the opera or to see a show. If you must, arrange to take a business contact. But do something other than business.

Essential Links

www.wwescapes.com/
aboutus/index.html
An internet-based travel company that plans add-on trips to your business trip so you get to do something fun as well as work.

Keep it simple

- Don't try to do too much.
- Expect to feel more tired than usual – especially if you are crossing international time zones.
- Leave plenty of time between meetings in case they over-run (better to sort it out than have to make another trip).
- Allow for the time difference.
- Build in some downtime.
- Get out of the hotel – even if it's just to walk to a bar.
- Do at least one activity that isn't business related – schedule an afternoon to see the sights, for example, or a show in the evening.
- Allow yourself some time for gift shopping (and don't burden yourself with a huge list from friends who say while you're there can you just bring me back …).
- Get some exercise. Many hotels have gyms and swimming-pools, use them sensibly – you'll feel better.
- Try to chill out..

Savvy traveller: James Healy-Pratt

Nationality: American

Job: General counsel Amlin Aviation

Financial back-up: Always carry a back-up credit card with a sufficiently generous limit. In 1998 I flew into New York from Paris one Sunday evening. I got to the hotel and when checking in, discovered that my corporate credit card had been summarily cancelled. A quick call to a London colleague did not confirm that my then-employer had lost faith in my abilities, but that an administrative error at the corporate credit card offices had resulted in its cancellation. However, it was not possible to rectify the situation there and then on the Sunday evening. The hotel wanted a credit card for the four-night stay, I did not have enough cash and did not have a back-up card with a sufficient limit to placate the hotel. My guardian angel then went into action, and a colleague from Los Angeles breezed into the foyer fortuitously to save the situation – so I narrowly missed a free night in Central Park. It then took a further three full days to get a replacement corporate credit card, in spite of the promises of seamless service, and in New York of all places. You have been warned.

Chapter 7 | Which airline? The loyalty behind the miles

In the airline business the customer is king and the business traveller is God. Building loyalty among business travellers (or 'commercially important passengers', as they are known) has taken on an entirely new dimension – it is something companies pursue with obsessive fervour.

The stakes are undoubtedly high. Disenchanted customers are bad enough but, when it comes to air travel, dissatisfied customers tend to have stories to tell and re-tell to potential customers. There are a huge variety of apocryphal air travel stories – baggage that ends up in different continents, nightmarish transfers in Bombay, hours spent sitting on the tarmac waiting for air traffic controllers 3000 miles away to clear the skies. The punchline is invariably 'I won't fly with them again' – and neither will the people who hear the story, however embellished it may be.

To engender customer loyalty, airlines have traditionally sought to make flights as comfortable as possible. With limits to how much pandering passengers can take and airlines provide, the airlines have had to look for other means of enhancing what they offer customers in an effort to build long-term commitment and loyalty. The solution that has swept the world is frequent flyer programmes (FFPs). The first was introduced by American Airlines in 1981. European airlines then followed and, later, airlines in Asia and elsewhere.

Today, you are hard pressed to find an airline that doesn't offer some sort of customer loyalty flight incentive. Their numbers are only matched by the heavy-handedness of some of their titles – Czechoslovak Airlines scheme was labelled OK Plus while Japan Airlines has the JAL Mileage Bank (with over 5 million members), American Airlines AAdvantage (40 million members and counting) and British Airways has Air Miles. There are 67 million members of FFPs in the United States alone – of these over a quarter are active travellers. The average year sees a staggering 500 billion frequent flyer miles clocked up by travellers.

Programme	Members (million)
American Airlines AAdvantage	40
United Airlines Mileage Plus	38
Delta Airlines SkyMiles	28
US Airways Dividend Miles	20
Northwest Airlines WorldPerks	18.4
Continental Airlines OnePass	17
Trans World Airlines Aviators	12
Korean Airlines Skypass	7
Japan Airlines JAL Mileage Bank	5.2
Air Canada Aeroplan	4.2

Source: www.webflyer.com

Table 1.1 Frequent flyer programmes

Initially, this was an innovative and imaginative means of differentiating what airlines actually offer to customers. The more air miles clocked up by passengers, the more rewards they receive. The principle is brilliantly simple – it rewards customers by giving them free tickets on other flights. For the airlines this solves two problems – it rewards customer loyalty and fills otherwise unfilled seats (on average, flights are one-third empty). As programmes have developed, other benefits have emerged – they enable, for example, airlines to build up a huge amount of information about their passengers.

It usually doesn't cost anything to join a programme, and you can enroll in the programmes of any number of different airlines. Indeed, it may not work to your advantage to put all your eggs in one basket by accumulating a high mileage balance with one airline if you find out later that another airline's programme suits you better.

Although similar in thrust, the precise terms of FFPs vary, so read the small print. Be aware, too, that although the number of frequent flyer miles awarded each year has increased exponentially, the number of seats available for those who want to travel for free has not. Warns *InsideFlyer* magazine: 'Free travel is a dream come true. But it could turn into a nightmare if you don't pay attention to the programme's details. Blackout dates, off-peak periods, origination points, length of stay restrictions, and expiring miles make award travel more difficult to use.' There's no such thing as a free lunch – even at 30,000 feet.

Increasingly, airlines are offering tie-ups with other airlines (see the box 'Frequent flyer programme partnerships' on p. 33). This means that passengers who fly with these airlines can still count their air miles. A survey by the *Official Airlines Guide* found that 70 per cent of European business travellers would choose an airline linked to their particular frequent flyer programme.

Despite the success of mileage schemes, drawbacks are now emerging. The most obvious one is that their sheer profusion means that they are no longer an effective means of differentiating one airline from another. Also, the fact that airlines have a complex web of reciprocal arrangements rather defeats the object. In effect, airlines can find themselves rewarding people who fly with other airlines.

Another problem is that the sheer success of air mileage schemes has produced planeloads of non-paying passengers. In one case, the late and little-lamented airline, Pan Am, found that its summertime flights to Hawaii were entirely filled with people making use of their free air miles. Airlines are now wise to this and on some schemes it is made clear that, no matter how many miles you have clocked up, you can't actually insist on a ticket to the destination of your choice.

At worst some business travellers are now more concerned with maximizing their points than with getting from A to B in the best way. Indeed, in some bizarre cases, travellers actually double or triple their journey times, and pay full-price fares to clock up the miles. Research suggests that buying unnecessary full-price tickets has actually added $5 billion to corporate travel budgets.

Essential Links

www.webflyer.com
Everything you ever needed to know about frequent flyer programmes but never got around to asking. The creation of frequent flying guru Randy Petersen.

www.frequentflier.com
Full of info on the frequent flier world and includes a weekly e-mail newsletter, the *FrequentFlier Crier*

www.ukflyer.com
British-based website.

www.eliteflyer.com
Canada-based frequent flyer site.

The obvious solution – for airlines and companies paying the travel bills – is to offer something other than free air tickets to loyal customers. The jet-setting business man or woman who collects enough air miles to fly to California for a holiday is probably a little tired of flying anyway. In response to this issue, at one stage Swissair was offering an hour in a flight simulator, two nights at a hotel or a spot of deep-sea diving, rather than taking up the other option – a free flight to New York. Other airlines offer hotel accommodation, a European break, restaurant meals and flowers, rather than flights.

As well as offering a range of rewards, airlines are also imposing stricter rules to the air mileage game. Members of schemes may not be able to get on heavily booked flights or may find that there are time limits to when they can use their free tickets.

Even so, airlines are still attempting everything possible to differentiate their frequent flyer programmes from those of competitors. For customers, it is incredibly complex. If you make two transatlantic trips with one airline, you earn a free trip to anywhere in Italy, Spain, or central or northern Europe. But, if you join another scheme when you make your transatlantic flight, you receive a bonus that is worth two return trips to Paris. Alternatively, you have to make five trips with yet another airline for one London-Paris ticket.

There are other curious quirks to the system. In the USA, where frequent flyer programmes began, points can be accumulated on discount tickets. An American buying a discounted, economy San Francisco–London ticket can earn their points. A customer in the UK flying the same route with the same-priced ticket would not be able to do so.

With such complexity, it is little wonder that the new emphasis does not portray air miles as a giant bonanza. This is now regarded as a rather tacky promotional approach. Instead, airlines emphasize building long-term relationships, based on all-round service quality, not freebies. So, rewards come in the shape of membership of various clubs, which offer quicker check-in facilities, more comfortable lounges and a wide range of other activities. With BA, for example, a small number of transatlantic flights brings membership of the Silver Tier Executive Club, and you have to be a member of the Executive Club to begin collecting BA's Air Miles (2.7 million people are members).

Such developments actually fit in with what customers want. Though 54 per cent of business travellers view free flights as 'very important', 72 per cent put moving to the head of the waiting list for overbooked flights as the top priority. After a tiring business trip, businesspeople just want to get home.

The truth about air mileage schemes is that, now most major airlines have them, it is difficult for any of them to find a way out. Yet, they still have to find innovative ways of differentiating themselves from their competitors and of building customer loyalty. The answer seems to be in links with other companies and, once again, through pandering.

The first of these elements can be seen in the tie-ups airlines are developing with car hire companies, credit card organizations and many others. The message is that membership of frequent flyer clubs has its advantages outside the airport terminal. You can now rack up frequent flyer miles by buying flowers, using certain hotels, car hire, using your credit card, using your mobile phone and in a variety of other ways.

Clearly, such extensions of frequent flyer programmes have their attractions. Customers are continually more aware of the company's name – when they buy petrol they ponder on the excellence of the in-flight service and consider how many litres are required for a free ticket to Paris. They make collecting points and miles a continuous rather than an isolated activity.

There are also risks. If the aim is customer loyalty, companies may be in danger of confusing the issue. Who is the petrol-buying miles accumulator expressing loyalty for? How can companies measure the success of such schemes? There is also the risk of diluting the brand and of being associated with companies, products or services that don't meet the exacting standards of the airline.

It is easy to point to the excesses, complications and risks attached to all these initiatives. But the fact is that airlines – probably more than any other business – have realized that building customer loyalty is a vital means of achieving competitive advantage.

Choosing a frequent flyer programme

Find Freddie

Since 1988, *InsideFlyer* has run the Freddies, the frequent flyer equivalent of the Oscars or Grammies. Inspired by Sir Freddie Laker, the man credited with introducing affordable transatlantic air travel, the Freddies are awarded to the frequent traveller programmes that offer the best combination of service, bonuses, awards, benefits and opportunities for their members. They are based on the votes of frequent flyers. For the past three years, SAS's EuroBonus scheme has scooped the award for the top international frequent flyer programme.

Right airline?

There is no point joining a programme for an airline that you are unlikely to use. Best to look first at the programme on offer from the airline you use most frequently. Then start looking at alternative airlines that fly to the routes you use most frequently.

How many miles do you need to fly?

Identify the reward that is most important to you and calculate how many miles you would need to fly to receive it. Is this viable and sensible?

How flexible is the programme?

Some are more flexible than others. Some programmes have a host of tie-ins with credit card companies, hotels and car hire firms, as well as other airlines.

Keep up to date

Once you're signed up, it is worthwhile keeping abreast of the airline's latest deals. Programme rules change regularly. You also need to keep track of how many miles you have travelled and whether it tallies with your statement.

Frequent flyer programme partnerships

A number of airlines have joined forces to create frequent flyer programme partnerships. These may have unfortunate names, but offer the business traveller more flexibility. They include the following.

Oneworld

The current members of the Oneworld alliance, which was launched in 1999, are: American Airlines, British Airways, Aer Lingus, LanChile, Cathay Pacific, Finnair, Iberia and Qantas. Members of the individual airline FFP plans can earn miles by flying any Oneworld partner. Covers 550 destinations and offers access to 340 lounges. www.oneworldalliance.com

Qualiflier

A joint FFP between Swissair and partner airlines Air Europe, AOM French Airlines, Crossair, Sabena, LOT Polish Airlines, TAP Air Portugal, Air Littoral PGA, Air Liberté, Portugália Airlines and Volare Airlines, with 2.5 million members. www.qualiflyer.net

Star Alliance

The Star Alliance has nine member airlines: Air Canada, Air New Zealand, ANA All Nippon Airways, Ansett, Austrian Airlines, Tyrolean Airways, Mexicana Airlines, British Midland, Lauda Air, Lufthansa, SAS Scandinavian Airlines, Thai Airways, United and Varig. Members of the individual airline FFP plans can earn miles by flying any Star Alliance partner. Covers over 815 destinations with 9557 departures every day. www.star-alliance.com

Worldperks

A shared FFP between Northwest, Midwest Express Airlines and KLM Royal Dutch Airlines. www.nwa.com.

Chapter 8 | Which airline? The comfort factor

Timing

When selecting a flight, remember a departure early in the day is less likely to be delayed than a later flight, due to 'ripple' effects throughout the day. If you book the last flight of the day, you could get stuck overnight.

If you have a choice between two connections and the fares and service are equivalent, choose the one with the less-congested connecting airport. This reduces the risk of a bungled connection. Also consider potential adverse weather when choosing a connecting city. Blizzards do not make ideal flying conditions. Hurricane warnings – in hurricane season – can also be a downer.

Look out for: Weather forecasts, timings, busy airports.

Lounging

Pampering is part of the flying experience – if you pay enough. It begins before you board the plane. On the ground, airline lounges are more inviting than they used to be. You can expect an onslaught of add-ons – free drinks, access to stock quotes from Bloomberg, newspapers, free local phone calls, copy and fax machines, conference rooms and speaker phones for conducting business on the ground, even a full travel desk to book upcoming flights.

Typical of the lavish lounge lizardry on offer is Cathay Pacific's business class lounge at Hong Kong International Airport, which provides passengers with amenities such as a laptop/cordless phone, Reuters financial information and access to the new Elemis Day Spa.

Airlines may be on the point of forgetting that what most people want is peace and quiet.

Look out for: Size of lounges, distance from boarding area, sharing facilities with other airlines.

Essential Links

www.prioritypass.com
Gain access to airport VIP lounges worldwide.

In-flight pampering

And then you get on board. Once again the emphasis is on pampering. Stewardesses ache from smiling, while airline finance directors have sleepless nights at the costs involved. The comfort factor is big. So big that upgrading Singapore Airlines' Raffles Class cost $300 million. The end result is cabins designed by the Givenchy fashion house and the usual panoply of frills including on-demand audio/video entertainment systems. The airline spent $27,000 per seat on the fibre-optic technology for these entertainment systems, which were launched on flights departing from JFK and Newark International airports. The airline has also just added a new international culinary panel, and passengers can choose when and what they wish to eat. (It recognized a while ago that its traditional silver service approach in first class often meant interrupting sleeping passengers, who were not best pleased at the disturbance.) Business class passengers also get more private storage space with new amenity receptacles located seat-side and personal privacy screens with individual fibre-optic reading lamps.

For all the boasts of greater comfort, though, space remains the issue. According to *Consumer Reports Travel Letter*, coach (economy) seats have actually shrunk since the 1970s, even as the average passenger has grown. In 1977, for example, a 747 usually had nine seats across – today it's ten seats. Likewise, DC10s and L1011s have gone from eight to nine across. In addition, leg room (called 'pitch' in airline parlance) has shrunk from about 34 to 36 inches in 1990 to about 31 to 32 inches today. Business class offers around 50 inches of pitch, although this varies from carrier to carrier and aircraft to aircraft.

Some flights are a lot more business-traveller friendly than others. British Airways, for example, now offers flat beds in its Club World class, taking the 'air-bed' concept out of first class and ushering in a new era of competition with arch-rival Virgin Atlantic. Virgin has responded by rolling out its own business class beds.

Competition is intense. In the USA, Delta boasts a BusinessElite service, while Continental's BusinessFirst is available to transatlantic and transpacific fliers. Other airlines such as Sabena, US Airways, Cathay Pacific and Swissair have all recently launched new first and business class services.

Elsewhere, All Nippon's SuperStyle Service is now available on flights between Tokyo and both Los Angeles and New York, featuring audio and video on demand, a fully equipped business centre, a bar counter and the airline industry's first onboard rice cooker.

Not to be outdone, Malaysia Airlines' Golden Club Class features an onboard business centre on all B777-200s and new B747-400s, with facilities such as laptops, printers, telephones, fax machines, stationery and mini multimedia library.

Of course, all these things are very nice, but what is more important is whether the plane is on time and whether the airline covers the route you want to travel. Fripperies get you nowhere.

Look out for: Seating plans, leg room; how useful are all the extras?

Arriving on time

None of this matters, of course, if you miss the flight in the first place. Helpfully, Continental and United offer flight paging: the carrier's Flight Status Notification system e-mails alphanumeric pagers, text-ready mobile phones or e-mail in-boxes at a prearranged time prior to the scheduled departure or arrival time of the flight. Passengers receive a message stating the current schedule as well as gate information in selected airports. Travellers can register for this service online.

And if you're worried about your luggage going astray, Delta's Business-Elite offers priority bag handling and check-in. In fact, ground services such as designated concierges are a growing trend among airlines. Professional and courteous ground personnel go a long way towards making a business traveller happy before he or she ever hits the runway.

Look out for: Airlines have corporate cultures and market niches. Their extras tend to reflect where their preferences and interests lie. Air New Zealand, for example, offers an aromatherapy amenity kit during flights that's designed to combat jetlag. It includes a floral-scented eye compress and foot massage gel. To some this is flaky nonsense, to others a refreshing change. But it does reflect where Air New Zealand's emphasis lies. Take your pick.

In transit: Alex Knight

Nationality: British

Job: Director of consulting at Ashridge

Best hotel: Lucknam Park near Bath, UK

Favourite country to visit on business: Malaysia – I love the Far East and Malaysia is such a great mixture of cultures and diversity.

Favourite airport: Hong Kong to arrive in, and believe it or not, Heathrow for a return, as it means I am home again.

Frequency: Varies from year to year: minimum 10, maximum 100.

Always takes: Sony Discman, pictures of the family and corporate credit card!

Chartering

You don't have to take a scheduled flight. Once the domain of the rich and famous, charter carriers are convincing more business travellers to travel in style. Admittedly, convincing your company may not be so easy. But think of the benefits. There's no standing in check-in lines, and no waiting around for a plane that was delayed on an earlier leg of its journey. Instead, the plane waits for you. All you have to do is climb aboard, sink into the leather upholstery, and relax.

Some itineraries are simply too condensed to allow you to use ordinary flights. Charter companies suggest the price differential is not enormous. Indeed, on certain routes this may well be true. Consider the case of three people travelling business class on a round trip from Chicago to Greebrier, Maryland. The trip takes eight and a half hours and costs $4315. The comparable trip on a charter flight takes only three hours and costs $5988.

Buying your own

Owning your own corporate jet may sound extravagant. And it is. But it remains the ultimate in executive oneupmanship. There comes a point when even the most lavish of company cars no longer hits the spot, and the corporate chauffeur has to be upgraded to a corporate pilot. Traditionally, it has been the domain of US presidents, business emperors and a few meglamaniacs, but it's worth considering.

The business aviation industry went through a lean patch after the corporate excesses of the 1980s. Today, it is booming again, with more and more companies owning, leasing or buying shares in corporate aircraft. In recent years, for example, the number of US companies with their own flight departments has soared to 8778, from 6584 in 1990. The number of business jets in use worldwide has more than doubled since 1980 to more than 10,000. And the trend looks set to continue its upward trajectory. According to one forecast quoted in *Aviation Week*, manufacturers will deliver 6800 new business jets valued at $90 billion in the next ten years.

Manufacturers are only too keen to pander to their growing market, adding a panoply of new and ever more luxurious touches. The modern corporate jet is better furnished – and sometimes bigger – than a luxury condo, and business aircraft have access to 5400 airports in the United States. If you have a few million dollars to spend, for example, you can pick up a BBJ, Boeing's airliner-sized business jet, or a GV-SP, the latest General Dynamics Gulfstream that will fly nine passengers from New York to Tokyo non-stop at Mach 0.83.

And if you don't have the money yourself – or access to the corporate coffers – the good news is that the corporate jet is being democratized. Today, a growing number of companies use their aircraft to shuttle middle management teams, and even hourly paid employees, between corporate hubs. As the theme of a recent business aviation industry convention stressed, a business aircraft is a tool, not a perk. We almost believe it.

> ### Essential Links
>
> **www.FlightTime.com**
> US air charter service.
>
> **www.flightserv.com**
> Business travellers can buy individual seats on chartered private jets flying between New York's Teterboro Airport (seven miles from downtown Manhattan) and Atlanta's Peachtree DeKalb Airport (15 miles from downtown Atlanta). The round-trip cost: $1280.

Trains

In the USA, business travel generally means air travel. But in other parts of the world the advent of high-speed rail networks now makes travelling by train a viable alternative. The original high-speed bullet trains (Shinkansen) were introduced in Japan in 1964, and have now spread to many other countries.

In Western Europe, high-speed trains offer a practical – and often more scenic – alternative to air travel. The Thalys high-speed trains, for example, link Cologne, Amsterdam, Brussels and Paris, making them an attractive option for an increasing number of business travellers. High-speed trains have even succeeded in connecting the UK to the European mainland.

Eurostar now whisks travellers between London and Paris via the Channel Tunnel in three hours. More than half the business traffic between these cities now goes by rail. (**www.eurostar.com** has information on these trains and includes schedules.)

Elsewhere in the UK, however, travelling by train remains an unappealing prospect. Privatization of the railway network has done little to improve the service and punctuality of British trains. More worryingly, a series of fatal train crashes in recent years has caused widespread public concern. Today, the UK, which led the railway revolution in the 19th century, is in a state of crisis. Large parts of the rail infrastructure are creaking from lack of investment over many years. This is highlighted by the smooth running efficiency of much of the rest of the European rail network.

In the USA, too, the railways have failed to keep up with the competition. Although the railroad has a special place in American history – blazing an iron trail, which opened up the country to business – in more recent times the railways have been largely eclipsed by the airlines. Despite the dominance of domestic air travel, however, some believe the railroad can regain some of its former glory.

Amtrak (**www.amtrak.com**) is launching a new high-speed service in the Northeast, replacing its tired Metroliners with the new Acela Express, which should clip an hour and a half off the Boston–New York journey time. The new high-speed trains were scheduled to enter service in 1999, but were delayed because of wheel problems. Amtrak has so far introduced a half-way house – Acela Regional – over the Boston–New York–Washington route. With updated Metroliner cars, the new service has reduced the Boston–New York run by 30 minutes. But until the new high-speed network is in place, rail is unlikely to take business away from the airlines.

The states of Oregon and Washington have bought high-speed trains for use in the Pacific Northwest corridor, even though those trains are currently restricted to 79 miles per hour due to track speed limits. Several other states and groups of states around the country are looking at developing high-speed rail corridors. Unlike most parts of the world where public investment in the rail network is the norm, the use of public money to build these systems remains controversial.

In transit: Pradeep Jethi

Nationality: British

Job: Head of FTDynamo.com

Favourite hotel: Paramount, New York; Hotel Adlon, Berlin

Favourite country: The Netherlands

Favourite airport: Have yet to find one but possibly JFK T4 (the only bar where you can smoke in the USA!) or London Stansted (a pig to get to, but hugely stress free)

Frequency: Around 18 times a year

Essentials: Laptop, diary/filofax, cell phone, vaseline (for my lips!), spare glasses (I've learned the hard way) – you can buy almost anything else easily enough.

Advice: Don't drink too much on the plane; travel light – take as little clothing/stuff as you can possibly get away with; and use hotel laundry.

Advice for the uninitiated: Always, always ask for an upgrade on flights and in hotels – you'd be surprised how often it works! You can use ATMs within most countries for foreign exchange. Don't stay stuck in offices or hotels – take at least some time to see the city you're in, even if it means eating in a local café or restaurant in the city centre on your own.

Travelling claim to fame: The man who saved his company 10 francs by taking the helicopter from Nice to Cannes instead of the taxi. Nobody believed me, of course!

And finally: You know that great-looking woman at the hotel bar who starts talking to you? Remember it's her job and that you're not really as good looking or interesting as you think!

Chapter 10 | Choosing your hotel

The National Business Travel Association reports alarming statistics on the psychological and physical stresses of business travel. Business travellers who prioritize choosing a hotel that nurtures and comforts them have come to realize that good choice is an excellent start in reducing some of the inherent stresses of being away from the familiarity of the home environment.

While some travellers might elect to stay in very modest hotels because they are 'just going to be sleeping there', it's best to recognize that hotel rooms in essence serve as homes away from home. Choosing hotel rooms that do not optimize our well-being does not put us at our best when conducting business. Tossing and turning on sub-standard beds, feeling stressed because of planes overhead, enduring bright lights shining through our windows, or listening to sirens blaring on nearby streets are not recommended options. Choosing quiet, safe havens that meet our basic needs for security and comfort is a wise investment both personally and professionally.

Sometimes businesspeople find themselves in the situation that their corporations dictate where they must stay. Women particularly are vulnerable when they find themselves being booked by their companies into questionable hotels in, say, industrial areas of large urban centres. According to one *Wall Street Journal* report, women who lodge in bargain-rate motels are more prone to being victims of crime. Putting employees in harm's way is not acceptable and employees travelling on business for their companies who find themselves in this situation should feel free to ask their employers to make other more suitable arrangements.

Women especially might think of staying in hotels where they may pass into a lobby in full view of the desk and into an elevator, rather than to opt for the anonymity of a motel where they are entering their rooms from the outside. Bear in mind, however, that staying in hotels is no guarantee of your personal safety. The facts are that hotel, elevator and parking lot crime are on the rise in many parts of the world.

Wherever you go in the world, you will find a big-name hotel chain. There will, in all likelihood, be a Marriott, Holiday Inn, Sheraton, Hilton, Ritz Carlton or another recognizable name. At one level this is reassuring. You should know that the experience will be much the same in a

Essential Links

www.worldexecutive.com/index.html
World Executive Hotel Directory

branded hotel in one place as it is in another. This is generally true, but is not foolproof. With the best will in the world, individual hotels may not meet the highest standards of a particular chain. Some hotels are better than others, even if their owners are the same corporate names. It is always worth checking out the reputation of an individual hotel.

'I once attended a book conference in New Orleans and I had chosen to stay in a chain hotel partly for safety reasons. When I got there it quickly became obvious that I was in a compromising position. Guests getting on the elevator were very inebriated, etc.,' recounts one female business traveller. 'By the second night I insisted that the desk clerk walk me to my room, assist me in getting my bags and checked out of the hotel in favour of one a colleague recommended. I insisted that they credit me for the second night, and they honoured my request. I later learned that the "chain" hotel had somehow secured the name of the hotel chain but was not really obliged to maintain the standards of that particular hotel. This was a good lesson that I could not make assumptions about the quality of a hotel merely because of its name. Now I ask around and try to get good advice, also make the booking myself, so I can assess the quality of service I will probably be getting by the way my reservations are handled.'

There's nothing like developing a good relationship with a reputable travel agent for choosing good hotels. You might also rely on your automobile insurance company, such as AAA in the USA, which has reliable travel information, staff and services. Or perhaps you can get a friend or colleague familiar with a particular area to recommend a hotel if you find yourself going to a city new to you. Do your homework. Use the net. Seek out hotels that have a variety of services that bring flow and comfort to your business travel. Look for quiet, quality hotels that offer restaurants, gyms, swimming-pools and jacuzzis on the premises.

Jack Journey, a California realtor, says when he travels for business he always tries to stay in a Courtyard by Marriott because the floorplans are always the same in each city, so he can easily adapt to his 'new' environment, as he knows where everything is. He even tries to book the exact same room number from city to city, so he knows the way there, the way back to the front desk, etc. Choosing continuity and familiarity can minimize the impact of the stress of travel.

When you arrive at your destination, if you discover your accommodations are not what you were expecting and you feel in any way jeopardized, don't take chances. Listen to yourself and get the assistance you need. You might ask someone to walk you to your room. Call for help in getting your bags back to the lobby. Those who have hired cars should feel free to ask to have their cars brought to the front of the hotel by a valet or be walked to their cars.

Never compromise your safety out of fear of asking for what you need. Tips for choosing a good hotel for your business travel:

- Use a reputable travel agent or automobile insurance company travel services for selecting your hotel. Look up that hotel on the net prior to going.
- Choose hotels that have shuttles to and from the airport.
- Choose clean, safe hotels with amenities that are close by, including quality restaurants, gyms, swimming-pools and jacuzzis, and quiet safe places to walk.
- Ask for non-smoking rooms if you don't smoke.
- Feel free to change hotels if your safety and comfort needs are not being met.
- Consider staying in a chain of hotels that have similar floorplans to maintain continuity and familiarity, if that would serve you.
- Consider the safety advantages of staying in a hotel with a lobby as opposed to the anonymity of a motel.
- Arrive a half-day early if possible to have time to adjust to your new environment.

In transit: G. Bruce Friesen

Nationality: Canadian

Job: Independent organization design/development consultant

Best Hotel: The Grand Phoenician (Phoenix, Arizona) – a real monument to comfort.

Favourite country to visit on business: USA. Everything in US hotels generally works.

Favourite airport: Is there such a thing? Maybe the new airport in Denver, CO.

Frequency: Highly variable – maybe 30 per year over the past five years.

Always takes: Laptop, electric razor, toothbrush, a least one change of clothes.

Chapter 11 | Car hire

If you want freedom of movement on your trip, then, short of a local friend or colleague with a spare set of wheels, renting a car is often the best option. Costs vary greatly from place to place. The dilemma for the business traveller is whether to book before you leave home (limited choice and poor local knowledge) or find a good deal once you arrive. There can be benefits on both sides. But, given that you're likely to be on a tight schedule, and that a convenient drop off is probably more useful than shaving a little off the cost, it makes sense to sort out car rental before the trip.

For service and peace of mind, the big rental companies like Hertz and Avis have a lot going for them, although you can probably get a car cheaper if you shop around.

Generally speaking, there are four basic rates for car rentals:

- a daily rate with a mileage charge
- a daily rate with a limited number of free miles
- a daily rate with unlimited mileage
- a rate with free mileage over an extended period.

For a longer trip, weekly rates tend to be better than accumulated daily rates – most companies offer five-day to seven-day weekly rates. If you're not sure exactly when you'll be back, or if there's a chance you could be delayed, you're probably better off with the weekly rate than with rate charges, often levied per hour (as much as $12–15 per hour). Companies usually offer a one-hour grace period for late returns. Rental car companies usually charge a drop-off fee if you don't return the car to its original location, either in the same or a different city. But it's well worth paying for the flexibility it provides.

If you don't have a credit card, most companies require a sizeable cash deposit that may exceed the estimated charges.

Underage drivers

Youth may be no barrier to the executive suite these days, but it can be a problem if you want to rent a car. You may be a consenting adult in new economy terms, but be aware that many car rental companies, especially in the USA, require that drivers be at least 25 years old (although some allow drivers as young as 21 with an additional charge, and a few companies allow 18-year-old drivers).

Discovering that you're too young to rent a car can cause red cheeks, and considerable disruption to your itinerary.

Insurance

Insurance can add substantially to the cost of car rental. Check to see if your insurance covers you. If your personal insurance doesn't cover rental cars, you need to sign up for coverage when you rent the car. Otherwise, you'll be responsible for damage ranging from a few hundred dollars up to the value of the car and third-party damages. Some level of insurance is a legal requirement in most countries.

In the USA, most rental companies will offer four coverages (check with your own insurance provider to see what cover you might already have): the basic cover is Collision Damage Waiver (CDW), or Loss Damage Waiver, which insures you against loss or damage up to the full value of the car. Personal Accident Insurance (PAI) provides accidental death and medical coverage for renter and passengers. Personal Effects Coverage (PEC) covers loss of personal belongings from the rental car. Additional Liability Insurance (ALI) protects renter and other authorized drivers from claims by third parties for bodily injury/death and property damage.

In addition, you'll have to pay taxes. In the USA, these vary from state to state and are added to the cost of the rental. For international car rentals, taxes can add as much as 30 per cent to the bill.

International rentals

Many countries require an International Drivers Licence; these are valid for a year and can be obtained before you leave home. You require two passport-sized photos and a valid drivers licence from your country of residence. Carry both your national and international licences when driving abroad.

Simple enough? Be reassured. Hiring a car was once a bureaucratic nightmare. The paperwork was overwhelming, the small print as long as a Russian novel. Standing by the car hire desk in an airport terminal was a sure route to hand cramp and disillusionment. And then, tired, confused by the exact meaning of the Collision Damage Waiver you had just signed, you headed out into a strange city, abiding by rules of the road you barely understood.

Times change and the first part of this nightmare scenario is rapidly disappearing. Only the second, the reality of driving, remains problematical.

The paperwork has not been totally eradicated – you are, after all, hiring a valuable piece of merchandise – but is increasingly notable by its absence. Hiring a car is easier than ever before. As in so many other areas, technology is the saviour. It is now possible to arrive and drive away in your car without signing a single piece of paper. Computer Reservation Systems (CRS), such as Amadeus, Galileo, Sabre and Worldspan, are increasingly used by airlines, hotels and car rental companies. The fact that the three are linked is obviously a major step forward.

Car rental companies are realizing that what customers want is a minimum of bureaucracy, combined with a maximum of speed. They want to arrive at an airport, walk straight to their car and drive off. Making life easier, as part of its partnership with BA, Hertz has its own BA check-in counter at Heathrow Airport. Avis has invested up to $1 billion in a system called Wizard which integrates its reservations, rental and billing systems throughout most of the world.

The growing number of partnerships between rental companies and airlines is recognition that the car rental business is dependent on the success of airlines and that customer loyalty is now a key competitive weapon. And, as companies are discovering, loyalty is more than just offering the cheapest rates. The new emphasis is on offering a complete service. Hertz customers may, for example, be offered information about their route, tourist information, and details of weather and traffic conditions, as well as medical and legal assistance.

Of course, some things appear to defy simplification. Take insurance. All advisers agree that you can't have too much insurance. Collision Damage Waiver – a fee paid to absolve the driver of any personal costs in the event of a crash – and Personal Accident Insurance, covering the driver against injury in an accident, are essential. But so too, in some countries, is a bail bond. European laws remain steadfastly unstandardized and car driving is one of the areas that defies pan-European consistency. Perfectly acceptable behaviour in Athens is highly dangerous in Lisbon; sensible driving in London is deemed suicidal in Bonn. You may be insured to the hilt in Italy, but inadequately covered in Germany.

While the car rental companies are offering broader-ranging services at increasingly competitive prices, life is not necessarily any more straight-forward when you make your uncertain way out of the terminal. The mechanics of renting a car have never been more straightforward but, once inside the car, the same challenges are still there, only more so.

Look at parking, the perennial *bête noir* of the hire-car driver. The potential for psychological scarring is large. You are trapped in a steel box that you are not entirely sure how to work, in a city that is totally unknown to you. Little wonder that motorists lose control – a term has even been coined for their aberrations, 'road rage'.

Some people are lucky. They cruise down the Champs-Elysées, take off down an obscure side street and park their hire-car without paying a centime, blocking an entrance or facing the wrath of an outraged concierge. Most people are not. Driving a hire-car they are unused to, they lurch from crisis to crisis. They wouldn't find a parking space if they drove all day. Often, this is precisely what they do, driving in ever-increasing circles in pursuit of a few metres of spare, cheap, tarmac. If time is money, seeking out an elusive car parking space can cost a small fortune.

The well briefed may carry an invaluable travel guide to help them secure their elusive space. Unfortunately, their helpfulness is limited. Look up any major city in a travel guide and it will lay claim to be the worst place to find a parking space in Europe. London? Expensive and all but impossible. Florence? Extremely difficult. Athens? Made all the more complicated by the regulations forbidding half the city's cars to drive on specified days. And then there is Paris with its intricate network of alleys and gendarmes on every street corner.

It is not only that drivers have to contend with their ignorance about *exactly* where they are on the street map. Regulations differ madly from country to country. In Prague parking in a no parking area will quickly result in your car being towed away. It may prove difficult to explain in Czech that you only popped into a shop for a minute and are deeply sorry. In Denmark you need a parking disc – *parkeringsskive* – which you obtain free from police stations, garages and post offices and many banks. This leaves you open to a parking fine when you park outside the police station to collect the disc. In France you need a blue-zone parking disc (*disque de station-nment)*, obtainable from police stations and tourist offices, though rented cars should come complete with a parking disc in the glove compartment. In Switzerland most cities have parking meters and blue zones where parking is limited to one hour and red zones where you can park for up to 15 hours. To make things a little more demanding, Swiss law demands that if you wear glasses you have to have a spare pair with you.

As a result, no matter where you park, you are never quite sure if it is safe or legal. In Paris things are made all the more challenging by parking being alternated from one side of the road to the other depending on the time of the month. A secluded side street close to a city centre may be legal, but it is probably not the safest place in the world. And what happens if you return to find an empty space? Indeed, car theft is so common in Italy that if you hire a Mercedes or BMW in Switzerland you may not be allowed to take it into Italy.

There is also the small matter of parking fines. Here, at least, the ruling is clear: if you are in charge of the car, you pay. Well, at least that's the theory. In practice, a car rental company confided, parking fines are usually written off – pursuing miscreants who have left the country is highly expensive. If you double park in Dublin you can probably rest easy when you return home to Dusseldorf – though you may still be having nightmares about finding a parking space.

Of course, the challenges of driving will remain – and may, with more cars on the world's roads, worsen. While car rental companies have made the process of renting a car far easier, during the next decade the emerging competitive battlefield will be on providing the extras – the information and support – that make driving more enjoyable and safer so that drivers don't feel they are entering a combat zone.

The European driving maze

Austria

Parking restrictions are clear, but then again all countries claim theirs are clear. One added complication is that street lights sometimes carry red bands – this means that they are switched off during the night and cars must have parking lights.

Belgium

A rigorous regime of on-the-spot fines and inner-city driving is made more challenging with the presence of trams which have right of way.

France

Increasingly expensive for drivers, as well as tourists. On-the-spot fines for speeding can reach 5000 francs and drink driving can bring an immediate fine of up to 30,000 francs. In Paris illegally parked cars are towed away and roads often have signs with 1–15 or 16–31 denoting the days of the month when you can park on that side of the road.

Germany

The biggest car rental market in Europe, due to the fact that when a vehicle is damaged in an accident a replacement car must be provided. Beware of on-the-spot fines for speeding, which are strictly enforced.

Holland

In Dutch towns and cities, space is at a premium and parking regulations reflect this. Some streets have a system of parking on the left on odd dates and on the right on even dates.

Iceland

While parking is unlikely to pose too much difficulty, if you go off the beaten track you need a two-way radio.

Italy

Driving is a free for all in Italy, and so too is parking. It is possible to park virtually anywhere, in spite of the usual restrictions. Hiring a car may require an international licence – a temporary version is available from the Italian Automobile Association, ACI.

Luxembourg

There are free car parks located just outside of central Luxembourg which help drivers get round the problem of finding a space. On-the-spot fines are euphemistically known as 'taxed warnings' and can cost up to 3000 Luxembourg francs.

Spain

A bail bond is an essential part of car rental in Spain. If you do not have a bond you may be imprisoned if involved in an accident in which someone is injured. Cars should also carry spare fuses and headlight bulbs.

UK

Driving on the left makes life for most visiting drivers a formidable challenge. In cities illegally parked cars are towed away or wheel clamped. Double yellow lines signify no parking at any time; single yellow lines mean parking is restricted.

In transit: Alan Briskin

Nationality: American

Job: Author of *The Stirring of Soul in the Workplace* and co-author with Cheryl Peppers of *Bringing Your Soul to Work*

Favourite places No. 1: I'm not sure I have a favourite country but one of the most extraordinary places I have stayed was in the Phinda Game Reserve in Zululand, South Africa. This is an upscale setting in the midst of a game reserve. A truly once-in-a-lifetime experience. I spent three days in an open Land Rover with lions, cheetahs, elephants and rhino. The food was wonderful and accommodation extraordinary.

Favourite places No. 2: Orcas Island between Seattle and Vancouver. I stayed at Rosario Spa and Resort and had dinner at Christina's.

Favourite places No. 3: I've also enjoyed my travels to Canada. Victoria is a great city with Butchart Gardens 13 miles to the north. If one has reason to visit Tofino, on the western coast of Canada, be sure to travel to the rain forest on a small island off the coast.

Favourite places No. 4: San Francisco, just a short way from where I live in Oakland, is always wonderful. The dining is the best in the world. I often stay at the Nikko Hotel.

Favourite places No. 5: In the Santa Fe, New Mexico, area, the 10,000 Waves spa and resort is tops.

Favourite airport: My favourite airport is all about practicality and convenience. I fly out of Oakland, California airport rather than San Francisco whenever I can. It is small, easy to get to and has access to an increasing number of locations.

Always takes: I travel light but always take a pair of slippers with acupressure nodules and ylang-ylang, which is an aromatherapy essence of oil.

Chapter 12 | Packing

Deciding what to take with you on business trips can be a soul-searching task. You are what you pack. There are no easy answers. But remember, she who travels light, travels fastest – and loses her baggage less frequently. Climactic factors should figure in your calculations. Turning up in Boston in January in a lightweight suit is not advised (minus 20 with chill factor). Accept, too, that no matter how well researched, global weather patterns are a law unto themselves. Freakish weather conditions – the hottest/coldest/wettest spell in 400 years – have a tendency to dog the unwary business traveller. You can't cover all the bases. That's why God created credit cards.

The secret is to prioritize. The best people to learn from are those who have spent more time in transit than any sane human being should. Management writer Tom Peters is better prepared than most. He gets around. A typical month sees him performing in the UK, Sri Lanka, Norway, Denmark and home in the United States. And that's a relaxing month. His luggage when he's on the road includes three watches, four alarm clocks, a ruler, a pair of binoculars, nine baseball caps, a bolt-cutter (he uses this in his seminars), an extension cord, an extra pair of shoelaces, flashlights, a hockey puck, cricket ball, Swiss Army knife, books, magazines, t-shirts, computer supplies, scissors, stapler and much, much more.

Most people can probably dispense with the boltcutter. The rule of thumb is to take half as many clothes and twice as much money as you think you'll need.

Packing essentials

- Passport
- Visas

- Extra passport photos (for visas you might require along the way)
- Vaccination certificates
- Copies of important documents
- Driver's licence (possibly international version)
- Health insurance information
- Charge and ATM cards
- Cash
- Traveller's cheques (though increasingly unfashionable)
- Business/calling cards
- Membership cards.

Business tools

- Pens
- Calculator
- Notebook
- Address/contact book
- Telephone access numbers to low-cost services
- Laptop (with potentially an adapter, transformer, phone-jack or a telephone-line adapter).

Local information

- Restaurant lists
- Contact details of people you are meeting
- Maps, guidebooks, phrasebooks.

Clothing

- Business wear
- Non-business wear.

Accessories

- Hair dryer (non-essential)
- Electric shaver (non-essential)
- Luggage lock(s)
- Alarm clock/watch
- Multipurpose tool (e.g. Swiss Army knife, Leatherman tool), scissors
- Safety pins, rubber bands
- Detergent, spot remover
- Earplugs
- Security pouch
- Camera (film, extra batteries)
- Gifts.

Medical

- See Chapter 24.

Your luggage

Jan Ziff, a former correspondent for the BBC, now host of SoundBytes, a nationally syndicated radio show on CBS, tells us, 'My husband and I are both 100K plus travellers, and sad to say, we do this every year. The airline loves us. So my first tip of business travel is if you have to do it a lot, stick with one airline, even if you have to change in Chicago or Dallas to get to someplace when you could have flown directly with another airline. The fact that the airline knows you does help, and when bags go astray and you're a top tier flier, the service and help you get finding them and getting them back is *very* different, as is the amount of money the airline is authorized to give you to buy replacement clothes and how quickly they do that.'

Ziff also recommends investing in the baggage delay option with American Express, as once your bags are gone 'you have $500 to spend, which is definitely worth the $5.95 they slap on the plane ticket'.

As for the luggage itself, she recommends buying the best. She buys Tumi, as it has a lifetime guarantee. 'If you travel as much as we do, within two years you will need it! Tumi stands by their promise. They fix bags for free, and if the bag is badly damaged, they replace it with a new piece – no questions asked. My Tumi bag has over 500,000 miles on it and it still looks presentable.'

Bear in mind that if you are travelling in Europe the size of the allowed carry-on is smaller by about two inches than the size in the USA. 'It's a royal pain in the behind,' states Ziff, 'when they won't let you take your bag on board in Europe because you have the 22-inch trundler and their rules stipulate 20 inches, even if you travel business class. If you are travelling a lot in Europe, buy a European sized trundler.'

Lastly, she advises, 'Oldie but goodie. Travel with your medication in your handluggage. Yes, really. Try buying something for asthma in Russia. No can do.'

Basic luggage tips include:

- Buy the best, most durable luggage you can afford. Read the warranty.
- Clearly label all luggage with your name, address and current phone number. Use leather tags that cover this information from the public eye, available at good luggage or leather goods stores.
- Do not overpack your bags, putting undue stress on your baggage, and risking losing contents or theft.

- Only check in bags that were designed to endure that treatment – never check through your carry-on bags.
- Place a coloured strap with a lock around the bag prior to checking it through to your destination, providing instant recognition when you arrive at the baggage claim and discouraging theft while it's not in your sight.

KH

Savvy traveller: James Healy-Pratt

Nationality: British

Job: General counsel Amlin Aviation

Must take No. 1: Tri-band mobile telephone: any serious business traveller needs a means of communicating. Tri-band handsets provide the most practical comprehensive global coverage, unless there is sufficient justification for a satellite phone. I have had a tri-band handset for two years – it has served me well in the USA, Far East, Europe and Africa. The last time I was in Tanzania, the internal land-line phone network was completely unreliable, so I found myself in the middle of the bush calling my London office on the mobile phone, which was a little surreal.

Must take No. 2: Laptop/palmtop computer: very useful business tool in conjunction with tri-band mobile phone. Again, where local conditions make faxes difficult or impractical, e-mail is a perfectly acceptable substitute. I recall investigating an aircraft accident in a remote location in northern Tanzania in September 1999, and being amazed at being able to use the laptop and mobile phone to obtain relevant technical information while en route to the accident site. Development of palmtop computers is now so advanced that I would probably choose to take my Psion palmtop rather than laptop on many assignments.

Must take No. 3: Alarm clock: time zones disrupt the traveller's bodily rhythms, so waking in time to prepare for the day's/night's appointments can be tough. A reliable alarm clock always gives me a sense of security, so I can sleep without having to rely on someone else to wake me up. In the past, too many hotel wake-up calls have failed to materialize.

Must take No. 4: Medical/first aid pack: I have carried a small but comprehensive pack with me on international trips for some nine years. It contains sterile syringes, swabs and dressings for use in areas with dubious health facilities, as well as the usual traveller's selection of painkillers, Imodium, etc., together with a goodquality pen-knife.

Must take No. 5: Smoke hood: not particularly obvious, but not the preserve of the paranoid either. In the event of a fire, whether it be on an aircraft, vessel or in a hotel, it is well documented that smoke inhalation causes most fatalities. Smoke hoods can assist in providing less-impaired vision to the wearer, thereby assisting in a swifter evacuation.

Savvy traveller: Martin Houston

Nationality: British

Job: Works for BG Energy Holdings Limited (a member of BG Group)

Frequency: I have spent the greater part of my 20 years in the energy business travelling. At peak, I was on the road over 200 days a year and took 230-plus flights.

Why travel?: It can become self-serving but, at best, a three-hour, all-afternoon lunch in a Madrid restaurant can do more to foster cooperation and business understanding than any form of indirect communication could achieve. At worst, an overseas meeting solves an issue that could be dealt with on the telephone. It is a fine line and a hard management call. The would-be traveller (who wants to make the trip) will lobby the approving manager with a well-worded and trusted set of phrases – 'I am the one making the sacrifices' (i.e. time/energy/commitment); 'You wanted me to do this deal – now you are denying me the tools'; 'I need to look into his eyes when I make the proposal/announcement, etc.'

Key questions: Will you check in baggage? Are you playing golf? Are you leaving from the office direct to the airport? Are you flying back overnight and straight to the office? Where will you shower in the above case? What is the airline baggage policy? Suit/shirt strategies, i.e. how many of each? How much non-business attire is required? Are you taking gym wear? Laundry facilities on trip?

Top travel solution No. 1: A Travelpro (US-made) 22-inch Rollaboard Wheelie Bag with an attachable soft briefcase (same make) which can take a laptop in a padded area. Plus a lightweight folded suit cover. I can travel for up to two weeks with this configuration: -

- 2 suits
- 4 shirts
- 2 pairs of shoes
- casual wear (2 sets)
- sleep/underwear, etc.
- computer and communications kit
- lots of business paper

Typically, long-haul, long trip, carry on.

Top travel solution No. 2: A leather soft Mulberry bag with briefcase. A short European trip:

- shirts
- 1 suit worn, 1 suit folded in bag
- computer and communications kit
- 1 pair of shoes

Typically one or two nights in Europe – easy to carry on.

Top travel solution No. 3: Delsay Hard.

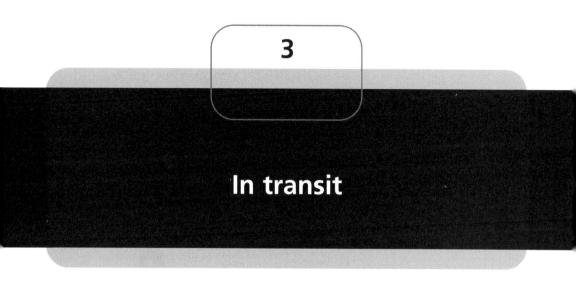

3

In transit

'There is not much to say about most airplane journeys.
Anything remarkable must be disastrous, so you define a good flight
by negatives: you didn't get hijacked, you didn't crash, you didn't
throw up, you weren't late, you weren't nauseated by the food.'

PAUL THEROUX, WELL-TRAVELLED WRITER

Most business trips involve a sojourn at an airport. These citadels of international travel are monuments to the transient nature of modern business life. They have become a sort of corporate limbo, places where even the most high-powered executive is impotent to change the course of events, unable to impose his or her will or make things happen any faster. From the most senior to the most junior in the organizational pecking order, airports disenfranchise us all. Whether you're waiting in the business class lounge or among the hordes outside, you're still waiting.

The fact is that business travellers have less time to cover more distance, which makes travelling by air often the only option. There are some who steadfastly refuse to countenance leaving the ground in a cigar-shaped cylinder loaded with highly inflammable aviation fuel. They include at least one famous soccer player, whose employers accept that he takes a lot longer to get to some away matches. Fortunately for him, his talents mean that he remains an important member of the team. For mere mortals, however, the fear of flying can create aerodynamic drag on your career.

Whatever misgivings we might harbour, the time efficiency of flying means that most of us are content to trust the statistics. They indicate that air travel is much safer than just about any other form of transport. That doesn't mean we like it, although some people even enjoy the experience. Others have simply grown accustomed to it. In the USA, where domestic flights are more common, boarding an aircraft is regarded in much the same way as hopping on a bus. In Europe, too, many business travellers now spend as much time at airports and on flights as they do at their desks. Unfortunately, most airports are considerably less inviting than the average executive suite or office cubicle.

'It can hardly be a coincidence that no language on earth has ever produced the expression "as pretty as an airport",' the late Douglas Adams, author of *The Hitch-Hiker's Guide* noted. It's an observation most frequent business travellers can confirm.

Checking in

Experienced business travellers go to great lengths to avoid checking in bags, preferring to carry on their luggage at all times. That way, they argue, the risk of parting company with your essential travel accessories is minimized. It also makes it a lot easier to switch flights or airlines if there are delays. The carry-on strategy also means they can avoid the scrum at the claims carousel, saving time and hassle.

Travel light and carry on, then, is the business traveller's preferred choice. But sometimes that just isn't possible. If you've got a full complement of executive paraphernalia – laptop, palmtop, suit carrier, bag of gifts for the kids, and miscellaneous reading materials – a more cunning approach may be required.

You may be able to charm your way past the flight attendant, but don't count on it. They have a job to do, after all, and have seen every charm gambit known to businessman or woman. The question is whether to risk it or play it safe and check in? Carry-on limits exist for passenger safety. No one is suggesting that you should flout them. However, even though airlines are cracking down, it is easier to get extra bags on board when the flight is less full, and you board early. Full flights mean that you are less likely to be allowed a larger carry-on bag and will then also have a lengthier wait for your luggage on arrival.

Another tactic is to send essential but bulky paperwork and presentation equipment under its own steam. The concierge at your hotel can handle this for you and you can still carry on your bag.

If you have to check in a bag, ensure that it does not contain anything you will need during the flight or anything essential for your business when you arrive. Equally, medication, glasses and other valuables should stay with you.

Upgrades

Some business travellers claim that they have the knack for getting upgraded. Perhaps they are among the world's great charmers, irresistible to their fellow human beings. Talking to airline staff, however, suggests that, as with life in general, there is no secret way to move effortlessly to a more expensive class. It's always worth a try. No harm in asking. Wear a suit and mention that you belong to the frequent flyer programme and really need a break. But don't expect to get one. Pop stars and other celebrities who have inadvertently bought economy tickets expect to get priority over business travellers – and usually do. If you get upgraded, it will be because the flight is half empty rather than any cunning stratagem.

Security issues

Thefts among and from travellers are common. Airports in particular are a rich hunting ground for thieves. Business travellers, with their penchant for expensive laptops and credit-card-packed wallets, are an obvious target. Americans have a variety of names for those who prey on innocent travellers. There are shoulder surfers, pickpockets and smash-and-grabbers. Their styles vary from sleight of hand to outright violence, but their motives are similar: to relieve unsuspecting travellers of their worldly goods.

The best way to avoid becoming a crime statistic on your next business trip is to use some common sense. A little paranoia goes a long way. The US State Department advises travellers to be especially cautious in or avoid altogether areas where you are likely to be victimized. These include crowded subways, train stations, elevators, tourist sites, marketplaces, festivals and marginal areas of cities.

Watch out for pickpockets in particular. They often have an accomplice who will jostle you, ask you for directions or the time, point to something spilled on your clothing, or distract you by creating a disturbance. A child or even a woman carrying a baby can be a pickpocket. In many parts of the world, groups of children may create a distraction while picking your pocket.

Wear the shoulder strap of your bag across your chest and walk with the bag away from the road to avoid drive-by purse-snatchers. Scam artists – strangers who approach you, offering bargains or to be your guide – are best avoided, too.

Try to appear purposeful when you move about. Even if you are lost, act as if you know where you are going. (For the average executive this should present no problem, as it is one of the skills of the job.) If you must loiter, do so with intent. When possible, ask directions from someone in authority.

Security checkpoints are another danger zone. Watch your bags like a hawk. If there is a commotion, watch out that someone else doesn't pick up your wallet or laptop. For this reason you should be pleased rather than annoyed if a security officer asks to see your baggage claim ticket. (Few airports actually match the bag to the passenger, so theft is common in this area.) And when you reach the bar in the airline club room, don't let your guard down, either. If you have to leave your possessions for even a few seconds, try to find a locker to stash them.

On arrival, don't dawdle on your way to the claims areas, as the early magpie can make a fast getaway. Once you've collected your luggage, there are other hazards. Passengers who aren't carrying any luggage should be regarded with caution. They may get off a shuttle bus before you – and grab your bags. To avoid embarrassing mistakes, it's a good idea, too, to attach something identifiable on the outside of your luggage, since so many bags look alike. At roadside check-ins, it doesn't hurt to watch your bags until they disappear on the conveyor belt. This provides peace of mind that the bag is on its way inside the terminal, rather than on its way somewhere else.

A final piece of advice for business travellers: if you have irreplaceable data, a client-compelling multimedia extravaganza, or a even simple Power-Point presentation that has taken days to create, always backup your laptop before you leave. That way, a thief may get away with your hardware but won't deprive you of your hard-earned intellectual capital. Senior civil servants, in particular, should beware. A number have become embroiled in national security issues when they parted company with their laptops containing the military strategy for this or that peace initiative.

The cautious traveller

- Do not flash large amounts of money when paying a bill.
- Make sure your credit card is returned to you after each transaction.
- Bring travellers cheques and one or two major credit cards instead of large amounts of cash.
- Don't carry irreplaceable items.
- Deal only with authorized agents when you exchange money, buy airline tickets or purchase souvenirs.
- Do not change money on the black market.
- If your possessions are lost or stolen, report the loss immediately to the local police.
- Keep a copy of the police report for insurance claims and as an explanation of your plight. After reporting missing items to the police, report the loss or theft of travellers cheques to the nearest agent of the issuing company, credit cards to the issuing company, airline tickets to the airline or travel agent, passport to the nearest home embassy or consulate.
- Carry the minimum amount of valuables necessary for your trip and plan a place or places to conceal them.
- Your passport, cash and credit cards are most secure when locked in a hotel safe. When you have to carry them on your person, you may wish to conceal them in several places rather than putting them all in one wallet or pouch.
- Avoid handbags and outside pockets, which are easy targets for thieves. Inside pockets are safer.
- One of the safest places to carry valuables is in a pouch or money belt worn under your clothing.
- Pack an extra set of passport photos along with a photocopy of your passport information page to make replacement of your passport easier in the event it is lost or stolen.

In transit: James Pickford

Nationality: British

Job: Editor

Favourite hotel: The Brora House Hotel on the north-east coast of Scotland. Formerly a large family home, it has simple rooms, most of which offer spectacular coastal views. It remains relatively undiscovered, though it has been known to golfers for many years. It sits beside the town's links course, and several other courses lie nearby up and down the coast. Not great for international business meetings, though.

Favourite country: I'd say Denmark is my favourite country for business. The business culture is civilized, friendly, open and constructive. Most businesspeople are highly educated and – important for a monoglot like myself – speak impeccable English. The transport infrastructure is good and hotel standards are, well, Scandinavian.

Favourite airport: I have no favourite airport. The modern airport is part waiting room, part shopping centre, neither of which tends to inspire great feelings of attachment. The one I regard as 'least bad' is Heathrow, on the grounds that its Express shuttle gets me out into the city in 15 minutes.

Chapter 14 | Sitting comfortably

Those who regularly take to the air confirm that getting a centre seat on a long-haul flight is bad news. No one wants to play piggy-in-the-middle on a long-haul flight. Indeed, frequent flyers say that it's worth putting in some effort to secure the seat of your choice. For the airline neophyte, here are some tips.

Seat assignment on most airlines starts 30 days in advance of the flight and with other carriers, up to 90 days (except Southwest Airlines and some shuttle flights, which do not assign seats at all). Aisle seats are usually the first to go, followed by window seating. The longer you wait to book your flight plans, the greater the chance you will have of ending up with a centre seat.

Bulkhead seating is generally reserved for frequent flyers. (It's worth signing up to the airline's frequent flyer programme to improve your seating prospects.) Passengers in the seats near the centre and rear tend to suffer more from engine noise. Seats near the rear are the most likely to experience turbulence. If you can slumber through engine noise and turbulence, book window seats in the back of the plane. You will have somewhere to rest your head while sleeping.

For the long-legged business traveller exit seats offer more space. But, these seats cannot be reserved, so if you covet the extra leg room, get to the airport extra early. And if, despite all your best efforts, you do get stuck with the middle seat, go for first mover advantage. Grab as much personal space as you can immediately. Dominate the armrests. Be polite, but capture your territory. Don't feel bad about your travelling companions; they have space on either side.

More generally, the seating lottery is more likely to go your way if you:

■ Book as early as possible. The early bird gets a choice of seat assignments (but book too early and seats aren't assigned and you have to take your chances when you check in).

- If you don't get assigned the seat you want, try calling just after midnight. That's when expired reservations clear and seats become available.

- Use your status as a member of the frequent flyer programme. If the flight is not full, most airlines will keep the seat next to you empty if you are a top-tier member.

- When making a reservation, confirm your seat assignment over the phone. Travel agents don't always follow through even when you've explicitly told them to.

- When you receive your ticket and boarding pass or e-ticket confirmation, check that you have been assigned the seat you wanted.

- If you haven't managed to confirm a seat, get to the airport early. Bulkhead and exit rows seats are kept on hold. (Remember though, bulkhead seats are frequented by babies, and exit rows on certain planes do not recline.)

- Abuse it, and you could lose it. If you do have an assignment for your preferred seat – don't check in too late.

- If all else fails, the gate check-in attendant could be your seating saviour. They have discretion to change your seat allocation. Ask politely. Remind them of your elite frequent flier status. Grovel.

In transit: Kathryn Hall

Nationality: American

Job: Author and publicist

Favourite hotel: The Acapulco Princess (without a doubt!). *And*, I have only gone there on business – a conference – even though it sounds like a holiday … They have *the* best service you can imagine. I *love* that hotel!

Favourite country: Mexico!

Favourite airport: San Francisco (SFO)

Do you work on planes: Sometimes I read books I'm working on.

Route to upgrading: I complain if there's something 'wrong'.

Bare essentials No. 1: Though I have travelled extensively in my life, somehow I find that travelling becomes increasingly more edgy. Perhaps this is a function somewhat of my ageing, but I think it's mostly because travel is simply more cumbersome and complicated than it used to be. To counter this, I always take a few things that will humanize my experience and help me to relax. These things include a very soft, rather flat down pillow that can be scrunched into the top of a suitcase if need be, but more often I carry it under my arm and use wherever I find myself, be that on a plane, in an airport or in a strange hotel.

Bare essentials No. 2: I also always carry a tiny bottle of Simpler's pure essential lavender oil which every traveller should avail themselves of, to add to bath water to wash away the travails of the traveller's day, or to dot on to one's pillowslip to sleep better or to use on one's wrist or temples on planes to balance the stress of flight.

Bare essentials No. 3: I also carry an assortment of tea bags in a plastic pouch, including camomile, peppermint, liquorice root and some favourite black tea, so I know I can easily counter indigestion, the inability to sleep, and the inability to stay awake.

Bare essentials No. 4: In the pocket of my suitcase I also always carry photos of my family and a very, very small white teddy bear. The photos I place in my hotel room where I can easily see them, and the bear always goes on the pillow in my room, where he's there to greet me when I return to my room. He always makes me smile and feel comforted. (I especially loved that at the Princess Hotel in Acapulco, housekeeping was always sure to replace my little bear on my pillow whenever they tidied the room.)

Chapter 15 | In flight

Once in the air, the choice for most business travellers is whether to work during the flight, or kick back and take it easy. Sleep can come in handy, too. A balance of the three is often the most useful way to while away the time. Breaking up the time into chunks of work, punctuated with periods of idle day dreaming and sleep, is often the most productive and least unpleasant way to pass a flight. The odd alcoholic beverage can also be inspiring. Dehydration in pressurized cabins is a relatively slow process. And the more you drink, the more you are likely to get up and walk to the lavatory – which may annoy the person in the next seat but is believed to reduce the risk of deep vein thrombosis.

A growing number of business travellers now use gruelling international flights to catch up with their workload. In these time-hungry days, well-organized executives designate certain tasks to be completed during a flight. The finishing touches on many a client presentation, speech or report is now added with altitude. Some businesspeople claim that they are more creative with their feet off the ground. The more upwardly mobile even target colleagues, customers and bosses as travelling companions. You can do a lot of networking in a ten-hour flight.

But don't underestimate the value of some thinking time. Different surroundings away from the office can stimulate different thoughts. Bold new strategies can materialize as you hurtle through foreign airspace. (As yet, there is no mile-high strategy group, but it's a possibility.) Ideas can simply pop into your head – executives report that Eureka moments have occurred at 35,000 feet. All this can be done with your eyelids in the open or shut position.

Getting wired

These days it's hard to find a business traveller who isn't toting a computer with more processing power than NASA. Laptops and palmtops abound. To date, much of that technological wizardry has lain idle. Pent-up Pentiums, though, are about to get a new lease of life. What has acted as a block on the activities of thrusting young executives is the inability to plug their micro-PCs and midget-Macs into the internet during a flight. Until recently, sending and receiving e-mail was off limits. That is all now changing. For those who run their business empires by sending copious e-mails, internet-wise things are looking up – literally.

As we write, the Scandinavian airline SAS is testing a wireless internet system developed by Seattle-based Tenzing Communications that runs on board aircraft. This will give laptop users access to an internet server when onboard. In turn, the server will link to a ground station when the aircraft is airborne, with content being transmitted and updated regularly.

More will certainly follow. Developers believe they will be able eventually to implement broadband connections on board aircraft, using advanced satellite technology.

Even so, a lot of work needs to be done before e-mail and internet access become ubiquitous on passenger aircraft. Safety fears have been paramount in the minds of the regulating authorities, pending a proven system that separates flight communications and controls from the passengers' use of computers.

In transit: Solon Ardittis

Nationality: French and Greek

Job: Co-founder and CEO, Tradeyoursite.com

Favourite hotel: I have been travelling to all the continents for the last 25 years (usually on business and hence staying at four- or five-star hotels) and my favourite hotel is, without a doubt, the Hotel Maya in Tegucigalpa (Honduras). It has impressive Mayan architecture and breathtaking views from the rooms.

Favourite country: Asian countries – this is where I experience the greatest cultural shocks.

Favourite airport: It depends from which point of view. If it is about shopping, London Heathrow and Frankfurt are impressive, but these are also the two airports where one faces the greatest probability of losing one's luggage (especially when in transit). Otherwise I quite like the airport in Havana, for its lively atmosphere and its non-stop (and full volume!) salsa music.

Frequency: Approximately eight to ten trips a year.

Essentials: Other than the basics, I always make sure I have enough reading material.

In-flight worker: I usually do not work, except when I have a meeting planned shortly after landing, in which case I simply read my notes for that meeting. Otherwise, I just read non-work-related books or magazines.

In-flight power games

You're sitting comfortably. Your reading for the flight lies in front of you. You are a senior executive, used to making things happen. Here, despite your hefty first-class fare, and the attentiveness of the flight staff, you are powerless. Think about it: you have precious little power, and this is not just based on your technical inability to fly a plane. First off, you are allocated a specific space (seat). In fact the organization of space on the craft would seem to be key to making power operate generally.

When do you sit down? When you are permitted. When can you stand up? When you are permitted. When can you smoke or take off your seat belt? Again, when you are permitted. This is not just for the sake of safety in whose name, of course, such power relations are wielded. Let us go further. What type of food can you eat? What seat can you sit in?

These are determined by the contract into which you have entered with the carrier, but the organization of seating is the way in which the power relations determined by the contract are actually expressed. This is an important point. The allocation of seating not only reflects the contract with the carrier; it is also the way in which the carrier leverages power over you once you are on-board. You have more control over the stewards when you book first than when you book coach. True?

Let us go further still. When can you sleep? Any time, but on long-haul, the carriers often run warm air through the cabins to make you drowsy (giving the stewards a rest) and run fresher air through the cabins (for example on the overnights) when they wish to serve breakfast.

Being on an airplane is a true experience in entering into quite an extreme form of power relations. The issue of safety, which would on the face of it warrant many of the personal restrictions you encounter, is in fact only responsible for some. There are other economic and operational reasons why you get treated the way you do. For example, to allow the stewards to serve all the passengers adequately and the carrier to put the minimum number of staff on each flight.

This is not a criticism of the flying experience. In fact, these power relations are necessary for the complete and commercially successful functioning of the carrier.

What is also interesting is that these extreme forms of power are exercised over us without any coercion, and without any show of superior strength. You see those pretty ornamental ropes sectioning off the different flight classes: first, business and coach? These ropes do perform a simple function in demarcating the various zones. They also act as symbols (this time economic) of what is and what is not permitted to you the traveller.

Ask yourself the question: are you on the inside or the outside of the braided cord? Is it permitted for you to step outside but not step inside? As a business traveller can you go down into coach (without permission) to have a conversation with a friend? In coach, can you enter into business (without licence) and have a conversation with a friend in business? The space begins to take on varying values and this indicates how the space on board is being used to leverage power over you.

While talking symbols, let us also remark on the military-type uniforms of the captains. Of course they are not really military personnel, but the title and the uniform act as symbols of the power invested in them by the airline with which you have entered into contract.

In mid-1998 a captain working with one low-cost airline held his passengers on board after landing for an hour until the person who had been smoking in the toilets owned up to the 'crime'. In fact the captain himself was later arrested for 'false imprisonment'.

Gerry Griffin, author of *The Power Game*

In transit: Sandra Harris

Nationality: British

Job: Writer, broadcaster and editor of Concorde's in-flight magazine

First trip: I was sent to Paris by BBC Radio to investigate whether Paris was boring or not! I couldn't believe that someone would pay for my ticket and hotel. Now it has become a mantra.

Favourite hotel: Chipriani in Venice and, in terms of business travel, Hotel du Rhône in Geneva, beautifully finished with art deco surroundings. It is very professional. It has everything you could possibly want in your room or at the front desk. I don't want faxes in my room. The general manager makes a hotel and it buzzes with life. It also has a good restaurant which is used by locals so you get lots of people doing deals and flirting.

The perfect room: A hotel room must have two phone lines. Also it needs a central switch beside the bed to turn everything off. The last thing you want to do is to trail around looking for switches. I object to exorbitant mini-bar prices for mineral water. It should be free.

The comfort factor: Travelling with a no-frills airline on a short-haul flight can actually be a good experience. They don't try to give you everything the way they do in business class. Basically, you want good coffee, bright people, punctuality and a comfortable seat.

Aisle or window: I'm a window person. You have to look outside and wonder about the miracle of flying.

Essentials: A spare pair of knickers and a toothbrush. You never know when you might have to stay over. Also basic make-up. There's nothing vital for business. I don't use my mobile and hotels provide everything. I don't carry a laptop: I'd rather pop into a café. I rely on the professionalism of the hotel. They should be able to produce anything. You just need to get on the plane.

Favourite airport: I rather like London Stansted – it's small. Frankfurt is quite good and Perth in Australia is lovely: it is very easy, modern and you get everything very quickly. You are immediately in Australia. I also like the drive from Singapore's airport into the city. It is totally unlike the drive into any other city.

Chapter 16 | Soft landings

The next challenge awaiting the business traveller, as he or she emerges from in-flight purdah and steps blinking into the cultural glare of a foreign land, is getting to their hotel as quickly and painlessly as possible. Stereotypically, this involves the time-honoured ritual of finding a taxi and being ripped off royally by the individual who pilots it. Those on a tight budget might consider the option of public or free transport (courtesy coaches, for example, often provide an efficient and cost-effective way to get into the city centre, even if you're not actually staying at that particular hotel). But most business travellers are sufficiently fed up by the time they touch down to simply jump in the first available taxi. This is often their first real brush with the local entrepreneurial culture.

Taxis say something about a place. Often it is not what the tourist board would like to hear. Taxi drivers the world over are renowned for talking straight, voicing opinions on subjects they know virtually nothing about and offering reactionary jibes in the unlikeliest of directions. In many ways, their links with the besuited businesspeople sitting in the back are strong.

So, travelling by taxi can be a very useful quick introduction to a city and a culture. Arrive at Stockholm's Arlanda airport and you face a 45-minute trek into the middle of the city. Your taxi driver will be fluent in English, will give his opinions on the weather (cold, but not as cold as it has been) and will usually drive a formidable and neat Volvo. It is life in the taxi lane, but not as it is usually understood by the maniacal cab drivers of Manhattan or elsewhere.

There is also the cost. The same journey in New York can cost twice as much as an equivalent in Sydney. A taxi in Bangkok is cheaper than one in Singapore, which is cheaper than one in Brussels, which compares favourably with those in Milan. Generally in North America and Western Europe taxis are an expensive means of getting around – research by UBS found that the average taxi trip in these areas cost $8.30, compared with $4.75 in South America and $4.35 in Asia.

The most expensive cities for taking a taxi

1 Los Angeles
2 Tokyo
3 Zurich
4 London
5 Amsterdam
6 Stockholm
7 New York
8 Berlin
9 Vienna
10 Milan
11 Copenhagen
12 Paris
13 Montreal
14 Buenos Aires
15 Brussels
16 Sydney
17 São Paulo
18 Hong Kong
19 Cairo
20 Johannesburg

Source: Prices and earnings around the globe, UBS, 2001

In transit: Tony Cram

Nationality: British

Job: Programme director at the UK business school Ashridge and author of *Customers that Count*.

Best hotel: My favourite hotel of all time is the Hotel Internacional Iguazu on the border between Argentina and Brazil overlooking the falls of Iguazu. Strung out over a crescent-shaped cliff, 4 kilometres long, 270 separate cataracts tumble up to 70 metres to create the most impressive waterfall in the world. Everywhere, you have the roar of the water and every room has a balcony view. Thunder and lightning are frequent, so at night, you may see the falls naturally illuminated from your balcony. The hotel is surrounded by primitive jungle, so butterflies, toucans and ring-tailed coatis greet you as you walk on the path from the hotel to the falls. You may even hear the cough of a jaguar late at night. After a lecture tour of Argentina, this represented perfect relaxation and a reminder of nature's superior might.

Favourite county to visit on business: The country I most like visiting on business is Cyprus – it has a unique combination of an international outlook and a heritage of hospitality extending back three millennia. Communications like telephones and e-mails function properly and there is a work ethic that gets things done, yet there is also a real spirit of enjoyment when the work is complete.

Favourite airport: My favourite airport has to be Changi in Singapore. The first time I visited Singapore, I was astonished to find my luggage already in the baggage hall. I wondered how they could unload an aircraft so swiftly. So on a couple of subsequent visits, I tried to race my suitcases to the carousel. Picture me running along the corridors, from plane to passport control, and down the escalators into the baggage hall! Finally on my most recent visit, I was lucky enough to be seated in the front row of business class, and was the first to emerge from the plane. I was well prepared: I had no hand luggage to encumber me and my feet were shod by Nike. Disregarding all conventions of dignity, I sprinted the entire distance, breathlessly showing my passport to an amused official en route. Half-way down the escalator into the hall, I saw bags beginning to appear from the jaws of the carousel. Three steps at a time and I was there just as my own bag popped out. I declared a dead heat.

Frequency: I take around 20 business trips per year.

Always takes: St Christopher always travels with me. He protected me from the ravages of dysentery on an overland trip to India in student days and he has watched over me ever since.

4

Home from home

'Take a little of home with you, and leave a little of yourself at home.'

MARK McCORMACK, SPORTS AGENT AND AUTHOR

'I travel for travel's sake,' writer Robert Louis Stevenson averred. That was back in 1879 before airports and jetlag were invented. Today's business travellers take a more pragmatic view. For them, the journey is just a means to an end. The usefulness of their business trips is defined by what is achieved while there.

Arriving in one piece is a good start, but now what? It may be late and you may be tired. Your flight may have been delayed. You may have had to fight for a cab to get you from the airport to your hotel. It may also have occurred to you that tomorrow's breakfast meeting wasn't such a great idea after all.

You sign in, collect your key and head to your room, giving the bar a wide berth, and noting where breakfast is served – and between what times. Bed beckons. But you have one more task to complete before you sink into slumber. The first step for the practised commercial explorer is to take stock of the situation – starting with your hotel room.

A few safety and security checks, and a quick inventory of your home from home will help you get a better night's sleep. If nothing else, getting your bearings will save you time in the morning – and could save your life.

On entering your room, prop the door open with a bag, turn on the lights, and give your quarters a quick once over. Check the closets and bathroom, to make sure they are empty. Someone else could have been assigned to your room (this is more likely in suites with adjoining bedrooms that can be sold as separate rooms). There could be a thief lurking. Next, check that the connecting doors, windows and sliding doors are secure.

Once inside, before you lock the door and attach the safety chain, check the diagram on the back of the door to review the nearest exits and plan your escape route. The few seconds that this takes can save your life in the event of a fire, earthquake or other emergency. Pace out the distance to the nearest emergency exit. When they stay in hotels, airline crew are trained to do this. In the event of a fire, you may have to find your way along a smoke-filled corridor.

Next, check the basic equipment – heat, air-conditioning, lights, phone, radio and television – are working. Check that the mini-bar is stocked. Turn on the shower to test the water pressure and temperature. If they aren't working, you should insist on changing rooms straight away. Don't rely on a plumber coming out the next day. It won't happen. Plumbers offer reassuring continuity between cultures.

Turn back the bed and lift up the pillows to ensure the sheets are clean. The bathroom also merits attention. Are the towels fresh? Is there soap? Is there toilet paper? These will come in handy in the morning. If you depend on them, also check equipment such as hair dryer, iron, electric razor point, to be sure they are working. Hang up whatever clothes you need for the next morning.

If you really have to deal with your e-mail, then go ahead and set up your laptop. Otherwise it can wait until the morning.

Set your alarm clock to the correct local time. Use the wake-up call and hotel alarm as back-up. And finally, before you hit the pillow, place your valuables – passport wallet, and room key – on the table next to the bed. Make sure you can find your shoes and something to put on in a hurry, just in case you have to get out of your room quickly in an emergency. A small flashlight, if you have one, could also come in useful, so place it somewhere you can reach it.

Now, with help from the mini-bar, if you must, you are ready for a good night's sleep.

Savvy traveller: James Healy-Pratt

Nationality: British

Job: General counsel Amlin Aviation

Preparation: The essence of successful business travel is being able to perform consistently in environments outside your usual office/business location. Travelling creates more opportunities for things to take unexpected courses. Preparation is probably the most important element in a successful business trip, followed by common sense and good luck. Preparation really means researching the place that you will travel to, and the best means of getting there, as well as having a contingency plan if things really do go badly wrong. There is also an element of self-sufficiency that should be noted – relying on others for assistance invites extra opportunities for things not to go to plan. However, do not be isolationist, because in some circumstances you will inevitably need to seek out local assistance and advice.

Luggage: Travel light – it is never fun hod-carrying a suitcase round foreign parts. More importantly, if you have packed say just one suit carrier, then you can carry it on board and not consign it to the twilight world of baggage handling, thereby ensuring that you will always have your belongings when you need them. This is especially so if you plan on changing planes, which is usually an invitation for hold baggage to part company with traveller.

Jetlag: My particular experiences of business travel happen to be of the long-haul nature, which means having to manage 'jetlag'. I do believe the anecdotal medical advice that it takes one day to adjust for each hour's time zone change. Plenty of research has been completed into how flight crews are affected by jetlag, and the best manner of minimizing the effects appears to be through the use of cat-naps of up to 40 minutes in length, especially at the 3–4 o'clock time in the body's 12-hour cycle. Where this is not possible, then just try to get rest wherever you can, preferably not alcohol induced. For those fortunate enough to be able to travel business class, I welcome the introduction of bed-seats in long-haul business class flights, especially on overnight flights. Also, on the subject of business class, the flexibility to eat prior to a long-haul overnight flight, or in Virgin Atlantic's case, whenever you want (and whatever you want) while on board is to be applauded.

Savvy Traveller: Bruce Tulgan

Nationality: American

Job: Founder and CEO of Rainmaker Thinking Inc., and author of *Winning the Talent Wars*

Travel tips:

- Use airport time wisely. Stretch, walk, read magazines and newspapers at the news-stand in airports while you're waiting. And read books in bookstores while you're waiting. Make phone calls.

- Use hotel time wisely. Work out. Watch movies that your partner will never want to watch. Make phone calls. Ask for a nice view. If I am in a nice walking city, I always take a walk and check out the city. To wake up, because I have a hard time waking up, I always use those 'order breakfast the night before' cards because then I know someone is going to knock on my door (a wake-up call isn't enough to wake me up).

- Use plane time wisely. Sleep, read, sort receipts, sort business cards. I try not to do 'serious' work that requires concentration on the plane because I find I am about half as effective as normal.

- Use ground transportation time wisely. Make phone calls. Usually I make personal calls from cars because I lose the connection so often and I don't want to get cut off in the middle of a business call.

- When departing or arriving from/to your home city, always use the same proven car service(s). In travel cities, I almost always use a cab instead of a car service. With a cab, you know what you are getting. With a car service, it may be great and it may be a total failure.

- Stay away from amateur travellers whenever possible, especially in lines and on planes. Bring earplugs in case of children. Give very cold vibes to talkative passengers.

- Drink tons of water.

- Pack very light. Never check bags.

- The most important thing I've learned is to be Zen when travelling because so many things go wrong nowadays. Whenever there is a problem, I very methodically work my way through options – different flights, different airlines, different routes, different airports, etc. – but the whole time, it helps to be almost emotionless.

- Don't get angry with airline personnel, especially in the airport. Smile. Be excessively polite. They have a lot more discretion than you think and plenty of tricks up their sleeves that can help you or make your life miserable. You want them to help you.

- When things go wrong, get on line, and at the same time, get on the phone and stay on the phone with the airline or a travel agent. Often they can help you while you are in line before you get to the counter.

- In the airport, study the arrivals and departures screens. They tell you a lot about what's going on in the airport. Are a lot of flights delayed or cancelled? Are there good back-up flights? Is there a more convenient flight than the one you are on right now?

- Avoid Chicago.
- Avoid connections whenever possible – take direct flights.
- Book back-up flights whenever possible, in advance, as insurance against cancellations and delays. If you buy full-fare tickets (and someone else is paying), the tickets you don't use are fully refundable. Otherwise, as long as you travel a lot, you can change whatever flights you don't use for a small fee and use the tickets later on another trip.
- Always be aware of alternative airports in or near cities where you are arriving or departing, so you have more options if flights are cancelled or delayed. And use alternative airports whenever possible because they are less busy.
- For USA to Europe, leave in the evening whenever possible, sleep on the plane, wake up in the morning at your destination.
- Mix business and pleasure. If I have some notice that I'm going to be in a city where I have friends, I'll try to arrange to meet up. If I am going someplace nice, I try to bring my wife.
- Join and use frequent traveller programmes.

In the summer of 1951, the Wilson family of Memphis set off on a motoring vacation. There was nothing special about it, just a couple and their five children heading to Washington, DC. Mr Wilson, Kemmons Wilson, was a Memphis builder and realtor. He and his family became exasperated as their vacation progressed. It was not a great deal of fun staying in expensive and poor-quality motels.

'A motel room only cost about $8 a night, but the proprietors inevitably charged $2 extra for each child. So the $8 charge soon ballooned into an $18 charge for my family,' Wilson later recounted. 'If we could get a room with two beds, our two daughters slept in one, and Dorothy and I slept in the other. Our three boys slept on the floor in sleeping bags. Sometimes there was a dollar deposit for the key and another dollar for the use of a television.'

So, Wilson decided to build his own. 'I was seized by an idea: I could build a chain of affordable hotels, stretching from coast to coast. Families could travel cross-country and stay at one of my hotels every night.' Wilson envisaged 400 such motels. It sounded outrageously ambitious, but Wilson didn't hang around. He began work while still on vacation. He measured rooms and looked at facilities. His conclusion was that features such as televisions, telephones, ice machines and restaurants should be universal. In his imagined hotel chain, children would be free.

When the family returned home, Wilson got straight to work. He asked a draughtsman to draw up some plans. The draughtsman had seen a Bing Crosby film the previous evening and labelled the plan Holiday Inn, from the Crosby movie. Wilson liked it. The name stuck.

The first Holiday Inn was opened in Memphis in 1952. (This fared better than Wilson's first house, which he mistakenly built on the wrong lot.) The rest is motel history. Clean and cheap, Holiday Inns sprouted up throughout the United States and then the world. 'He changed the way America travels,' Senator John Glenn concluded of Wilson, 'Kemmons Wilson has transformed the motel from the old wayside fleabag into the most popular home away from home,' noted *Time*. By the time Wilson retired in 1979, Holiday Inn was the world's largest lodging chain. Today there are 1643 Holiday Inn hotels with 327,059 rooms.

The success of Holiday Inn marked the apotheosis of the industrial hotel, where service was cleverly systematized and standardized. Now, to the uninitiated, one hotel room can look very much like another. You could be in Bangalore, Beijing or Baltimore, and the hotel room will look eerily familiar. The great achievement of the modern hotel chain is to reduce the traveller's experience of any destination around the globe to a single uniform and uninspiring box.

But while Holiday Inn led the charge to mass production, the emphasis is now on mass customization. Hotel chains spend millions every year on focus groups to advise them just where to put that desk power point and reading light. Hotels pull out all the stops to attract the business traveller. Innovations abound. The Hilton Group, for example, recently tested its 'room of the future' at one of its hotels by seeking the views of corporate 'decision makers'. The desk, with its associations with work and stress, is directly behind the bed. Business travellers, it seems, don't want to be reminded of their travails when they slip beneath the sheets. Out of sight is out of mind. This is one of a number of startling revelations gleaned from 3000 Hilton guests across the world who were shown 'mood boards', in order to find out which they liked best.[1] The boards are filled with colours that provoke different emotions. Most opted for the 'cool sleep' board which had pale lilacs and pinks and was the most calming. Surprisingly, men and women, regardless of age, all liked the same colours.

Extra extras

Hotels worldwide are engaged in a constant war of one-upmanship:

Fitness

The JW Marriott Hotel in Seoul has a 50-ft-high rock wall, scuba-diving pool, 280-foot jogging track, underwater running machines and 22 indoor golf ranges.

Eating

Seoul's Hotel Lotte has 23 restaurants and bars. Delhi's Grand Hyatt boasts that all of the restaurants in the hotel feature innovative show kitchens 'allowing for an interactive dining experience'.

Room service

Residents of San Francisco's Nob Hill Lambourne can order food from 75 local restaurants which is then delivered to the room piping hot. The hotel offers free use of laptops.

Swimming

The Oriental in Singapore has underwater piped-in classical music in its swimming-pool.

Prayer

Tel Aviv's Carlton Hotel has a rooftop swimming-pool and an in-house synagogue.

Size

Big remains a hotel mantra. Shanghai's Grand Hyatt occupies the top 35 floors of the Jin Mao Tower, standing 420 metres tall. It is the world's highest hotel. A drink in the 87th floor cocktail bar, Cloud 9, is not for those who suffer from vertigo.

Ratings

There are no five-star hotels in Taiwan. Instead, the best hotels have five plum blossoms. After the defeat of the nationalist government, the country's new rulers dispensed with stars in favour of the now ubiquitous blossoms.

Jarvis Hotels is another company that pays close attention to what its guests want. Responding to women travellers' concerns, the company has installed spy holes in the door and better locks. However, when the group took this one step further and introduced its 'secret service', things didn't quite work out. Guests were told that a trapdoor (dubbed the catflap by staff) meant that their room service order could be left in a holding box linking the corridor to their room. When it was delivered in the box, a bell would be buzzed and the guest wouldn't have to interact with hotel staff. The idea was that women wouldn't have to open the door in their dressing gowns. The idea was good, but the fact that the waiter still had to knock to get a signature was overlooked.

Bathroom design is also a key concern for Jarvis. The company installed two-person 'love tubs', and showers modelled on the Japanese rain bath notion – complete with water jets – in some of its top properties. (The Rain Baths have since been removed because, the company says, 'they were too titillating'.)

The dutiful business traveller, of course, remains detached from such frippery. This is probably because research suggests that hotel guests the world over want the same things. Hotel groups report that customer feedback indicates a preference for white bathrooms with power showers, duvets not blankets, lighting settings than can be altered for mood, windows that open, and a layout where work areas, and other amenities like ironing boards and kettles do not impinge on the bed and relaxation area.

Business travellers have their own demands. An independent survey of US business travellers, who took a minimum of six business trips in the past year, indicated that road warriors are looking for hotels committed to keeping pace with their technology needs.[2]

The survey was commissioned by Cyberoom, a provider of guest technology services for hotels and resorts. It confirms what hotel operators around the world are hearing increasingly from their guests. Business travellers want fast, reliable internet services to keep in touch with their priorities while away from home.

It suggests that they are inclined to select hotels that offer superior internet resources in guestrooms. In terms of how they prefer to spend their hotel-room time, surfing the web appears to have caught up with surfing the TV channels – and it's significantly more appealing to today's business travellers than traditional amenities like pay-per-view movies.

Key findings of the survey include:

- A majority of survey respondents (53 per cent) project that within three years they will need or want to use a computer in their hotel rooms more often than they do today. A full two-thirds agreed it is already very important that they 'stay connected' while on the road. If hotels provided computers, 65 per cent said they would be likely to use them.

- Almost three-quarters of respondents (73 per cent) agreed that they'd like better options from hotels in terms of computer use, e-mail and internet access. And they want that technology in guestrooms. Eighty per cent of respondents expressed preference for using a computer in their rooms, rather than in hotel business centres.

- Two-thirds of respondents agreed they would choose one hotel over another if it offered superior in-room technology resources.

- Slow connections was the most popular choice among a list of frustrations travellers encounter when attempting to go online from hotel rooms today. In addition, two-thirds of respondents (63 per cent) agreed they would use a computer more often if hotel rooms supplied faster connections.

- Half of all business travellers surveyed indicated they would prefer to surf the web than the TV channels in their hotel rooms. And high-speed internet connections were twice as appealing as pay-per-view movies when respondents were asked to 'build' their ideal hotel – second only to newspaper delivery.

- When asked what types of online content areas would appeal to them when travelling, e-mail got the most votes. A two-way tie for second went to news and local entertainment/restaurants. Hotel guest services was another popular choice.

In transit: Sam Hill

Nationality: American

Job: President of Helios Consulting

Favourite hotel: Ritz Carlton, Naples, Florida or the Mandarin Oriental, Jakarta

Favourite country: Argentina

Favourite airport: Worldwide it's Sydney – pristine, easy in and out, and no weather problems. O'Hare in the States.

Least favourite airport: Dallas (impossible connections), St Louis (endless concourses and dingy brown 1960s decor) and anywhere in Central America (guns 'r' us).

Frequency: 50–70 trips per year

Essentials: Tissues – nothing worse than getting a case of the sniffles and being strapped in for take-off; also a stack of reading, which I usually avoid reading, but turns out to be a sort of substitute for a workout with weights.

Notes

1 Dinah Robinson, 'A Room with Your View', *Business Traveler*, 7 November 2000.

2 Cyberoom Survey, released at the Hospitality Industry Technology Exposition and Conference (HITEC), 1999.

Chapter 19

THE ALTERNATIVE BUSINESS TRAVELLER
Your room is your castle

It may seem futile to try to impose your personality on a hotel room. After all, hotels have cornered the market in sterile design and anonymity. But, since this is going to be your base camp for the duration of your trip, it's worth making the effort to try to make your room as pleasant and as personal as possible. It is a well-documented fact that people's mood and productivity are influenced by their environment. The more you can make your hotel room your own, the better you will feel.

One of the reasons travellers get burned out on the road is that they never think to personalize their hotel rooms and make them human-friendly. Most people appear to view hotels simply as generic bedrooms and impersonal bathrooms that function basically as pit-stops before rushing on to the next plane or next business meeting. What makes each individual person more comfortable is going to vary widely from person to person, but with a little forethought and minor planning, one can easily make being in that home away from home a much more enjoyable and even nurturing experience.

The first priority when you check into your room is to familiarize yourself with the little map on the back of the door that tells you how to get out of your room in case of an emergency. Once you've completed that important task you can feel a small degree more comfortable in your new surroundings.

A word to the wise: if upon entering your room you feel in your gut that there is 'something wrong', however inexplicable it may be, trust your gut instincts and politely ask the desk to put you in a different room. If the walls could talk, you'd realize in short order that hotel rooms are subject to a million different transactions and behaviours. Everyone has had the experience of walking into someone's home for the first time and sensing that the house 'felt weird' without knowing why. Your hotel room should be a place of safety and comfort. You will be sleeping in the room. To many the thought of being asleep is justification for settling for a room in nearly any condition. With a moment's thought, one would realize that being in a state of sleep is a very vulnerable time, a state of unconsciousness, and not a time to be compromising. It's imperative for a good night's sleep that you can relax and feel as comfortable as possible. Basic stuff. Be good to yourself and give yourself what you need. You deserve it.

To ease the dis-ease of continually being in unfamiliar environs, try carrying certain small favourite objects you can place in full view as you settle into your room, even if you are only there for one night. Examples might be a favourite stone or shell or crystal; a small, familiar clock; photos of your closest family members; even a small toy. You might also bring postcards with images that you find nurturing, be they images of favourite paintings, or images of faith. Whatever you decide is right for you, bring along a few small things that make you feel more secure and that nurture your heart. This is always a very personal decision.

Other things you can take to make yourself more comfortable include a small favourite pillow or neck pillow, and women, particularly, might pack a large lightweight colourful favourite shawl, such as a silk or wool pashmina in a favourite colour, that they can easily unfold, shake out and place on the end of their beds as a familiar, cozy touchstone of comfort in which they can envelope themselves or which they can throw over themselves when resting or when taking a power nap.

Lastly, to keep personal and private inner processing alive and well and current, invest in a particularly inviting journal you can jot thoughts and feelings into to share with loved ones when you return home.

KH

In transit: Michael Pitfield

Nationality: British

Job: Communications director

Best hotel: Shangri-La Kowloon (great hotel, spectacular views of the Hong Kong skyline)

Favourite country to visit on business: United States

Favourite airport: Hong Kong (state of the art)

Frequency: About 30 trips a year

Always takes: Dual-time, backlit watch (for night-time long-haul flights), a really good book (for inevitable delays/waiting), Handspring Visor (instead of heavy laptop), camera (for people and places), small Maglite torch.

Tips: Take as little luggage as possible and take it as cabin baggage. Smile and be nice to everyone – you make friends, get better service, etc. than if you are aggressive (e.g. if delayed).

Power napping

Even the most battle-hardened road warriors need to power down their laptop and recharge their batteries some time. Learning to take power naps on the road can greatly improve the quality of life and energy levels. Power napping can be deployed to good advantage during a lengthy flight. But it can also be usefully practised at other strategic points in the trip. Taking a planned power nap can also reduce the risk of an unscheduled one during a conference or meeting.

You can preprogramme yourself to take power naps by first telling yourself that this is what you are about to do. First, make certain you have 10–15 minutes of uninterrupted time. If this entails calling the front desk at your hotel or colleagues with whom you are travelling and saying you will not be taking calls for a quarter of an hour, do that. You might also put the Do Not Disturb sign on your door, or over your plane seat. Do whatever it takes to be sure you can give yourself this small block of time. Say, 'This is a power nap.' (Over time this will make sense to your mind and your body.) Lie down flat on your back on the bed without a pillow. You might even consider lying at right angles to the way you would normally lie, simply to distinguish for yourself internally that this is not a long nap or a night's sleep. (Again, over time this will also make sense to you. You are programming yourself.)

Cover your body with a light blanket or shawl. Put a silk eye pillow over your eyes to block all light, preferably scented with lavender and camomile herbs. (Eye pillows can be purchased at any good health food store.) Keep your legs outstretched and apart. Place your arms loosely at your side.

Tell yourself again, 'This is a power nap.' Allow yourself to go to sleep knowing you are getting up in 10–15 minutes. You will be amazed that you can easily train yourself to do this precisely, and you will awaken in this short period of time vastly refreshed. If you find you have overslept beyond this short block of time, repeat the process another day using an alarm clock (like training wheels on a bike) but aim for training yourself to do power naps spontaneously, at will. Don't be discouraged if you oversleep (you were probably really tired) and it takes a few tries to master the power nap. Trust that your mind and body can learn to do this with a little practice and enjoy the great benefits on the road.

KH

Chapter 20 | Wired for work

At some point, you'll probably want to set up the laptop to connect with the home office. This is getting easier as hotel chains get wired for the 21st century, but technology angst is by no means a thing of the past.

Futurist Arthur Esch has made predictions about the speed at which technology innovations will gain acceptance in the hotel industry. In Esch's view, 2001 will herald the era of digital TV, while 2002 will see major hotel connectivity as interactive TV, high-speed internet access and wireless phones become more common. For 2003, Esch sees tech-enabled meeting spaces becoming the standard, with wireless high-speed connectivity, digital displays and building-wide LANs.

In the meantime, most business travellers have to put up with what they can get. What's available at present varies from country to country and hotel to hotel. Capital cities lead the technology parade. Globalization, and more international business travellers, means that in the commercial hubs the top hotels – five star – adopt new technology and service levels faster. Reflecting the needs of the global business traveller, most now cater for laptop-toting cosmocrats. Whether in London, New York or Karachi, the business traveller can find a place to plug into the internet – although data transfer speeds vary. In more provincial places, however, services are patchy, and wired hotels are still in a minority. In Europe, for example, many three-star and even four-star hotels still don't cater for such seemingly basic needs as e-mail.

In the next few years, the global brandname hotel groups are likely to set the technology standard. In the US, hotel chains such as the Marriott and Hilton groups are now installing high-speed internet access in guestrooms to help attract business travellers, although most charge for the privilege. Marriott, for example, reports that more than half of its guests travel with a laptop and want to connect to an internet provider. The hotel group is rolling out high-speed internet connection to rooms, meeting rooms and business centres in around 500 of its US hotels. The system, it says, is up to

50 times faster than conventional data ports. Guests can also access the internet while simultaneously using the telephone.

The system permits the guest to easily connect to the internet using an Ethernet or USM cable, and works with any internet compatible laptop or computer without any special PC accessories. Guests can simply access the internet as they would at home or the office. Helpfully, Marriott also provides guests with a toll-free help line with 24-hour assistance to answer questions. In addition, guests have secure access to their private corporate networks' e-mail systems.

Hilton Hotels is installing high-speed internet access at what it claims are speeds up to 175 times faster than a typical dial-up modem. The OverVoice system is installed in approximately 85 guestrooms and meeting rooms throughout Hilton's US properties. Hawthorn Suites is another hotel group installing laptop computers and high-speed wireless internet access to all its guestrooms in the USA. But the service is not free and requires an Ethernet card. Marriott and Hilton both offer 24-hour internet access for $9.95 per day. Other hotels such as Hyatt, Sheraton, Choice Hotels and Holiday Inn are also investigating or testing the new technology.

Once IT backwaters, European hotels are also beginning to rise to the challenge. Business travellers will find a significant change from just a couple of years back when travellers on the continent struggled to send a fax to the home office. European hotel chains are debating which standards they should adopt.

But few have gone as far as the Sofitel hotel near the Arc de Triomphe in Paris. The hotel group Accor, which owns the Sofitel, is intent on taking the hotel room as work environment to a higher plane. The Sofitel boasts the concept room, equipped with what Accor claims is the most up to date in room technology for the demanding business traveller. For $350 per night, the road-weary business traveller can take advantage of ambient refreshment. At the push of a button, guests can 'create the effect of sunrise upon waking, scent the room with jasmine, and hear the sound of birds singing,' the company says. Guests can also dial up 'sea-breeze', 'exotic', 'anti-humidity' and Sofitel's own 'signature' oatmilk-based scents.

Such fragrant pleasantness may not be top of the business traveller's list, so the Sofitel room is helpfully designed to allow business travellers to send faxes, check e-mails and plug their computers straight on to the LCD TV screen and thereby into the internet. An infra-red keyboard is located next to the bed. The company reports that it is now planning to introduce similar concept rooms at many other hotels throughout their network of 145 hotels in 48 countries.

Alternatively, visitors to Geneva can remain connected while enjoying their ambience *au naturel*. Hotels of Switzerland offers Le Montreaux Palace, on Lake Geneva, where guests can plug in at a wired café, allowing them to stay in touch while sipping their afternoon wine.

Outside of such deluxe chain-backed hotels, however, Europe can still vex the peripatetic businessperson. Smaller hotels may have old world charm in abundance, but can be frustrating for the technology-minded business traveller. Yet, demand for the fully connected hotel room is growing as quickly in Europe as it is elsewhere, which will force hotels to add internet connections.

Research by OAG found that e-mail/internet connections are popular with two-thirds of travellers, while in-room fax facilities were seen as useful to only four in ten of the 1999 survey respondents. 'Only the Japanese seem to wish to send faxes anymore', the survey found. 'Overall, the Europeans are least interested in staying in touch by e-mail, executives from the Americas are the biggest fans of satellite/cable TV and travellers from the Asia-Pacific region are most likely to send an e-mail.'

The great majority want it all there in front of them, ready to go. At the Marriott's London outlets there is a standard US telephone socket as well as a UK one, so guests don't need an adapter to use a modem. There are also US and UK power sockets.

'Technology is changing so quickly and not at a universal pace across the globe,' says Nigel Underwood, senior vice president for technology at Hilton International in London. The first goal these days is pretty much the same around the world. 'We need to get the basics right,' Underwood says. 'Two lines in the rooms so you can have voice calls and handle e-mail.'

Beyond that, however, solutions can differ widely. Hilton, for instance, is 'in 50 other countries and we need to make a concerted decision on where to invest and what [technology] to go with,' he says. One growing demand, Underwood says, is for round-the-clock, on-call technology staff backup, as the Inter-Continental chain now offers. Underwood acknowledges that only a few Hilton business centres are open 24 hours but that 'business travellers now expect 24/7 service'.

Hotels also have to focus on what Underwood calls the 'little things' that often irritate business travellers, such as 'the kind of power socket' in a room. 'It is those kind of things we need to get right all the time.'

Messaging made simple

For the business traveller away from the office, keeping in touch with colleagues and clients used to be a nightmare. Checking e-mail and voicemail messages separately, and loitering by hotel fax machines to pick up that all-important missive from HQ wasted valuable time. Such tiresome shenanigans may soon be a thing of the past.

Most people know about Hotmail, the service acquired by Microsoft. It allows e-mail messages to be sent and received from anywhere in the world. The beauty of a Hotmail address – free when you register for the service – is that you can access it from anywhere and with any computer.

Today, messaging is becoming even easier. For a monthly fee, unified messaging services allow the business traveller to check messages sent via a variety of media through one convenient in-box. A number of companies now provide this service to simplify life on the road. The aim is to give control of the communication to the recipient rather than the originator. Before, the sender decided when and how the recipient would receive the message: as a fax, phone call, e-mail. But with a unified messaging service, you can pick up all your messages in a convenient format.

Services such as Octel Unified Messenger, for example, let travellers access all of their messages using a PC or telephone. The original form in which the message was sent does not matter. So messages can be received through a fax, through e-mail or phone by means of voicemail. Working with Microsoft Exchange, Octel Unified Messenger gives the subscriber flexibility to reply to messages any way he or she wishes, and 110 million mailboxes now exist in over 90 countries worldwide. www.octel.com.

More communications solutions are available through Cisco Unified Communications, which also offers voice, fax and e-mail services on a single IP network. Subscribers use the same communications tools (phone or PC) regardless of whether they are dealing with a fax, e-mail or voicemail. www.cisco.com.

Unified Messaging, the first internet messaging service, enables the road-weary to collect their messages from one in-box. In addition, with Unified Messaging you can set up a live telephone answering service in the company's name. This service includes trained and polite tele-receptionists who view a screen of your company information throughout each call they answer. An instant notification service lets the road warrior know the second a message arrives so that important phone call is never missed. http://unified-messaging.com.

Executive health and safety

'*One of the symptoms of an approaching nervous breakdown is the belief that one's work is terribly important.*'

BERTRAND RUSSELL, BRITISH MATHEMATICIAN AND PHILOSOPHER

Chapter 21 | The health basics

Successful business travel is not just about getting there – it's about being in good shape to do business when you arrive. So take some time to pamper yourself while on the road. Your body is a temple. It may be a shrine to the gods of commerce, but a dilapidated ruin is no good to anyone.

At the very least, you should attend to your physical welfare. That means travelling safely and staying well. To do so, you have to know what precautions to take before you go and while you are there. Muggings and malaria can be avoided by following a few simple tips. And, as *The Hitchhiker's Guide to the Galaxy* recommends, if all else fails, don't panic. There are steps you can take in a crisis.

The one thing you can't predict about business travel is whether or not you are going to get sick while you're away and whether you will face unexpected dangers – anything from unsavoury new acquaintances who want to relieve you of your wallet, to kidnapping and terrorism. But you can prepare for both.

The first thing to remember is that business travel is not like a vacation. You will probably be working to tight schedules, possibly changing venue frequently. Anything can happen out there. Business travellers are under pressure from a number of sources. Away from home and family, and alone in a strange – possibly very strange – place, they also have to deliver their job performance targets. The fact is that no matter how far you are from the corporate HQ, companies remain obsessed with the numbers. The bottom line is always the bottom line.

Stress levels are accentuated by business trips. A study by the Hyatt Hotels Corporation found that business travel lasting more than five days interferes significantly with a traveller's personal life. And a separate survey by the WorldClinic in the USA and independent research firm Leflein Association found more than 80 percent of respondents had concerns for their health and well-being while travelling on business to emerging markets.

The reason is more than just jetlag. Apart from all the other stresses and uncertainties, business travellers are likely to eat more unhealthy food and to drink and smoke more. So what do you do? Let's start with the basics.

Prepare

Smart travellers, notably international pilots and cabin crew, ensure their immunizations are always up to date. You should do the same. The box on p. 119 gives an indication of some the diseases travellers leave themselves open to.

Hygiene and diet

When you're away, even at a good hotel, don't assume the food must be safe. Diets and cooking regimes vary with the region and your body won't be as accustomed as the locals' bodies are. However much you love shellfish, try to avoid it (shellfish concentrates water pollutants). Make sure that food hasn't been reheated or re-served. The more complicated the dish, the more likely it is to have been handled several times by different people. Avoid. Peel your fruit yourself and steer clear of salads, which may have been washed in local water.

Water is a potential danger. Every smart traveller should know the dos and don'ts. Don't drink from a tap or other local sources, keep to bottled water, or bottled or canned drinks (carbonated for choice). Use bottled or boiled local water to clean your teeth. Ice is made from water so avoid it in your drinks. One good piece of advice is to cool your drinks *on* ice rather than with the ice in them.

Given the right climate you might have the chance to swim – but again water can be a health hazard. (We're in Catch-22 territory here.) Swimming-pools can cause eye and ear infections if the water is not properly treated, though in most good hotels there shouldn't be a problem. Fresh water swimming in tropical areas may expose you to a risk of bilharzia. Generally, seawater is infection free but watch out for sewage outfalls.

Proceed with caution

Before getting on to the frightening details of medical conditions that can affect the unsuspecting traveller, there are some general rules to observe.

- Wash your hands often: it doesn't hurt to take a bit more care with personal hygiene while you're away. Remember, your immune system may be pretty good on home territory, but in a strange environment you are more vulnerable to bugs than the local population.

- Stay alert when you're out and about, whether walking or driving. Road crashes are one of the main causes of injury among travellers, especially in developing countries.

- Watch out for fire risks. Make sure your hotel has smoke detectors and sprinkler systems. Always make sure you know the escape route from your room – rehearse it if you want. You may not feel cool but you will be safe. Nothing can match the absolute terror of a hotel fire alarm system going off in the dead of night.

- If you have a medical condition such as a heart problem or diabetes, then make sure you have enough of your regular medication and know where to get local medical help should you need it. You stand much more chance of exacerbating an existing condition when you are away than catching some exotic tropical disease.

Get a check-up

Get your company's medical department to give you a thorough check-up and vaccinations before you leave. If you're a regular traveller try to see them twice a year. Make sure you pack a first aid kit and appropriate medical supplies – we've made a list for you on p. 114. If your company is too small or too mean to have a medical department, then check yourself into a specialist travellers' clinic or see your medical practitioner (although usually they will require lots of advance warning, especially for exotic immunizations).

Get insured

If your company cannot guarantee to pay local hospital bills or have you flown out, you need medical insurance. As well as covering these eventualities, the best travel policies also provide telephone access to an emergency assistance centre through a 24-hour hotline.

Get help

Historically, the medical emergency kits on most airlines would have disgraced many a boy scout troupe. Airlines have traditionally relied on the time-honored ploy of calling on on-board doctors for help (apparently the statistical chances of finding one are quite high). But forget travellers' tales of heroic heart by-pass surgery using only a twisted coat hanger and a corkscrew. In this age of liability legislation, doctors are increasingly unwilling to become involved, especially if they have been plied with alcohol beforehand. Many doctors' groups are now campaigning for some sort of recognition beforehand – such as an upgrade – when they announce themselves at check-in. Otherwise many are increasingly likely to remain silent in their seats when the call comes over the intercom.

So if you're concerned, especially on long-haul flights, check with airlines what medical equipment they carry (some now have on-board defibrillators for heart attacks) and the medical knowledge of their cabin crew.

Rules about keeping healthy on board are fairly well known, though given even greater importance by recent cases of fatal deep vein thrombosis allegedly brought on by cramped long-haul flights. The basics are simple: drink plenty of water and not so much alcohol, and get some exercise. Walk around the cabin when you can or do simple muscle flexing, especially of the feet and legs, in your seat.

Get fit

One of the best ways to stay healthy while you're travelling is to continue your regular exercise regime (or start one if you don't exercise already). Most top hotels now have at least some form of fitness centre, though they can vary from a pretty basic rowing machine to set-ups that would put your local

Essential Links

www.fitforbusiness.com
Keeping fit on the road.

www.healthcentre.org.uk/hc/clinic/
websites/travel.htm
Health centre links to travel health
websites.

health club to shame. Make use of them. That means ensuring you take your gym gear and swimming costume with you. Most should be air-conditioned so the local climate can't really be used as an excuse.

If your hotel doesn't have a gym or a swimming-pool, there are lots of other ways to stay fit.

Walking and jogging are both good exercise for the heart and circulation, although the respiratory effects can be negative in areas of heavy air pollution. An early morning jog in downtown Athens, Mexico City or Los Angeles may do more harm than good. But many hotels have maps of local jogging/walking trails or you can simply plan your own brisk expedition around the local sights.

There are also simple exercises you can do in your hotel room.

Savvy traveller: Neville Thrower

Nationality: British

Job: International business projects director CGNU

Frequency: I travel mainly in Europe but do go further afield, and just to give you an idea of frequency of travel, I have been at home in the UK about ten days in the last six months. I live in Norwich so the first difficulty I encounter is where to get on a plane. London or Midland airports are a few hours away by car/train and both means of transport in East Anglia are predictably slow. My preference is to fly out of my local airport to Amsterdam where I can pick up either onward flights, or the train if I am going to Brussels or Antwerp, for example.

Tip No. 1: Try to use your local airport to avoid stress and time loss.

Tip No. 2: On intercontinental flights where time differences cause such serious fatigue, try to schedule arrival for late evening so you can go straight to bed. There is nothing worse than arriving dog-tired early morning and having to struggle through a business day.

Tip No. 3: Don't kid yourself that you can work effectively on a plane. Apart from the distractions of food, drink, duty-free sales and other passengers who want to talk, confidentiality is a real issue. I have heard real horror stories about travellers giving away secrets to a neighbouring passenger who finds your work much more interesting than his own and indeed might be a competitor! Similarly, if travelling with a colleague, be careful how you talk about business issues. Use airline lounges for the confidential stuff but if you can, do the preparation before you travel.

Tip No. 4: Be careful how you use the phone, for the same reasons of confidentiality.

Tip No. 5: Relax at all times. If the plane is late, or you are going to miss a connection, there is nothing you can do about it so stop fretting. Channel your energy into planning your way out of the situation in a measured way.

Tip No. 6: Drink a lot, but not alcohol, to avoid dehydration. Save the alcohol for the last leg home!

Tip No. 7: If you get into trouble, don't expect your secretary to sort it – she's not there. Talk to airline personnel as they are always very helpful and the odds are that they've experienced your problem before!

Tip No. 8: Keep patient, cool and level-headed at all times. Being otherwise alienates others and you do not get best advice.

Chapter 22 | Healthy flying

The jury is still out on the health hazards posed by aircraft cabins. Recycled cabin air is widely suspected of spreading bugs and other airborne nasties. Cramped seats may increase the risk of deep vein thrombosis (DVT). Exposure to cosmic radiation is said to cause cancer.

The facts, though, remain elusive. To date, the research into the effects of air travel on passengers has not been extensive enough to assess the level of risk or the most effective ways of minimizing it. What research has been done suggests that travellers can take some precautions to lessen the risks.

Recirculated air is often blamed by travellers for illnesses they develop, although other factors may also be involved. According to Dr Simon Janvrin, chief medical officer of the UK's Civil Aviation Authority, health concerns should not be dismissed, but should not be a cause for hysteria. 'After all, flying transports people who may be unfit or relatively unfit to the altitude of a low Alpine peak in five or ten minutes. If they have respiratory problems, for example, they are going to be magnified. Obviously, if you sit next to someone with a contagious disease, such as tuberculosis for ten hours, you are at risk of getting that disease. But I don't believe that recirculating air spreads those diseases around the cabin. The measurements I have seen suggest that cabin air is actually cleaner than the air you breathe in the airport terminal.'[1]

Airlines tend to down play the risk. Dr Mike Bagshaw, deputy chief medical officer at British Airways, points to World Health Organization reports saying there was no evidence that tuberculosis could be transmitted via cabin air systems. He says: 'The fact is that 50 per cent of the air is recirculated to stop it getting too dry. It passes through high-efficiency particulate filters which remove bacterial and viral particles.'

Deep vein thrombosis

Deep vein thrombosis (DVT) is a cause for some concern with controversy over whether airline passengers are at risk as a result of sitting still for long periods. The risk of actually dying from the condition is relatively small – it has been put at about one in 2.5 million compared with a one in 6000 risk of being fatally injured crossing the road on the way to the airport. But worries have grown in recent years. Although it was picked up by the media early in 2001, it is not a new issue. Prolonged sitting in cramped and uncomfortable conditions was identified as a possible cause of DVT as long ago as the 1940s. The problem was observed among Londoners who were sleeping in deck-chairs in bomb shelters during the Blitz.

More recently, research has focussed on examining a possible link with air travel. A recent French study compared some 160 hospital patients who had suffered DVT with a similar number who had not. About one-quarter of those in the first group had made journeys of more than four hours in the previous four weeks, compared with only about 6 per cent of the others. Of those who had travelled, however, only a minority had flown. Following a subsequent newspaper article about this, 110 people claimed to have suffered after flying. They were asked questions about their treatment to check that they really had experienced DVT – and 84 provided convincing evidence. Fifteen per cent of them had flown in business class. However, two-thirds of both groups combined were found to be at risk before they took off. Some were using the contraceptive pill, for example; others had varicose veins or were suffering blood abnormalities.

Among those conducting research into DVT in the UK is Dr Patrick Kesteven, consultant hematologist at the Freeman Hospital in Newcastle upon Tyne. He believes the risk should not be exaggerated. 'We asked 630 people living between the Tyne and Scottish border, who had suffered DVT, whether they had travelled more than 100 miles in the four weeks before it occurred. In all, 26 said they had, of whom two-thirds travelled by air.'

So what can you do to lower the risk? Moving around, even just standing up at regular intervals during the flight, is one measure that may help to reduce the risk of DVT. Some airlines now show videos demonstrating exercises passengers can do in their seats. Experts agree it is a good idea to keep flexing your calf muscles, wriggling your toes and walking about regularly. If you're aged over 50 and a bit nervous, some doctors recommend taking an aspirin, but you should always consult your own doctor first.

And if you are unfortunate enough to be taken ill on a flight, the good news is that your chances of survival are better than they used to be. A growing number of airlines now train flight crew to use defibrillators, which can be used to resuscitate passengers who suffer heart attacks. Some even have instant access to specialist medical advice on the ground.

In transit: Kjell A. Nordström

Nationality: Swedish

Job: Funkster

Favourite hotel: Soho Grand, New York; St Martin's, London; Sandersons, London

Favourite country: Switzerland

Favourite airport: If there is such a thing, Singapore

Frequency: 100 plus per year

Essentials: Mobile telephone, Swiss army knife, credit cards

Note

1 Bray, Roger, *Business of Travel*, Pearson Education 2000.

Chapter 23 | Beware burnout

Frequent business travel can exacerbate long-term work-related health risks. The phenomenon of burnout has long been recognized among executives. Managers who work too hard for too long can become demotivated, depressed and, in extreme cases, suffer nervous breakdowns. Comparative figures are hard to come by, but anecdotal evidence suggests that the problem may be getting worse.

Restructuring has added to job insecurity, reduced the number of employees and heaped higher workloads on those who remain. (In Japan, a small number of managers are believed to die from work-related stress each year.)

'Burnout is the outcome of a mismatch between workers and the workplace,' say Michael P. Leiter and Christina Maslach, authors of *The Truth about Burnout*. 'A critical point about burnout which is often missed is that it is a management problem, not simply an individual one. Too often managers side-step the issue as being either outside of their mandate or impossible to address.' In reality, they argue, it is a problem that requires management solutions. 'It should be front and centre on the management agenda.'

Burnout is usually associated with management positions. Employees suffer from stress. The difference between the two is unclear, although burnout is usually the result of long-term stress.

Professor Andrew Kakabadse at the UK's Cranfield School of Management has also investigated the phenomenon of burnout as part of a worldwide study of top executive performance. His data, based on a detailed survey of 6500 managers from ten countries, suggests all leaders are prone to burnout, but their organizations are often embarrassed by the phenomenon and don't know what to do about it. 'Corporate life requires deadlines to be met and inevitably workloads are unevenly shared, meaning that organizations generate their share of workaholics irrespective of the wishes of the individual,' he says.

'In addition, organizational chaos is rife, yet most workplaces still implicitly demand employees be corporate people, living and dreaming about attaining success in organizational life.'

Comments from one consultant sum up the way many managers feel. 'I'm bored, I'm tired, and I'm going nowhere,' he says. 'There are no more promotions. The work doesn't get any easier. Yet, what's pushed hard in the firm? More commitment! More drive! More time for work. Get the client! Keep the client! Maximize the chargeable hours. To think I have another 11 years of this, minimum; that is if I do not lose my job in the meantime. Sometimes it can seem just so pointless.'

Serious attention, Professor Kakabadse says, should be given to how burnout happens, how to recognize and cope with it and how to combat it. The symptoms include increasing fatigue, not listening effectively, feeling saturated with work, feeling unable to participate in routine operational conversations. Frequent travel can compound those stresses.

What make the tell-tale signs hard to spot, however, is that declining morale and feelings of personal vulnerability usually emerge slowly and insidiously. 'Increases in stress, job pressure, competition, higher work complexity, faster pace of life and the greater likelihood of redundancy all make for an inevitable drip, drip of negativity which leads many top managers to burnout,' says Kakabadse.

The problem is compounded in companies where a macho 'can do' culture means that delegating authority is viewed as a sign of weakness. Ambitious young managers can become obsessed with keeping their plates spinning to the detriment of their health. Flatter organizations mean fewer promotions, with people stuck in the same job for longer periods.

'Prolonged demotivation leads to an emotional deterioration which is worsened by a realization that to some extent current lifestyle traps us in our jobs,' says Professor Kakabadse. 'Age, difficulty in matching remuneration packages and the continuity needed to support family life contribute to a sense of being trapped.'

It is often worse for those further down the organization. Evidence suggests that stress is more pronounced among those who are not in control of their own destiny.

Nothing will change, however, until corporate cultures stop implicitly encouraging managers to become workaholics. You may not be able to change your corporate culture, but you can look after yourself better. The first step is to recognize that personal energy is the scarcest resource for the business traveller. Staying power is good, but not if it's at the cost of your health. Manage your energy wisely.

Some health experts also caution the need to take care of your mental and psychological state while you're away. Quite apart from the work stress, you will probably be lonely if your trip is of any length. Advice includes staying in regular touch with family, friends and the office, taking pictures of loved ones, taking a portable tape recorder with favourite music tapes, and a short-wave radio to listen to the news if you are out of range of CNN.

Common sense is the best protection against burnout. Too much work, as we all know, is bad for you. Take a break. Put your job in perspective. Remember, too, that you're in a different place, interacting with a different culture, with different customs, and new sights, sounds – and smells. So take time out to let your imagination and senses take flight. Chill out. Let the frescoes of the soul express themselves. Watch the world go by.

In transit: David Coles

Nationality: British

Job: Managing director DHL

Essentials: Paperwork/reading – good use of time; travelling alarm – hotel ones often very complicated and unreliable; swimming trunks/gym kit – exercise; contact details – in case of problem with schedule; mobile phone – to look important along with everyone else when mobiles are brought out on the bus to the destination terminal.

Key lessons: To regard travel as mobile work time. This makes you productive and reduces stress when there are the inevitable delays. I keep a file in my office of 'things to do/read when travelling'. Also keep your mobile in your briefcase – you will forget it at security otherwise.

Your first aid kit could prove vital. What you take is a matter of personal preference – or necessity. Here are some ideas.

Band aids/bandages

Something to cover foot blisters and minor cuts – don't assume you'll be able to buy them. And scissors to cut them.

Insect repellent

Essential where there's malaria (where repellents should contain DEET) and also useful in places like Canada, Scandinavia and Scotland during the summer. Some insect sprays, it is reported, also repel leeches.

Iodine

Iodine purifies water and is also useful for cuts.

Ear drops

Useful for ear infections caused by swimming in the sea or dodgy swimming pools. Also great for recovering from airplane-induced deafness. (Consult a doctor first.)

Pills and tablets

- Pain relievers
- Anti-histamines
- Vitamin pills
- Travel sickness pill or patches
- Fever tablets (paracetamol/acetaminopren)

Keep medicines in their original, labeled containers to avoid problems at customs and carry a copy of your prescriptions and the generic names for the drugs. If a medication is unusual or contains narcotics get your doctor to write a letter confirming you need it.

Condoms

Well, this isn't the Victorian age and they can be hard or embarrassing to buy, or strange, in some countries. Make sure you take a supply if you think you'll need them. Incidentally, some countries may look askance at contraceptive pills or contraceptive devices, especially if a woman is travelling alone. Sound advice for women is to always wear a wedding ring when travelling, whether or not you are married.

Glasses

Pack an extra pair.

Alternative remedies

There is always another way. Alternative medicine is a useful support for any business traveller. The following is an alternative list of various tools you might include when you pack to have on hand to counter the travails of road travel.

- Bring silk eye pillows to block out all light, for relaxation and to enhance power naps.
- Pack very small bottles of various essential oils such as lavender (relaxing), citrus or eucalyptus (stimulating), ylang-ylang (nurturing) to scent bathwater, or to dot on to one's pillowslip or wrists or temple.
- Carry arnica gel and arnica montana for bruises and sprains and backpain.
- Keep an assortment of tea-bags in a plastic baggie in your bag that includes herbals, such as camomile to enhance sleep, liquorice root to aid digestion, green tea as an antioxidant, peppermint as a pick-me-up, and stimulating caffeinated black teas. (Try ones with fruit additives, such as apricot or ginger peach for a special treat when you find your caffeine choices too pedestrian.)
- Use papaya enzyme tablets for indigestion.
- Try Bach Rescue Remedy and/or homeopathic ignatia amara to help alleviate extreme stress or for any unforeseen dire circumstances or big emotional distress.
- Note that nox vomica is a good homeopathic remedy for balancing that last drink you wish you hadn't taken the night before.
- Pack both eyemasks and earplugs to control light and reduce noise pollution.
- Drink bottled spring water. (Don't substitute mineral water; it has high sodium content and will not satisfy your thirst.)
- Bring relaxation tapes, favourite music and a compact CD player with noise-cancelling headphones.
- Carry Coenzyme Q-10 as an antioxidant, to assist with jetlag and to counter radiation in plane cabins.
- Pack 2 oz packets of soy protein powder to stir into orange juice in the mornings for an extra energy punch to start the day, or as an energy snack.
- Carry liquid echinacea and Vitamin C to take at the very, very first sign of a cold or flu to boost immune system. Bring melatonin to help with sleeping.
- Pack small arm and leg weights so you can exercise in your room.

Alternative resources

The Bach Flower Remedies by Edward Bach, MD, and F.J. Wheeler, MD, C.W. Daniel, 1997

Back to Eden by Jethro Kloss, Back to Eden Books, 1985

Everybody's Guide to Homeopathic Medicines by Stephen Cummings, MD and Dana Ullman, MPH, J.P. Tarcher, 1997

drweil.com – a useful alternative health website

Chapter 25 | When it all goes wrong

Even the best and most experienced traveller can get ill (in fact most business travellers, given their punishing schedules and often poor diet on the road, do get ill at some time), so what do you do when things go wrong?

It goes without saying, of course, that medical insurance should be fully up to date and hefty enough to cover likely charges wherever you are, including that of flying you back home. That said, the first stop has to be the front desk of your hotel. Most have doctors and dentists on call who will be able to examine you. The hotel should also be able to help with languages but may still be open to the vagaries of local medical culture.

Your embassy or consular office may also be able to help.

Many seasoned travellers find they get more piece of mind from dedicated travel health services such as US-based WorldClinic, which, at a cost, provides immediate access 24 hours a day to 300 US board-certified doctors for individuals who travel or work abroad. WorldClinic also provides travellers with secure electronic medical records and personalized prescription travel medical kits.

There are also nonprofit organizations dedicated to travel health. The International Association for Medical Assistance to Travelers (IAMAT) is based in Canada with offices in Canada, New Zealand, Switzerland and the United States. IAMAT (**www.sentex.net/~iamat/**) advises travellers of overseas health risks and recommends competent medical care around the globe.

Membership is free and includes a directory of approved doctors in 125 countries and territories.

There is also the US International Society of Travel Medicine (ISTM) whose website (**www.istm.org**) has a country-by-country list of 1200 clinics and doctors in over 50 countries. The site contains links to other travel and medical sites, including the World Health Organization.

What you could catch

Cholera

The International Certificate of Vaccination no longer has a space for details of cholera vaccination. According to the World Health Organization, current cholera vaccines are unreliable and it no longer recommends them. Some countries still need proof of vaccination if travellers are arriving from infected areas.

Diphtheria

Diphtheria is a disease of the skin and throat caused by bacteria. Skin diphtheria is most common in arid regions. Infection is caused by direct contact with contaminated dust or by inhaling droplets from an infected person. Wash regularly and keep the skin clean and dry.

Hepatitis A

Infection comes from contaminated food or water or from direct contact with infected persons. Most travellers from developed areas are susceptible and should be vaccinated.

Hepatitis B

Hepatitis B is a dominant disease in most of the developing world. Infection can occur in a number of ways, including sex, invasive medical treatment, blood transfusion, and tattooing. Vaccination is available.

Malaria

Malaria is common and serious, and widespread in many areas of the world, including Asia, the eastern Mediterranean, South America, Africa and Asia. Vaccinations and prophylactic drugs are widely available but none give complete protection. A key issue is to avoid being bitten by malaria-carrying mosquitoes in the first place. This means keeping well covered by clothes, and using mosquito nets and effective insect repellents.

Polio

Most travellers will have received immunization as a child. But anyone travelling to a developing country should consider further protection.

Plague

Don't laugh, plague is endemic in many parts of the developing world. As it is transmitted by the fleas of rats and other rodents, you may be at risk in areas where there is overcrowding and/or poor sanitation. Antibiotics are available and so are vaccines, though their efficacy is limited and side-effects can be severe.

Rabies

Rabies is common in many parts of the world. If you think you might come into contact with animals or rabies is endemic at your destination, think about vaccination.

Tetanus

Though common, especially in the tropics, infection is comparatively rare. But worth checking that your immunization is up to date.

Typhoid

Typhoid is endemic worldwide but the risk of infection depends to a large extent on hygiene. You're not likely to catch it in your hotel.

Yellow fever

There are two types: 'urban', transmitted via mosquitoes, and 'jungle', which affects animals but which can also be transmitted to humans by mosquito. The disease is restricted to parts of Africa and South America. Vaccination is available but usually at specialized centres.

Chapter 26 | Sleep

The entire underpinnings of our life as business travellers rests firmly on a good night's sleep – or lack thereof. Some of the sleep factors can be controlled or manipulated and others simply cannot. You probably know which ones are within your control. Jetlag, too, is closely linked with sleep patterns. Learning effective ways to reprogramme your body clock can greatly reduce its effects.

Pierce J. Howard, director of research at CentACS (Center for Applied Cognitive Studies) in North Carolina, and author of *The Owner's Manual for the Brain*, has done extensive research on sleep that will help the road warrior lessen the effects of being on the road.

His tips include:

■ Those rising before 6 a.m. to catch early flights should try to ensure their hotel room is dark and quiet, should go to bed as early as possible and upon rising turn on all the lights in their room, to simulate sunrise, which is what normally triggers our body clocks.

■ Exercise no later than several hours before bedtime, as exercise arouses the cortex and that will delay how quickly you are able to sleep. Don't awaken earlier than usual to fit in your exercise routine. The stress of having lost your sleep will cancel out the benefits of the exercise.

■ When flying across time zones, avoid coffee and alcohol in favour of milk, which stimulates melatonin production in the body.

■ Lose weight. Heavier people need more sleep than those who are slender.

■ When sleeping by day is your only option, use both eyemasks and earplugs to try to simulate the night.

■ Do absolutely everything you can in preparation for the next day in order to avoid awakening before dawn.

■ Schedule naps, optimally between noon and 3 pm whenever possible.

Those who nap consistently live longer and reduce heart disease incidence by as much as 30 per cent. Naps are critical for the sleep-deprived: studies indicate naps result in consistent improved performance.

Circadian Technologies, Inc. (www.circadian.com) is a world leader in helping companies and government agencies research and develop human alertness technologies and fatigue countermeasures for 24-hour transportation and industrial operations. 'Under normal circumstances,' says Dr Martin Moore-Ede, the founder and CEO of Circadian Technologies as well as an expert on jetlag, 'the human body's circadian [or biological] clock naturally runs on a 25-hour day. Each day, morning sunlight and other time cues reset our clock by an hour to keep it in synch with our external environment. When we travel across time zones, we can exceed the ability of our circadian clock to automatically adjust.'

We call this jetlag, and it is most likely to have an effect when we are travelling from west to east, where we are more apt to 'lose a day'. Since light is a key factor in resetting our circadian clock Dr Moore-Ede advises that west-to-east travellers seek bright light when departing in the morning but avoid light when departing at night. 'The brighter the light and the longer the exposure,' he counsels, 'the greater the resetting effect.' Conversely, east-to-west travellers departing in the evening can benefit from exposure to bright light, but if leaving during morning hours should avoid bright light by wearing dark glasses and perhaps pulling down their window shades on planes.

Alternative routes to nod

Camomile or sage-flavoured tea is reputed to enhance sleep. The Dutch add a little sage to warm milk to help them have a good night's sleep.

A hot bath with a little lavender oil at the end of your journey before climbing between those sheets will help you get that vital sleep you need for your work the next day.

But, don't be fooled into thinking that alcohol consumption is helping you sleep well! Try to limit drinking alcohol to several hours prior to bedtime, and follow with water.

Sleepy sources

The Pocket Idiot's Guide to Getting a Good Night's Sleep by Dr Martin
   Moore-Ede and Suzanne Le Vert, Macmillan, 1999

The Owner's Manual for the Brain by Pierce J. Howard, Bard Press, 2000

*The Twenty-Four Hour Society: Understanding Human Limits in a World
   That Never Stops* by Dr Martin Moore-Ede, Addison-Wesley, 1993

Websites

www. esrs.org (European Sleep Research Society)

www.sleepfoundation.org (National Sleep Foundation)

www.circadian.com (Circadian Technologies, Inc.)

www.centacs.com (CentACS Center for Applied Cognitive Studies)

www. med.stanford.edu/school/psychiatry.humansleep (Stanford
   University Center for Human Sleep Research) – This site has a fabulous
   links page.

www.sleepnet.com – This is the most fun of the sites, begun by someone who did sleep research at Stanford University.

The business tourist: Watts Wacker

Nationality: American

Job: Futurist

In short: Just think of 'a plane as a bus'. There is no magic in it any more.
   Business class should be renamed 'the bitter class'. The Park Hyatt in
   Chicago is world class … brand new, too. Also, the Four Seasons Hong
   Kong.

Favourite country: Netherlands

Favourite airport: None

Number of trips: 100 plus

Essentials: Laptop, cell phone, DVDs, PDA

In-flight worker: Yes … read, write.

Essential activity: I'm intrigued by different types of museum. I like Churchill's war rooms and traditional museums, but also there's something like five museums to the unibomber. What I love about the USA is that we're the only country that builds monuments to its failures – Custer's last stand has a museum; there's a memorial at Pearl Harbor. Going to museums is the cornerstone of learning about different cultures. One of the first things I always do when I visit somewhere is to see what the new museums are.

'Frequent business travellers' are more likely to suffer from psychological disorders than employees who stay put,' concluded a 1997 report by the World Bank. According to a survey by InfoCom, one in four business travellers say their stress is raised by business travel. Reasons cited included time away from family, arranging personal business, travel logistics and keeping up with communications via e-mail, faxes and voicemail. Add to this the personal impact of airport delays, rude people, sound and air pollution, culture change, lack of sleep, fast food and dehydration. The rigours of being on the road are endless and daunting.

A study of claims filed in 1993 by more than 10,000 staff and consultants at the World Bank (Washington, DC) found that men who travelled on business filed 80 percent more health claims than men who did not travel on business. Health problems included gastrointestinal flare-ups from changing diets, back pain from inactivity, and respiratory infections – possibly linked to recirculated air in planes.

The truth is that sustaining the demands of being a businessperson on the road is not unlike sustaining those of a person in training for any rigorous athletic event. Such a lifestyle requires some, well, training! Otherwise one will find oneself in a downward spiral of ever-lessening energy levels facing the mounting and overwhelming challenges required of such a lifestyle. In short, one will burn out.

Sophisticated business travellers who manage to ensure their Mercedes Benz has all its tune-ups, checkups and high-quality fuel and oil and water are sometimes slow on the draw to do the same for themselves. Your precious body is your vehicle (the only one you will ever get) and its require-ments are not unlike your beloved car at home. Annual checkups, paying attention to that weird noise under the hood, a thorough rubbing down and going over and the highest-quality fuel you can access are all requisites to an optimal journey on the road. What to do?

Removing the road

As we travel from location to location, door to far-flung door, plane to taxi, office to café, we are unconsciously picking up a wide variety of unseen baggage. We are collecting germs. We are affected by other people's stresses. We are accruing frustrations. We are picking up energies that are not, technically, ours. When we arrive at the final point in our destinations we owe it to ourselves to stop whatever we are doing and leave that collection of unseen various deposits, if not at the door to our hotel rooms, then shortly after entering, to send them on their way. But how?

Many travellers have found it very useful to wash their hands frequently while on the road. It is also highly recommended that each time you enter your hotel room from the street one of the very first things you do is to wash your hands thoroughly with soap and water. A brief review of all the doorknobs, monies and public objects you have touched in the previous few hours should sway the unconvinced. This single practice could easily spare you the discomforts of many a cold or flu you would otherwise have contracted.

Then what about the other unseen tensions we have collected that we might not think about? That baby crying on the plane? That shuttle delay? The rush hour traffic? That rude fellow at the desk? Did those events pass you by, or did you bring them with you? A good way to find out is to take a few minutes to decompress from the stresses of the day by sitting down in a comfortable chair with your feet flat on the floor, hands lying loosely on your lap with palms turned upward, eyes closed, and taking a nice long deep breath with a longer exhale. Try taking four short breaths in, holding your breath to the count of eight and then exhaling to the count of eight. Do this three times and you will immediately notice your body relaxing.

Now, with eyes remaining closed, focus on your feet, and do a slow conscious body scan, moving your attention slowly through your body, sensing for tensions held in any particular parts of your body. Move your attention from the bottom of your feet slowly upward to the head, pausing in each general area. As you sense any particular tensions you have brought with you from the road, take a slow, deep breath and imagine your exhaled breath moving into that particular part of your body and imagine that breath moving through that tense place. Notice how that part of your body now feels. You might also contract tight muscles and then release those muscles at the same time you imagine breathing through the tension. (Note that this is also a good practice while sitting in an airport waiting for a plane. Then you don't have so much to unload when you do arrive at your destination!)

Following the body review and releasing of tension you might also take the time to do a mental review of the events of the day and release any emotional tensions you might have collected as you interacted with people throughout the day. Forgiveness and acceptance are critical tools for this process. If you had a particularly gruelling exchange, don't expect that this one sitting will clear the air, but you might begin by acknowledging what happened, review from a more relaxed stance, and begin to now process more fully. Later you can return to such upsets or incompletions through deeper inner work through journaling, or in speaking with a trusted friend or boss or partner.

Another consequence of being on the road is tremendous dehydration. One way to counter this, other than drinking water whenever and wherever possible, is to give oneself the luxury of submerging oneself in hot water in the tub in your hotel, to soak amounts of water directly into the skin. One might even sprinkle a very small amount of essential lavender oil into one's bath for greater relaxation. If one is going out again during the day or evening it is better to use a light essential citrus oil such as orange or lemon verbena, or perhaps eucalyptus oil, any of which would promote an uplifting of the spirits, not prepare you for sleep, as lavender does.

If you are feeling particularly adventurous you might light a scented candle. Most good candle shops and healthfood stores now sell aromatherapy candles contained in very small metal containers with their own lids, which are perfect for travelling.

Many of the above suggestions might seem a bit 'far out'. Try one or two ideas and see if you get any results. Eventually you might find that taking the time to incorporate some or all of these tried and true practices will lessen the wear and tear of the road on your own dear self.

Food and water and air

Businesspeople on the run frequently find themselves severely limited on food choices because they are either stuck in airports, on planes, or in hotels or conferences or countries with different menus.

Solution number one? Get in the habit of carrying chewable papaya enzyme tablets in your briefcase or carry-on luggage to pop in your mouth for those inevitable times where you find yourself drastically compromising your diet and suffering dire digestive consequences. Papaya is a huge boon to digestion and these tablets blessedly offer almost instant relief. There are several teas you might also carry for the same purpose, if you have access to hot water. You can always soothe regrettable food choices with camomile, peppermint or liquorice root tea. All three will calm your stomach, and camomile will help you relax and sleep. Don't drink peppermint before bedtime as it could keep you awake: it's a stimulant. All three of these teas are now readily available in teabag form. It's a simple thing to put a few bags in a plastic bag to tuck into a briefcase or purse; they add no weight to what you are carrying and can make the difference between lying in bed in some hotel unable to sleep in stomach pain and getting a good night's rest. Many hotels come equipped with microwaves and cups in one's room, so it's a simple thing to make a refreshing cup of tea. You might also carry a black tea for a caffeine pickup if you do not drink coffee. Do not make the mistake of using the coffeemaker in your room for this purpose, however!

Bottled water is an absolute must for all business travellers. As inconvenient and heavy as it is, it's a good investment to carry a bottle of uncarbonated spring water on every plane you get on. Negotiate with your resistance by knowing it will be gone by the end of the flight.

As impossible to imagine as this is most air carriers still do not routinely stock plain bottled water. (Lufthansa is an exception.) You will end up with carbonated water at best, or soda water at worst, which is simply not the same and does not meet the needs of the body to rehydrate. Rehydration is critical to successful business travel. Those who make the simple commitment to remain hydrated on each and every business trip they make endure the road better. It's too much to ask of the body to travel without water. It is basic, as basic as it gets. Yet people forego water needs because they will have to carry it, it's too hard to get and because they might suffer the inconvenience of climbing over a fellow traveller to make their way to the back of the plane. (Is it any wonder our bodies suffer on the road?)

Speaker, author and well-known pianist Michael Jones, who yearly logs thousands of air miles, agrees. 'Drink lots of water to stay hydrated –

knowing this also involves reserving aisle seats in advance so you don't have to crawl over the two other passengers and the baby who has *finally* drifted to sleep if you have taken a window seat. Also order special meals. I hear kosher is ideal, but if you object for religious reasons, there is always gluten-free which gets you lots of vegetables, digestible meat and fruit for dessert! This may not sound appealing, but it will save your digestive system on long trips.'

It is worthwhile always to carry some healthy food alternative with you so that you do not put yourself in the position that you are an hour from arriving at your destination, stuck in traffic, stuck on a plane, stuck in a line and your blood sugar is plummeting because you had coffee and a doughnut for breakfast and it's all used up. You will feel awful and your body will pay. Instead, opt to carry protein bars (not the very tastiest, admittedly, but not bad) in a bag you can easily access so you have something decent to eat until you can arrive at a place where you can get a full meal. Another miraculous item to carry, generously and perfectly supplied by Mother Nature herself, is an apple. They carry well, are hard to bruise, come in convenient sizes and could become your best friend on the road in a pinch. Nuts and dried fruits also help in a pinch and are durable on the road, a fact known to world travellers for millenia, no doubt.

Though business meetings and schedules often determine how late we eat dinner, it really is best to eat on the early side. Some cultures will not support this practice and some will. Latin Americans are wise in eating the main meal at midday, and opting for lighter fare in the evening. It is not really wise to eat very late and go to bed on a full stomach, though some cultures are so inclined.

Recirculated air on planes has a bad reputation. Airlines reputedly close down some ducts to reduce the costs of the flight. If you suspect you might be on such a flight, feel free to ask the plane attendants if it would be possible to improve the air quality on your flight by making some minor adjustments. Some travellers have put vanity aside and placed dampened handkerchiefs over their noses to add moisture to the dry air to protect their lungs, and to screen germs that are invariably being shared by all on board.

K.H.

Savvy traveller: Richard Coltart

Nationality: British

Why travel?: No one would travel frequently these days who didn't have to. It is not fun, it is no longer comfortable, it is rarely enjoyable. If meetings with clients could be conducted via video conferencing (or whatever technologies may appear) they would already be happening. It is, however, impossible to measure the amount of travelling that is not occurring because of new technology.

Basics: Travel light, plan ahead.

Work: Now that hotels provide individual fax machines in a bedroom (and also connections for laptops), it is much easier to work in a hotel.

Chapter 28 | Keeping in shape

It pays to stay in hotels that offer gyms replete with exercise machines, tracks for walking, jacuzzis, massage therapists, saunas, and swimming pools. This affords one the facilities one needs to readily care for oneself out on the road. If you know you are going to be sitting on a plane all day, schedule a run before you leave for the airport. Or at the very least stretch. There is no better way to start a productive day than to get the body moving. The energy generated from an early morning routine will upgrade the tenor of your day and sustain you into the wee hours, if need be.

If your hotel does not sport these amenities, consider joining a health club that offers international facilities such as 24 Hour Fitness network, called Fitness Holdings Europe in the EU, and California Fitness in Asia. In addition to health clubs in 15 states in the USA, they have facilities in Norway, Denmark, Sweden, Spain, Germany, Hong Kong, Singapore, Korea, Thailand and Taiwan. (For more info on how to join and the availability of health clubs in your area go to **24hourfitness.com** and check out the Clubs page.) Health clubs not only offer exercise equipment but also ongoing aerobic and yoga classes you could tap into as you journey from town to town or country to country. Often membership in one club will be honoured at another. Check with sales to see if your membership can be used at other clubs. Also consider that the YMCA can be found throughout the USA and 120 countries worldwide. Visit their website at **ymca.net** for a listing of US facilities on the home page, or click on YWorld on the home page to find a listing of international facilities or affiliated facilities. Additional information can be obtained in the USA by calling 1-888-333-YMCA.

New York Times number one bestselling author and nationally syndicated business columnist Harvey Mackay, chairman of the $85 million Mackay Envelope Corporation, offers the following advice: 'Exercise is good for your mind as well as your body. I've always been active in sports, but one of the best decisions I ever made was when I became a runner over 25 years ago. Now, with ten marathons under my belt, I feel qualified to tell you what a difference it's made in my work life. I follow a pretty hectic schedule. Who doesn't? Being in shape keeps my energy high and my attitude positive. If your company has gym facilities or offers subsidies on health club member-ships, consider yourself fortunate indeed and take advantage of this valuable benefit.' Mackay's Motto? 'The human body is the only machine that wears out faster if it is not used.' In lieu of formal facilities such as gyms and health clubs, ask hotel clerks where you might safely run or walk near the hotel or on a local beach. Even a slow methodical walk after dinner helps restore the body. The Rand Corporation, a policy research organi-zation, estimates that for every mile an individual walks, society saves 24 cents in medical and healthcare costs. Public parks can also be taken advantage of, or schedule a round of golf where possible. Try to take full advantage of whatever the locale you find yourself in affords you. It takes extra effort, just when you might feel that the last thing you want to do is to track down a new place to be, but the restorative energies will make it all worthwhile.

Lastly, don't forget to explore day spas as you travel on business. These are a great way to nurture the body and soul on the road. You can access good information about day spas by going to **spafinder.com**. Note that Spa Finders does not make reservations for day spas, but they list those all over the USA on their Gift Certificate page. They plan to add listings for day spas throughout Europe and Asia as they have noticed that corporations are buying gift certificates to day spas for their employees, a good tip.

Spas are beginning to show up inside hotels. The new Fairmont Vancouver Airport Hotel offers soaker tubs in each room, in-room body treatments, and a full spa including just-for-men services, massage, hand and foot care, body scrubs and wraps and hydrotherapy (**www.fairmont.com**). Hopefully this is the wave of the future and road warriors, weary selves will be able to find respite on every desolate shore. Enjoy!

K.H.

Savvy traveller: Douglas Urquhart

Nationality: British

Job: Partner, Weil, Gotshal & Manges LLP, a leading New York law firm

Ticketing: Even if you are flying coach, which now seems to be standard corporate policy for US travellers on flights of under five hours, do not let your travel department buy a restricted ticket. You need absolute flexibility with refunds and exchanges. Also, opt for paper tickets over e-tickets, since currently only paper tickets can be quickly exchanged for use on another airline.

Flight times: Even if it means you are not getting air miles on your preferred airline, it is always preferable to fly non-stop. If you are flying eastbound overnight (particularly to Europe from the USA) and have difficulty sleeping on planes, select an early evening flight (arriving in the early morning hours), arrange for early check-in at your hotel, and try to sleep for a couple of hours before your first meeting. Traffic from the airport to your hotel should be light, and you will find that even two hours' sleep is better than none. For those who can sleep on planes, the late-night flight works better.

US immigration: If you make frequent business trips to the United States (over three trips a year) and are a citizen of an eligible country, apply for an INS pass. You can apply at major US international gateways and, if you are approved, the pass can be used when you next return to the United States. INS Pass is an automated system which enables you to proceed through US immigration without seeing an immigration officer (the pass is read by a machine which verifies your handprint). At busy times, for example in the summer months and especially if you are not a US citizen or green card holder, the INS pass can save you 45 minutes to an hour of waiting. The INS pass needs to be renewed annually.'

Y ou don't have to worry just about your health when you travel abroad – you need to be on guard to protect your own safety. In high-risk areas, the dangers can include the risk of being kidnapped, for ransom or as a political act, and being involved in terrorism.

Your company may have a corporate security arm and it is worth talking to them before you leave. But there are some basic precautions you can take when you are abroad.

In most Western countries, government agencies, such as the US State Department, publish information sheets for virtually every country of the world. These normally cover entry and currency regulations, health, crime and security information, political disturbances, areas of instability, special information about driving and road conditions and drug penalties. They generally also list addresses and emergency telephone numbers for embassies and consulates.

In some dangerous situations, such government agencies may even advise their nationals not to travel to certain areas or to leave them as soon as possible. These announcements are normally made over public broadcast media or in newspapers. They should be adhered to since your government may not be able to help if you ignore such warnings and get into trouble.

Safety and women

According to research commissioned by US hotel group Wyndham's Women on Their Way programme (www.womenontheirway.com) in 1999 men took only 3.6 more trips per year than women did. Men averaged 38.6 per year. Women averaged 35 trips annually. In 1997, men took 34.2 trips per year, women 19.3.

Wyndham suggests a number of steps women travellers can take to improve their safety.

At the hotel

- Place a Do Not Disturb sign on the door to discourage anyone from entering your room while you're away.

- Always check window and door locks.

- Check with the front desk before opening your door to determine if room service or a bellman is really on their way.

- Use your luggage to prop the hotel room door open and check the closets and shower before closing the door.

- Keep the room curtains closed.

- If it's late at night or you feel uncomfortable, ask that hotel security accompany you to your room.

- Order room service for two, and ask for a pair of keys upon check-in.

In cars, parking lots and waiting areas

- Check under your vehicle and those immediately around it.

- Put your luggage key on a ring with a small, high-powered flashlight.

- When arriving at night, prearrange for a car service to meet you.

- If you're renting a car, study a city map before you travel. Familiarize yourself with the town before you get there.

- Make sure you don't have the route to your hotel marked on a map and conveniently lying on the seat of that rental car for someone to see.

- Make sure the car you rent has in-state licence plates. Out-of-state plates signal that you're a visitor – and therefore more vulnerable.

On the plane

- If something goes wrong aloft, women are just as vulnerable as men. Like any good frequent flyer, know the emergency evacuation procedures, and consider carrying a smoke hood.

- When talking to the person in the seat next to you, don't talk about where you'll be staying. The conversation might be overheard by another person and put you at risk.

Stay safe

Don't

- Dress in flashy or ostentatious clothes, try to fit in.
- Carry expensive luggage.
- Leave money and other valuables in your hotel room while you are out. Use the hotel safe. But always carry a little cash. If you are mugged it's safer to have something to hand over.
- Make a show of large amounts of money. Make sure your credit card is returned to you after each transaction.
- Visit seedy bars or strip clubs. You're likely to be ripped off but even worse they have been known to spike customers' drinks.

Do

- Travel by non-stop flights where possible.
- Make sure your office and home know exactly where you should be at any time.
- Check government travel advice for the area you are visiting.
- Keep your hotel door locked at all times. Meet visitors in the lobby.
- Read the fire safety instructions in your hotel room and know where the nearest fire exit is. Counting the doors between your room and the nearest exit can be a lifesaver if you have to crawl through a smoke-filled corridor.
- Only exchange money at legitimate outlets.
- Report theft or loss at once to the police and keep any report for insurance purposes. Report loss of travellers cheques and credit cards to the issuing companies, loss of airline tickets to the airline or travel agent, and loss of passport to your embassy or consulate.
- Travel light. You will be able to move more quickly and are more likely to have a free hand. You will also be less tired and less likely to set your luggage down, leaving it unattended.
- Carry as few valuables as you really need. If you must carry your passport, credit cards or cash, conceal them in several places rather than one. Avoid handbags and outside pockets, which are easy targets for thieves. Inside pockets and a

sturdy shoulder bag with the strap worn across your chest are a bit safer. Consider a pouch or money belt worn under your clothing.

- Use travellers cheques and credit cards instead of cash.

- Take an extra set of passport photos plus a photocopy of your passport information page. This makes it easier to replace your passport if it is lost or stolen. Do the same for airline tickets, driver's licence and credit cards. Leave copies at home and at the office as well.

- Leave a copy of the serial numbers of your traveller's cheques at home and at the office.

- Generally it's safer to stay in larger, international, hotels. They usually have better security.

- Make sure you know the limits on your credit cards and don't overstep them. Some travellers have been arrested for going over their credit limit. Make sure you know how to contact your credit card company to report the loss of your card from abroad.

Terrorism and kidnap

Every business traveller is at risk from terrorist incidents or being kidnapped, though obviously the risks vary from country to country. A number of tragic incidents in recent years involving business travellers and ex-pat employees have highlighted the dangers. In more dangerous parts of the world, experienced business travellers report that they try to avoid leaving the relative safety of their hotel unless it is strictly necessary.

The rules for staying out of trouble are similar to those for avoiding crime or other violence. Travel non-stop where possible and avoid stops in high-risk airports; don't discuss your plans in public; avoid advertising yourself, by your clothes or behaviour, as a businessman or woman and stay away from possible terrorist targets such as places where non-nationals congregate; be alert for suspicious packages or unattended luggage.

Travel to high-risk areas is sometimes inevitable, but requires a high level of preparation and caution. The US State Department, for example, recommends: discussing with your family what they would do in the event of an emergency and making sure your affairs are in order before leaving home; registering with your embassy or consulate when you arrive; remaining friendly but being cautious about discussing personal matters, your itinerary or programme; leaving no personal or business papers in your hotel room; watching for people following you or people observing your comings and goings; keeping a mental note of safe havens, such as police stations, hotels, hospitals; letting someone you trust know what your travel plans are and keeping them informed if your plans change; avoiding predictable times and routes of travel; reporting any suspicious activity to local police and your embassy or consulate.

It also suggests that you should be certain to choose your own taxi cabs at random and never take a vehicle that is not clearly identified as a taxi. If possible, travel with others. Don't meet strangers at unknown or remote locations. And don't open your hotel door to anyone you don't know. Refuse unexpected packages and have a plan of action for what you will do if a bomb explodes or there is gunfire nearby.

If you are driving, check for loose wires or other suspicious circumstances around your car and make sure it is in good condition in case you need to resort to high-speed or evasive driving. Drive with car windows closed in crowded streets. Bombs can be thrown through open windows. If you are ever in a situation where somebody starts shooting, drop to the floor or get as low as possible. Don't move until you are sure the danger has passed. Do not attempt to help rescuers and do not pick up a weapon. If possible, shield yourself behind or under a solid object. If you must move, crawl on your stomach.

Top ten countries in total kidnappings, 1999

1 Brazil
2 Colombia
3 Former Soviet Union
4 India
5 Mexico
6 Nigeria
7 Philippines
8 Russia
9 Venezuela
10 Yemen

Source: Control Risks Group. (These results are based on kidnappings the Control Risks Group has confirmed and about which it has gathered information. They may not represent the full extent of the problem.)

In transit: Costas Markides

Nationality: Cypriot

Job: Professor of strategic and international management and chairman of the Strategy Department, London Business School

Best hotel: Hostellerie La Butte aux Bois, in Lanaken, Belgium in a virtual tie with Le Mirador Hotel in Vevey, Switzerland.

Favourite country to visit on business: USA (especially the East Coast)

Favourite airport: Copenhagen (especially the SAS lounge!) followed closely by Heathrow (for shopping)

Frequency: 20 business trips a year

Always takes: Academic articles to read on the flights!

Horrible discovery No. 1: Hotels charge anything they want on your bill. The bill usually ends up with your client without you seeing it first. The client pays without bothering to ask whether you really incurred those ridiculous charges that appear on the bill. End result: hotel gets paid for whatever they care to put on your bill (and believe me, they do get away with murder)!

Horrible discovery No. 2: Airlines don't really care who you are or if you are a Gold Card Executive Club member. At every opportunity, they will try to squeeze you.

6

Behaving yourself

'What affects men sharply about a foreign nation is not so much finding or not finding familiar things; it is rather not finding them in the familiar place.'

G. K. CHESTERTON, BRITISH WRITER

Chapter 30 | Travelling with an open mind

In a global economy, it's more important than ever to know how they do things in other countries. A basic grounding in the dos and don'ts of international business etiquette can prevent red faces and a deal-killing faux pas. For the business traveller, the famous business maxim applies: Think global; act local.

The key to successfully navigating cultural currents is a genuine respect for other cultures. When in Rome, try to see the world as an Italian might. It's not easy. It's natural to feel off-balance in unfamiliar surroundings. Understanding that we simplify in order to make ourselves feel less vulnerable is the key. It is a defensive reaction to impose simplistic explanations on the behaviour of others. In a sense, it is a way to cover our own discomfort. The business traveller who accepts his or her cultural inadequacies will fare better than one who tries to pigeon-hole people and rides rough-shod over their cultural sensitivities. We might not understand the language or the customs, therefore we seek simple answers to explain the differences.

Cultural stereotypes are rarely helpful when dealing with individuals. Not all Americans are pushy and loud; not all English people are reserved and formal; not all Frenchmen love wine and food. The same is true of any culture. There will always be individuals you meet who do not match up to the cultural average. It is also worth remembering that out of necessity even the best sources of information tend to generalize.

Once they take root, cultural misconceptions and myths can be stubbornly resistant to reality. In 1940, for example, an amateur linguist misinterpreted some 1911 research of Eskimo languages. The linguist, Benjamin Lee Whorf claimed that while English has only one word for snow, Eskimo has many, with separate words for falling snow, slushy snow, and so on.[1]

Whorf's article contained two major errors. First, English has several words for snow, including powder, sleet and slush. Second, comparing word-counts between radically different languages has little meaning. The

Inuits (the modern term for Eskimo) make extensive use of prefixes and suffixes, combining several concepts into a long, compound word. English speakers can say the same thing by using several words instead of one long one. For example, in Inuktitut (an Inuit language), the generic term for snow is 'aput'. In English we add an adjective to describe the concept of 'new snow'. Inuktitut expresses the same concept by adding suffixes to make the single word 'aputiqarniq'.

Whorf's observation that Inuits use many words for snow was misleading. But it became widely accepted. Some reports put the number at 50, or 100, or even 200 words. The linguists at Canada's Department of Indian and Northern Affairs now report 'over 30' variations of Inuktitut words for snow, all of them based on just a few root words.

Few of us are conducting business deals with the Inuit. But we've all heard misinformation about other cultures. We need to regard these preconceived ideas with scepticism before travelling internationally. Take another stereotype: you only do business with men in Muslim countries. While Muslim countries usually place more restrictions on the activities of women than they do on men, there are still women in positions of power in Muslim countries. Pakistan – a predominantly Muslim country – had a woman prime minister, Benazir Bhutto. Turkey, which is officially secular but is predominantly Muslim, has almost as many women executives as men.

Furthermore, everyone is an individual. There are undoubtedly Italians who don't gesture when talking, and Japanese who never apologize. So, when you embark on that business trip overseas, try to leave behind any preconceptions based on suspect sources such as jokes or movies. And, while books and articles by experts are useful, don't expect every individual to act in predictable ways. Take along some humility, plenty of respect and an open mind on your travels, and you will find that you encounter individuals far more often than cultural stereotypes.

Culture at work

A useful point comes from cultural diversity experts Fons Trompenaars and Peter Woolliams who have examined cross-border acquisitions, mergers and alliances. They estimate these are worth in excess of $2000 billion annually. Yet, two out of three deals don't achieve anywhere near the initially antici-pated benefits.[2]

They believe that relational aspects like cultural differences and lack of trust are responsible for 70 per cent of alliance failures. Building trust is a cultural challenge in itself. Lack of trust, say Trompenaars and Woolliams, is often caused by different views of what constitutes a trustworthy partner. In addition, intercultural alliances involve differences in corporate cultures as well as national cultures. Problems can be due to perceptions about each other, including perceptions of national culture.

In short, culture is pervasive. Trompenaars and Woolliams advocate that *cultural due diligence* should be a priority for companies just as financial due diligence is. The resolution of cultural differences, they say, should be based on the three Rs: recognition, respect and reconciliation. The message is one that the business traveller should also heed.

The fact is that cultural nuances pervade all aspects of global business. Platform speaking and presentations are an especially thorny issue for the business traveller. Giving a presentation to a roomful of prospective clients in a foreign country is a difficult task. Even as they stride toward the podium, exuding confidence, the cultural banana skins await for unwary executives. They may have a polished and well-rehearsed speech that goes down well at home, but that is no guarantee of success in another country.

Even thanking their host is riven with potential problems. Much depends on what part of the world they are in. They have to be sure that they use the host's correct title, get his or her name in the right order, and get the pronunciation right. Should they use their host's first name? While this is perfectly acceptable in the US, it is likely to be frowned upon in many other countries. In Latin America, for example, titles are very important and people should generally be addressed by their title alone, such as 'Professor' or 'Doctor'.

If they try to use humour to loosen their audience up, their cultural footing becomes even more precarious. Russians, for example, have an ironic sense of humour, but may not appreciate having their noses rubbed in their economic troubles. While in Germany, and other parts of Northern Europe, business is taken very seriously: a German business audience will not react well to someone cracking jokes. Humour is not usually part of presentations, negotiations or business in general. German executives, as well as those from Sweden, Switzerland and other Central and Northern European countries can appear stuffy to an Anglo-Saxon manager. What they respond well to are preparation, planning, knowledge, experience and competence. A presentation must be smooth and well rehearsed, from the very beginning. Assertions must be backed up by data. Comparison advertising – which attacks a competitor – is regarded as crass. Punctuality is important.

Graphical presentations, too, are problematical. If a multimedia presentation includes triangles and bold swathes of yellow, they may be unsuitable for many Asian clients. Triangles carry negative connotations for Koreans. In general, red is a good colour for graphics used in Asia. Red is considered lucky, especially among Chinese, but, confusingly, it can also symbolize death. To make life even more fraught, to make a good first impression anywhere with a graphic presentation, it is important to take into consideration whether the audience reads left-to-right, right-to- left or vertically: this could have a direct bearing on their understanding of what is pictured.

This may seem to be over-complicating matters in the opening moments of a presentation. But if you and your company have already invested a lot of time and money just to get to this point, then cultural trapdoors are best avoided. Unfortunately, there is no easy solution. The fact remains that the idea of a presentation that will be well received anywhere in the world is misconceived. It is much better to try to adjust your message to local circumstances. The best people to ask are your local contacts. Remember, navigating cultures requires the three Rs – recognition, respect and reconciliation.

In transit: Jan Lapidoth

Nationality: Swedish

Job: Publisher, talent spotter

Best hotel: Triton in SFO (San Francisco), central, funky and reasonable (Jerry Garcia Suite)

Favourite country to visit on business: UK – never boring

Favourite airport: Copenhagen – big, well designed and with a certain ambiance

Frequency: 10 trips per year – wish they were fewer.

Always takes: A good book – I hate to be left alone with an airport magazine.

Blunders and faux pas

Every country has its cultural no-nos. Unwary business travellers can unintentionally insult their hosts without even realizing it. What makes this such a difficult area is that the cultural subtleties are so idiosyncratic. Here are some examples:

Germany

Always knock before you open an office door. Office furniture may seem far apart, but moving your chair closer is insulting to your host.

Saudi Arabia

Everyone is subject to strict Islamic law. Alcohol (and pornography) are strictly taboo.

Mexico

The family is central to every aspect of life. Nepotism is an accepted part of the culture; criticism of it is taken as an insult.

China

Business leaders are highly sensitive to sovereignty issues. Things must be done their way or not at all. For Westerners this can be frustrating, but should be respected. Chinese people put a lot of store in business relationships; to rush this process is insulting. Business is built on a solid relationship between the two parties. You should plan your trip accordingly, allowing sufficient time for getting to know contacts before moving on to try to clinch a deal.

India

Combines many different cultures and cultural taboos. Be alert to your surroundings. Hindu tradition reveres cattle; do not wear leather. The caste system is also taken very seriously.

United Kingdom

Change is not necessarily a good thing in the UK. Many businesspeople prefer old, well-made clothes to new fashions. You can't always tell a book by its cover.

Egypt

As in all Islamic countries, use the right hand in preference to the left (which is considered unclean).

Argentina

Manners in Argentina maketh the businessman or woman. Informality and casualness can make a very poor first impression.

Notes

1 *IndustryWeek*, 24 March 1998
2 *Economist*, 9 January 1999

Fons Trompenaars's research over almost two decades – involving thousands of employees in more than 50 countries – makes him a leading expert on cultural differences. His work indicates the existence of four broad types of culture, giving rise to four styles of management, which he has called:

- the Family
- the Eiffel Tower
- the Guided Missile
- and the Incubator.[1]

Family model

This is typical of cultures as seemingly disparate as France, Italy, Japan and India. The result is a power-oriented corporate culture in which the leader is regarded as the caring head of the family who best knows what should be done and what is good for subordinates. Japanese companies re-create aspects of the traditional family. The idealized relationship is called *sempai-kokai*, that between an older and younger brother. The relationship to the company is long term and devoted. The head of the family encourages discussion about issues and decisions, because that is the way he ensures agreement.

Eiffel Tower model

This model is typified by the approach of German companies where authority stems from the occupancy of a given role with prescribed decision-making powers and areas of accountability. Job specifications with clearly defined areas of responsibility form a superstructure within which the members of the organization operate. Each successive level in the hierarchy has a clear and demonstrable function of holding together the levels beneath it to maintain the management edifice. Subordinates obey not because of emotional ties reminiscent of a family, but because it is their role in the scheme of things to obey the person immediately above them.

Guided Missile model

This model is so-called because it is based on a view of the organization as a missile homing in on strategic objectives and targets. British companies as well as many American and Swedish companies are typical of this type of organization. The culture is oriented towards tasks and objectives, usually undertaken by teams or project groups. It differs from both the Family and Eiffel Tower models because roles are not fixed. The over-riding principle is to do whatever it takes to complete a task or reach a goal. This is reflected in the decision-making style, which is often time-rather than issues-driven.

Incubator model

Typified by the companies of California's Silicon Valley, this is distinctively Californian in outlook. These organizations, which now include many new economy companies, are structured around the fulfilment of the individual members' needs and aspirations. In this model the management framework of the organization exists to free individuals from routine tasks so they can pursue creative activities. The only legitimate management function is to protect and enrich the efforts of individuals. These organizations are made up of knowledge workers who demand a high level of discretionary decision-making power.

It is where these four sets of cultural assumptions play against each other, says Trompenaars, that things can go wrong. Where problems occur it is often because the decision-making style or formula used does not take account of the different cultural values.

Terry Brake, author of *The Global Leader*, is another who has researched the impact of cultural differences on business. He notes that contact among cultures is of more than anthropological interest. 'A clash of cultures affects the bottom line directly and can destroy a potentially rewarding joint venture or strategic alliance.'[2]

The business press is full of stories in which highly successful companies have suddenly become grounded on the hidden sand banks of international cultural differences. As Brake points out: 'On paper, Corning's joint venture with the Mexican glass manufacturer Vitro seemed made in heaven. Twenty-five months after it began, the marriage was over. Cultural clashes had eroded the potentially lucrative relationship.' What happened? American managers were continually frustrated by what they saw as the slowness of Mexican decision making. Compared to the USA, Mexico is a hierarchical culture and only top managers make important decisions. Loyalty to these managers is a very high priority in Mexico, and to try to work around them is definitely taboo. The less urgent Mexican approach to time made scheduling very difficult. The Mexicans thought the Americans wanted to move too fast, and vice versa. Communication was also problematic, and not simply because of language.

'American directness clashed with the indirectness of the Mexicans. The Americans often thought that the Mexican politeness was an attempt to hide problems and faults. Corning also thought Vitro's sales style was unaggressive. Over time, the differences were felt to be unbridgeable.'

Corning's experience is by no means unique. Disney's experience in France is another high-visibility example. EuroDisney was referred to in British and French newspapers as Corporate America's cultural Vietnam or Chernobyl.

In another case, the sportswear manufacturer Nike withdrew a line of sports shoes. The original design included a motif that resembled the symbol for Allah, and was deemed disrespectful to people in the Arab world, especially since the shoes would inevitably become dirty. Clearly, the designers at Nike could have made an earlier decision to remove the offending emblem had they had a better understanding of that culture.

Procter & Gamble had a rocky start in Japan, too. Its decision to use an aggressive style of TV advertising (which knocked the competition) offended the Japanese taste for surface harmony, or wa, and damaged P&G's initial credibility.

In transit: Fons Trompenaars

Nationality: Dutch

Job: Consultant and author

Best hotel: I love the New York Palace Hotel, because it is centrally located, has a great cuisine and fitness room. Superb service and my wife likes it.

Favourite country to visit on business: USA because the audience is so enthusiastic and has my sense of humor.

Favourite airport: Singapore

requency: Approximately 100 trips a year

Always takes: My Dell laptop with two batteries lasting eight hours in total.

Notes

1 Trompenaars, Fons, *Riding the Waves of Culture*, Nicholas Brealey, 1993.

2 Brake, Terence, *The Global Leader*, Irwin, 1997.

Chapter 32 | Dress to impress

Behaving yourself is not just a matter of attitude. It is also about how you look. We all know that first impressions are important. Research among job interviewers indicates that most people make up their minds about someone they've just met within the first couple of minutes. Once that impression is made it is very difficult to change. How you present yourself matters.

The first and most obvious impression is how you dress. It speaks volumes about you and your attitude towards those you are meeting. Business dress codes are changing, but don't assume that they have changed. The right clothes can help close the cultural gap. In Western countries, the advent of the new economy has accelerated the introduction of casual wear around the world. Even the British prime minister is looking to escape. Tony Blair recently observed: 'It's one of the tyrannies of modern life that men have to dress in conventional suits the whole time. I am trying to get out of suits.' Many companies now allow 'dress-down' Fridays or have gone the whole hog and allow employees and managers to wear casual clothes all week. However, even these organizations often specify traditional business dress for meeting clients, customers or suppliers. (Some have now also introduced dress codes for casual wear – jeans are OK but not if they're scruffy jeans.)

In some Western countries, the suit may be dead as a workaday corporate uniform, but dressing for success has never been harder. The demise of collar and tie has introduced many more permutations. These changes are not welcomed by everyone. The chief executive of the UK subsidiary of a multinational works open necked. He relates a salutary tale. On a recent visit to a once austere investment bank, he was greeted by a pin-striped executive who, much to his evident disgust, had just been told by memo that dressing down was now acceptable in his firm. The investment banker was clearly not impressed by what he regarded as a decline in corporate standards. He is not alone.

For the traveller the rule of thumb must be to assume that dress will be formal unless it is known to be otherwise. Some countries, especially in Northern Europe, would be shocked if a visitor (man or woman) turned up in anything other than a suit. Even in hot climates, ubiquitous air conditioning means that the same rules apply.

In some religious countries formality also implies modesty. In many Islamic countries, shorts are not acceptable even as casual wear. Even in cosmopolitan cities such as Istanbul women should ensure that their upper arms and shoulders are covered at all times. As a rule, women should wear loose rather than tight clothing.

In Saudi Arabia, for example, air conditioning is common, so businesspeople should expect to wear full business suits to a first meeting. If it seems appropriate, men can dispense with ties and jackets at subsequent meetings. Despite the heat, legs and upper arms must be kept covered. Shorts are a no-no, even for casual wear. Many foreigners have fallen foul of the Matawain (religious police). Clothes may not be tight; women, especially, should wear loose-fitting clothes. Baggy clothes also make sitting on a floor or cushion more comfortable.

In transit: Bruce Tulgan

Nationality: American

Job: Founder of Rainmaker Thinking

Best hotel: I can always recommend The Ritz Carlton – the Ritz Carlton Naples is pure luxury. The Fairmont in San Francisco is the best city hotel I know. The Inn at Spanish Bay has an awesome gym and really wonderful outdoor fireplaces on the patio, as well as the most beautiful golf course that follows along the Pacific coast. The Four Seasons in Georgetown is great because the treadmills in the gym each have their own television and VCR and they have a video library. All of the above on the condition that someone else is paying, of course.

Favourite country to visit on business: The UK (so I can fly British Airways first class, which is the best flight I know of: I am pretty sure that's where people go when they die if they have been good on Earth).

Favourite airport: Schiphol for design; Pittsburgh for shopping; Washington Reagan for ease of in and out.

Frequency: 150 trips per year

Always takes: Credit card, book, picture of my wife.

Chapter 33 | Meeting and greeting

How you introduce yourself is also important. Today, in almost every country around the world the common rule in business is to shake hands on meeting and leaving. In a group, you should shake hands with everyone present. Keep handshakes gentle. Few people are impressed by having their knuckles crushed. Those tempted to dismiss such formalities might consider that the reasons for shaking hands go beyond good manners. The handshake is a symbolic offering of the hand of friendship. Psychologists have also found that appropriate tactile contact is an acceptable way to move into another person's personal space, and can help break down barriers.

The onus here is on what is culturally appropriate. It is unlikely that men will have to experience a kiss from other men. Even when this is common practice, in Russia for example, it is usually reserved for friends. Similarly, women generally kiss only other women who are friends. Male to female kisses in a business context, even among close associates, should be brief and chaste.

In Asia, a handshake may be preceded by a brief bow from the waist. In some Asian countries the degree of politeness offered may depend on the status of the visitor.

Using an appropriate level of familiarity with names is also important. Though globalization is leading to many countries adopting the informal business practices of the Anglo-Saxon world, travellers can still find themselves caught out by the cultural minefield of forms of address. The general rule is to be formal until invited to do otherwise. In Europe outside the UK (and even there often) early use of first names is seen as over-familiarity and is frowned on. (Likewise, do not use familiar forms of the second person singular – *tu* and *du* in French and German, for example – until the other person suggests you might like to.)

Names are, of course, a potential source of trouble for innocents abroad. Most people are probably aware that Chinese names come in the opposite order to those in the West, with the family name first followed by the given name (sometimes with a middle name in between). Hence Wu Jichuan is Mr Wu. (But watch out for 'westernized' Chinese names, notably in Taiwan, where a Western first name may precede the Chinese family name.) Names are also in 'reverse' order in some other Asian countries such as Thailand and South Korea though not in Japan, where given names precede family names.

Essential Links

www.xe.com/ucc/
Universal currency convertor

Hispanic cultures frequently use the family names of both father and mother (father's first). Both are used in writing but generally only the father's in spoken address. In Latin America, people with professional or academic titles such as doctor or professor may prefer to be addressed by those titles alone.

Russian names follow the Western style but the middle name is a 'patronymic' derived from the father's given name. For example, Anna Arkadyevna Karenin is Mrs Karenin though it is also respectful to call her Anna Arkadyevna. Note that in Russian women take a feminine form of their husband's name – strictly it is Anna Arkadyevna Karenina but non-Russian speakers can probably ignore this with impunity.

Arabic names are similar, with a middle patronymic denoting son of, *bin*, or daughter of, *bint*. The title sheik is widespread and may denote either a princely ruler or someone versed in the Koran. This title is used in conjunction with the person's given name. Non-titled individuals may be addressed in a variety of ways and it is polite to ask how they wish to be referred to.

Business in the UK is almost as informal as in the USA with first names used easily and without waiting to be invited. However, a number of leading UK businessmen have received titles as a mark of respect for their business success and this can be a quicksand for foreigners.

The British system of hereditary or bestowed titles deserves a book in itself – indeed there are many such guides. A knight is referred to as 'Sir' plus the given name – 'Sir John'. His wife is Lady Anne. The female equivalent of a knight (a dame) is also Lady Anne though sometimes Dame Anne, but her husband is *not* Sir John. A lord is referred to as 'Lord' plus family name – Lord McDonald – or assumed or family title – Lord Cranberry. Never 'My Lord'.

The intricacies of baronets and baronesses and the rest are too involved to go into here. If in doubt, smile politely and use 'sir' or 'ma'am' (pronounced marm or mam). You may if you wish give a 'court bow', a slight downward inclination of the head, to anyone above the rank of knight, but this is not expected. Only bow properly or curtsey to royalty.

In transit: Barnett J. Fletcher

Nationality: British

Job: Chairman of Langmoor Communications Group

Favourite hotel: W New York

Favourite country to visit on business: USA

Favourite airport: Grantley Adams, Barbados, because I know when I arrive I'm on my way to my house!

Frequency: Too many (20ish trips per year). Investing in video conferencing.

Always takes: Photos of my kids, mobile phone, laptop, clean shreddies.

Business cards

It may seem an obvious point, but on any trip make sure you have plenty of business cards. Many cultures expect to exchange cards on first meeting and you may be embarrassed if you don't have any. (You will also go down in the respect of the people you are meeting.)

Ideally, you should have your business card translated into the local language of wherever you are visiting on one side, again as a mark of respect. The other side should be in your own language. Keep card design simple and straight-forward and avoid colours. In many Asian countries, for example, red is considered a 'lucky' colour though it can also, confusingly, be associated with death. In South Korea triangles have negative connotations. Other colours such as green and yellow may have specific connotations in certain areas. So if your company logo is a riot of colour, best consult an expert. Remember, too, that many cultures read from right to left or vertically and this can affect their interpretation of logos and other graphics.

Some cultures regard business cards as an extension of the person's status. Respecting the card shows you respect them. When exchanging business cards:

- Take your time. It's impossible to convey respect if you fling your card at someone. In Japan, and some other Asian countries, it is respectful to present your card with both hands and hold the card you receive with both as you read. Don't forget, either, that in many Asian and Middle Eastern countries the left hand is regarded as 'unclean', so avoid giving or receiving business cards with that hand.

- Make sure you read the other person's card carefully as soon as you are given it; in most Asian countries this is expected as a mark of respect.

- While you may write on your own card, never write on someone else's business card.

Not all communication is verbal and gesturing is a common practice in every culture. This, too, can lead to misunderstandings. Inevitably, some gestures common in the Western world have confusing or even opposite meanings in other cultures. Here are some examples:[1]

The 'A-OK' sign

With the palm out, the thumb and forefinger are curled into a circle, while the other fingers are extended upwards.

This means OK or everything is fine in North America and the UK. But in France it means 'zero' and in Denmark or Italy it can be taken as an insult. In most of Latin America it is considered obscene.

The peace sign (also known as 'V for victory'):

With the palm out, forefinger and index finger are pointed upwards and split into the shape of a 'V.'

Though used by Winston Churchill during World War II to signify 'V for Victory', it is now universally accepted as a sign indicating 'peace' (it achieved this meaning among the US hippy movement in the 1960s and has never really been out of fashion since).

If it is done backwards (with the palm in rather than out) it takes on an obscene meaning in the UK (much used by Oasis's Liam Gallagher) and some other countries such as parts of Canada and Australia and New Zealand.

Thumbs up

With an outstretched fist, the thumb is extended straight up.

'Thumbs up' as a positive gesture quickly gained popularity in the USA, especially as a visual signal in noisy environments. Pilots unable to shout 'All's well!' or 'Ready!' over the noise of their engines used it frequently. With a slight backwards tilt, this gesture is used for hitchhiking.

However, in most of the Middle East and parts of Africa (notably Nigeria), this symbol can be obscene. In Japan, the thumb is considered the fifth digit; a raised thumb will order five of something!

The 'come here' gesture

With the palm up, the forefinger wiggled at the person summoned.

This gesture is rarely made to a superior, but is commonly used among peers, or in summoning service personnel (such as a waiter or porter). It is also sometimes used in sexual situations, when it is archaically referred to as a 'come hither' gesture. It is confusing to some foreigners, since most of the world uses a full-hand scooping motion to summon a person.

Pointing

A single outstretched finger (usually the index finger, sometimes the thumb) to designate an object or person.

Although 'it's not polite to point', children – and many adults – frequently do. Pointing at objects is not considered rude, and can be useful for foreign nationals who don't know the name of something. Pointing at people is not polite, perhaps because of its use in court, to point out wrongdoers. In many cultures, pointing is done with a toss of the head, a thrust of the chin, or even a pursing of the lips. In Asia, the entire open hand is used, except in Malaysia, where the thumb is preferred.

Notes

1 *SwissAir Gazette*, July/August 1997

Timing is everything in business. Western executives, in particular, are obsessed with it – after all, time is money. Each and every move is mapped out in their personal organizers. Their diaries are divided into half-hour segments. They rush from meeting to meeting, pausing only to read *The One Minute Manager* on the plane. The trouble is that though time is universal, our attitudes to time differ wildly. One executive's nine o'clock prompt is another's around half past nine if I can make it.

As in so many other areas, national stereotypes abound. Germans are sticklers for punctuality, as are the Swiss. Indeed, it is no coincidence that Switzerland is renowned for the quality of its watches. If they say nine o'clock, do not arrive a minute later. And any country anywhere near the Mediterranean is populated by people who often don't care when you arrive or what the time is. There's always tomorrow.

Attitudes to time keeping can be regarded as local customs. 'To some extent national stereotypes do fit,' says international consultant Kevin Barham, who lives on the France–Switzerland border. 'In Germany or Switzerland you do not turn up 15 minutes late while in France that would be quite acceptable. Things are changing. With business becoming more global, larger companies do tend to put greater emphasis on punctuality. In smaller French companies, however, attitudes are much more casual.'

In Germany, Switzerland and Scandinavia punctuality is expected. A few minutes late and you can wave goodbye to the lucrative contract. Lateness is strictly for amateurs and who wants to do business with them? Mark McCormack, a serious and unremitting globetrotter, advises business travellers to Geneva: 'Here, more than anywhere else on earth, be on time.'

Somewhat strangely, the British appear to defeat stereotyping. Renowned for their fastidious good manners and their emotional caution, the British are surprisingly casual about time keeping. This is ironic for a nation that numbers a clock, Big Ben, among its landmarks. Indeed, the only piece of time keeping the British are passionate about is that their time should be an hour different from the rest of Europe.

'I've been to many meetings in the UK and found that when I've arrived I have been the only one there,' admits one bemused executive. 'The others eventually arrive with various excuses. It's strange when you consider that meetings are the most important management activity in the UK – they are where the work gets done. Contrast that with Italy where meetings are for posturing and eloquence and the real work gets done later.'

When it comes to time keeping, the Italians remain a glorious law unto themselves. 'For Italians punctuality is simply not in their culture,' says Alex Knight of Ashridge Consulting, regular visitor to Italy. 'They live for the moment. If you agree to meet at 12 o'clock and your Italian colleagues arrive half an hour late they will invariably not have an excuse but a great idea. They'd be affronted if you didn't celebrate with them. The fact that you've been sitting there is irrelevant.' One cynical executive observes that the British pretend to be German but would, in fact, love to be Italian.

In Spain straightforward honesty overcomes a less than Germanic adherence to punctuality – if they are going to be an hour late, Spanish executives will quickly inform you of the fact. It can't be helped. The *Berlitz Business Travel Guide* observes that 'morning can stretch into mid-afternoon in Spain'.

Once outside Europe, punctuality becomes ever more complex. Europeans would generally accept that time is money and, therefore, a valuable commodity. A few minutes doesn't really make much difference, even if it may be slightly annoying or mystifying at the time. But, what if time isn't money? It isn't in Japan where it is more important to make the right decision. The Japanese arrive well prepared and on time, because they want to make sure that they make the best possible decision for their business. And that can take some time.

Different approaches come to a head when companies are involved in mergers and acquisitions. Here, the reliably punctual and the casually late often end up in fierce arguments. Mergers made in hell often feature French and German, or Italian and Swedish, combinations. The big question becomes not whether the deal makes business sense, but whether both sides will actually arrive at the same time to sign the contract.

Nine on the dot ... or not

If you are requested to be at a meeting at nine o'clock what do you do in:

Germany: Arrive at least 15 minutes early.

UK: Arrive before half past nine armed with an excuse ('I had to check some numbers just in from Tokyo').

France: Arrive up to 15 minutes late.

Spain: Telephone if you are going to be late.

Italy: Enter at nine o'clock to an empty room and order a coffee.

Switzerland: Sleep overnight in the meeting room.

Iceland: Arrive some time ('Punctuality isn't observed in Iceland,' observes Berlitz).

Greece: Arrive on time and discuss life before moving on to business and lunch.

Netherlands: No more than five minutes late.

Scandinavia: Arrive at least one minute before.

One merger made in corporate heaven is the Swedish–Swiss conglomerate, Asea Brown Boveri. Here, you can be sure, everything works like clockwork. Indeed, the only worry for the company's customers must be whether an extremely large turbine will arrive early. Examples of such timely relationships are rare. In a world of clock watchers, persuading two companies to synchronize their watches remains a major feat. But arriving at the appropriate time should not be beyond the well-organized business traveller.

What day is it?

Holidays, especially religious holidays, are an important part of life in many countries. It is worth consulting a local calendar if you are scheduling events or meetings.

Many cultures use a lunar calendar rather than the solar calendar familiar in the West. In this system a month is roughly 29 days from one new moon to the next. This also affects the number of days in a year. In Islamic countries, for example, a year is 354 days. Most societies agree that there are seven days in a week but the 'weekend' – i.e. rest periods – vary, usually based on religious observance. In Islamic countries Friday is a holy day and the working week begins on Saturday.

In some countries sporting events can also be elevated above business, so check with a local contact. In some parts of the world, especially South America and Europe, you may be disappointed at the turnout to your presentation or cocktail party if the local or national soccer team is playing an important match.

In transit: Gerry Griffin

Nationality: Irish

Job: Communications director joose.tv

Best hotel: The 'W' hotels in New York

Favourite country to visit on business: Spain

Favourite airport: City Airport, London

Frequency: 20–30 trips per year

Always takes: Psion (has an alarm clock)

Chapter 36 | Gift giving

Cultural differences surrounding gift giving probably cause more problems for business travellers than anything else. The potential for misunderstanding is immense. What might seem tantamount to bribery in one culture is viewed as harmless and entirely appropriate in another. Choosing appropriate gifts is tricky. US presidents have been known to get it badly wrong. Executives from famous corporations, too, have caused red faces by giving inappropriate gifts to their foreign counterparts.

Cultures view gifts very differently. In Anglo-Saxon and Western European countries, for example, gift giving is not expected and anything beyond small corporate gifts such as pens carrying a corporate logo would be looked at askance and cause embarrassment. But in Asia, particularly Japan, and also in the Middle East, gifts have a much greater importance and are seen as cementing a personal and business relationship. Even so, they need not be overly expensive but should be of a high quality.

In Japan, for example, gift giving has been part of the traditional chain of favour-and-obligation that has underpinned relationships for centuries. To the Japanese, gift giving is a way of communicating respect, friendship and appreciation. In Islamic countries, where generosity is an admired quality, avoid alcohol and products made of pigskin (and in India avoid leather). In both regions, downplay the importance and value of the gift and expect a polite refusal at first (you are expected to insist whereupon the gift will eventually be accepted).

Gifts are normally exchanged at the end of a business meeting or series of meetings. Group gifts are acceptable in Asia. Individual gifts should be tailored to the seniority of the recipients, but it is considered rude to leave anyone out of a round of gift giving. Gifts should always be wrapped. Whether they are unwrapped immediately or not depends on local customs.

In the Middle East it is not appropriate to offer a gift to the wife of a business contact. Elsewhere, if you are invited to a contact's home for a meal, a small gift – flowers, chocolates – for your hostess is generally appreciated. (Choose flowers carefully, though. In some cultures, especially in Latin America, certain types are reserved for funerals.) If you are entertaining foreign guests in your own country, remember they will have to transport your gift home in their luggage – avoid heavy objects, including over-large books.

What is considered an appropriate gift in Hawaii may be entirely inappropriate in India. How do you know that you are not committing some dreadful faux pas? To make life easier for the business traveller, the Internet gift store Netique Gift Boutique has compiled a list of tips on international gift giving.

Japan

Gifts are given frequently. Business gifts should be given at mid-year (15 July) and at year-end (1 January). Politeness may require that the recipient first decline the gift; the giver may have to offer it three times. Since gifts are never opened in the presence of the giver, the presentation is of equal importance. Proper gift wrapping is vital, but avoid white and brightly coloured wrapping paper: white symbolizes death and bright colours are too flashy. Gifts need not be extravagant, although expensive gifts are not viewed as a bribe. When meeting with a group of Japanese professionals, be sure to give higher-quality gifts to those with more senior rank within the company.

Never surprise the Japanese recipient with your gift. Subtly let them know that you would like to present a small memento. When presenting a group gift, be sure to allow time for the entire group to gather before making the presentation. When meeting with a group of Japanese colleagues, either present a group gift or a gift to each individual within the organization. It is considered extremely rude to present a gift to one individual in a group, without giving gifts to the rest of the ensemble.

Downplay the importance of the gift. This is common in the Asian culture. It conveys the message that the relationship is more important than the gift. And always present the gift with two hands. (Avoid giving gifts in sets of four. The word 'four' in Japanese is 'shi', which is also associated with the word for death.) Avoid giving monetary gifts or gifts displaying company logos. Be certain that gifts are of unquestionable quality.

Products that are difficult to obtain in Japan make good gift ideas for Japanese contacts. Gadgets are popular gifts, and could be something not sold in Japan, or something that is extremely expensive. Gifts that reflect the recipient's interests and tastes are good. Pens are highly appropriate gifts – the pen is a symbol of knowledge in the Japanese culture.

China

Communism brought scepticism to gift giving, and offering gifts to government officials became illegal. The importance of gift giving in China is slowly returning, however, but no set guidelines have been established. In order to avoid your gift being perceived as a bribe, it is wise to: present group gifts (this is seen as a 'company presenting a gift to a company', and not as a bribe to one individual from that company), display your company logo on the gift, and avoid giving highly expensive gifts.

In the Chinese culture it is normal to refuse a gift, sometimes repeatedly. It is expected, however, that the giver will persist and the recipient's acceptance will eventually follow. As in the Japanese culture, it is proper etiquette to present gifts with two hands.

Avoid giving clocks as gifts. The word for 'clock' in Chinese is similar to the word for 'death.' Colours such as white, blue or black are associated with funerals. Do not wrap gifts in these colours. Red, yellow and pink are seen as joyful colours, and are perfectly acceptable for gift-wrap. Just remember not to write anything in red ink, as this symbolizes the ending of a relationship.

Sharp objects such as knives, letter openers, or scissors also imply the severance of a relationship. Giving gifts in single or odd numbers suggests loneliness or separation, while gifts given in pairs equates to good luck.

Taiwan

Avoid giving a gift originally made in Taiwan.

Thailand

Thais love bright colours, and it is acceptable to wrap gifts in brightly coloured gift-wrap and ribbons. Ripping open the wrapping paper is offensive. 'Three' is considered a lucky number.

Korea

Generosity is viewed as a valued personal trait. Whenever possible, present an expensive gift. Gifts between business associates are viewed as symbols of appreciation. Four of anything is considered unlucky.

Malaysia

Pay special attention to the Muslim culture. Avoid pork, knives, alcohol and highly personal gifts. Present gifts with the right hand only. In Indian sections of Malaysia, avoid black and white colours. Yellow, red or green symbolize happiness.

Middle Eastern countries

Gift giving is important in the Arab culture. Arabs will normally be the first to present a gift. Whenever possible, reciprocate with gifts of similar quality and value. Avoid alcohol and leather products made of pigskin, which are offensive to Muslims. (Also avoid giving gifts to the wife of an Arab colleague, and never enquire about her.)

Ideas of gifts to present to your associates in the Middle East include the highest quality of leather (not pigskin), silver, precious stones, cashmere, crystal or porcelain.

Latin American countries

Don't present a gift at the first business meeting. As in most cultures, however, when visiting a home for dinner, it is important to present the hostess with a small gift of flowers, chocolates or wine. Thoughtfulness in gift giving goes a long way in Latin American countries – it demonstrates your awareness and respect. Choose gifts carefully by taking into consideration the tastes and interests of your Latin American business colleague. Avoid leather gifts, since most of the world's finest leathers come from South America.

USA

American businesspeople give out many promotional items, which are not gift-wrapped. Formal gift giving among US executives is usually limited to Christmas/Hannukah and commemorative events. Some US executives who deal with foreigners have learned to give gifts on other occasions. Gadgets are popular, and gifts may display a corporate logo. Gifts are opened immediately.

Switzerland

Gift-giving habits vary among Switzerland's three major linguistic groups. Quality and craftsmanship are appreciated, but gifts must not be mistaken for a bribe. Small, tasteful gifts are preferred over the large and ostentatious. Crafts or folk art from your home region are respected. Gifts are usually opened immediately.

South Africa

By and large, gift giving is infrequent among businesspeople. However, when invited to someone's home, you can bring something edible, especially to informal gatherings. South Africa's various cultures have very different traditions. In the Black and Coloured (Asian and mixed-race) communities, do not present a gift with the left hand – use the right hand or both hands. Gifts are usually opened immediately.

In transit: Carl Hamilton

Nationality: Swedish

Job: Author (of *Absolut: Biography of a Bottle*), broadcaster

Best hotel: My favourite business hotel would be Hallstabacken in the small town of Sollefteå in northern Sweden, situated in the middle of a ski slope. The vista at night is unparalleled. If I could recommend a hotel for leisure and recreation, it would be the San Roque on Tenerife, in the charming village of Garachico. It's arty, classy and very traditional.

Favourite country to visit on business: My favourite country for business I guess would be the USA, as you can always get good food and drink, no matter when. Or my home country Sweden because IT connections, etc. are usually quite good.

Favourite airport: Barcelona

Frequency: 5–10 trips per year

Always takes: Always two good books, one classic, one modern, in case of delays, long flights, boring companions, etc.

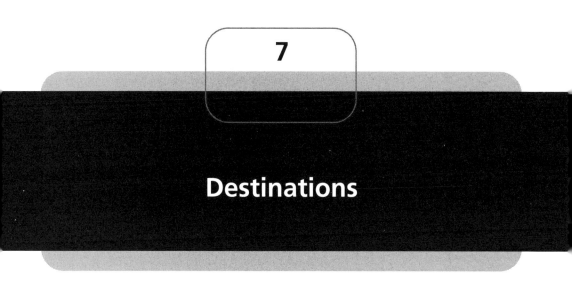

7

Destinations

'*Location, location, location.*'

MUCH-QUOTED SECRET OF RETAIL SUCCESS

Chapter 37 | This year's places to do business

Business fashions come and go. Today's gold mine is tomorrow's deserted town. The dominant goldmine over the last decade has been America's Silicon Valley, a few square miles of technological and financial tumult in and around Palo Alto, California.

Silicon Valley companies are now valued at four times those of Detroit, and their value almost equals that of the entire French stock market. Palo Alto, California, a place formerly known for its bowel-looseningly delicious prunes and raisins, is now home to 7000 electronics and software firms. While major cities around the world routinely fight to stage the next Olympic games, Palo Alto seems to have hosted the entire technological revolution.

The beneficiaries can be seen in the Mediterranean-style splendour of the Westin Palo Alto (**www.westin.com**) – where rooms come with the latest in T1 lines and in-room television access to the internet. Alternatively, they can be viewed beside the palm-bordered rooftop pool of the Fairmont Hotel San José (**www.fairmont.com/Hotels/Index_SF.html**).

The success of Silicon Valley highlights a paradox. Technology was supposed to make it possible to work from anywhere in the world. But in the technology business, face-to-face contact still matters. This is counter-intuitive: despite the spread of technology that enables people to work remotely, location matters more and more.

Every movement needs a symbolic home. Silicon Valley was the right place at the right time. The myth endures. But others are catching on. The next Silicon Valley could, it must be said, be virtually anywhere on earth. After all, in the Far East there is Silicon Island in Taiwan and Silicon Plateau in Bangalore (the city with 150,000 software programmers). Then there is the cringingly entitled Softopia in Gifu, Japan, and Media Valley now being developed in Inchon, Korea. Spotting the place to be has never been harder. The top tip seems to be to relocate to a place with the word silicon in its name. (There are plenty to choose from.)

Every red-hot cluster eventually meets its maker – look at the demise of one incredibly successful cluster of the past, Detroit.

As fashions change, Silicon Valley remains at the head of the pack, but only just. The new places to be seen include the following.

Cambridge, UK

Silicon Fen (or the Cambridge Phenomenon, as insiders call it) is home to around 1500 high-tech firms, employing 40,000 people. An estimated 25 new businesses are formed every month in the high-tech sector. The annual turnover of the cluster is estimated at around £5 billion, of which 40 per cent is exports.

The Cambridge area has a strong technology pedigree. It was home to one of the UK's first science parks, and pioneer companies included the electronics company Pye and the Acorn Computer Group, from which the microprocessor company ARM is derived. A number of leading US and European technology companies have established a presence in the region, including Microsoft which invested $80 million in a research facility, and Olivetti Research Laboratories. Cambridge University also has an alliance with MIT. Backed by £70 million of UK government funding, the Cambridge–MIT Institute aims to be a catalyst for entrepreneurial activities in the region.

Home-grown high-tech stars include Autonomy and ARM (both FTSE 100 companies), Zeus and the Generics Group. The region also benefits from a growing network of angel investors and venture capitalists, including Armadeus, the investment vehicle of Hermann Hauser, the founder of Acorn. Cambridge is a multi-species cluster, including software, scientific instruments, and technology consulting firms. Cambridge also has a significant biotechnology cluster, which dates back more than 100 years.

Cambridge could be Europe's best prospect of a cluster to rival those in the USA. Some in Cambridge also have designs to expand to create a super cluster, taking in the universities of Oxford and Cranfield, and the region around Milton Keynes. In 1997, the British government announced its ambition to develop Cambridge's knowledge-based economy, highlighting clusters of computing

> ### Essential Links
>
> **www.citysearch.com**
> For guides to local lodging, dining, sports and entertainment. Some of the city sites are much better than others (e.g. San Francisco's is excellent), but a great resource overall.
>
> **www.expatfinancial.com/links.htm**
> Links to expat websites – a great way of finding out the lowdown on cities/countries.

and biotech companies as the key to future prosperity.

Links: www.gwydir.demon.co.uk/cambridgeuk/sect2.HTM (extensive links to businesses, business parks and jobs); www.siliconfen.com

Sophia Antipolis, France

Sophia Antipolis in southern France is home to the largest science park in Europe (and there are now more than 300 such parks on the continent). It is home to more than 20,000 engineers and technicians, and some 5000 researchers and students. Located on the French Riviera, between Nice and Cannes (15 minutes from Nice airport), it covers 2300 hectares – or one-quarter of the size of Paris. A planned extension to the north will double its size to 4600 hectares.

The region's ambitions date back to the 1960s when the French government declared its intention to create 'the great European city of science in the sun'. Sophia Antipolis has been a slow-burning project. For years it has made steady progress without grabbing the imagination. Some say that it is now reaching critical mass with development likely to accelerate. Job creation at the park has been rising, lending some credence to the claim. There are currently 35 companies employing more than 100 people each. A number of leading companies have established research centres there, including Siemens, Lucent Technologies, Compaq and SAP.

Sophia Antipolis is a multiple-species cluster. The main technologies on the park are information technology (electronics and advanced telecoms); medical and chemical sciences; and natural sciences.

Links: www.businessriviera.com (a great one-stop resource); www.sophia-antipolis.org

Dublin, Ireland

Ireland, an island with a population roughly the size of Connecticut, now exports more software than any other country in the world. The US is second. Most of the high-tech industry is based around Dublin, which has been reborn as a high-tech Mecca. A number of technology parks have been established, including Citywest, located on the western fringe of the city, which covers 330 acres, and has been designated as Ireland's National Digital Park.

Ireland's current economic boom is well documented. The Irish economy is growing faster than any other European economy – expanding at three times the rate of the USA. Total output has grown at more than 8 per cent for each of the past five years. Unemployment has tumbled from 15 per cent in the early 1990s, to below 5 per cent.

Recent arrivals include Compaq, HP, Microsoft, Oracle, Gateway and SAP, which have all set up shop in the region. But the influx of high-tech multi-nationals began in 1989 with Intel's decision to site its first European plant at Leixlip, a former stud farm in County Kildare, just west of Dublin. Intel employs 4600 people at the 270-acre site, and the company has invested more than $3 billion, with a future $2 billion planned. An additional 600 home-grown software companies, including the NASDAQ-listed Trintech, have also blazed a trail across the Irish economy. (Intel's venture capital arm helped finance some start-ups.)

'We've moved from a vicious to a virtuous circle,' David Duffy, an economist at Dublin's Economic and Social Research Institute, recently observed. Obstacles remain. The country's infrastructure still lags behind many parts of Western Europe. However, head to the lobby bar at the Morrison Hotel near the River Liffey and you will feel the buzz (and if that builds your appetite, there's always the networking-rich restaurant downstairs).

Links: www.visitdublin.com; ww.dubchamber.ie; www.etradebusinessireland.com (a database of companies); www.finditireland.com (extensive links to businesses and all things Irish).

Kista, Sweden

Kista is the high-tech hub of Stockholm. Situated to the north-west of the city, Kista Science Park is a centre for wireless R&D. By European standards, there is a good supply of venture capital and the area is a hotbed of high-tech, especially internet-related, start-ups. Sometimes called Kiselsta ('kisel' is the Swedish for silicon), or Wireless Valley, around 700 companies are located on the park, employing a total of 28,000 people. Several multinationals, including Compaq, HP, IBM, Microsoft and Sun Microsystems, have their Scandinavian headquarters there.

But Kista is best known as one of the world's leading telecoms centres, especially in GSM technology. Ericsson is the largest employer and Nokia has a development centre on the park. In 1999, Intel established a research centre for mobile technology, the Wireless Competence Centre. The new IT University – dedicated to information technology – was established in 2000 by the Swedish Royal Institute of Technology. A recent (2000) survey of opinion formers, by *Wired Magazine*, placed Kista number two next to Silicon Valley among the locations that matter most in the digital economy. Another survey identified Kista as the world's fifth-hottest IT area.

The much trumpeted hope is that Kista will be a new Florence, somewhere where both business and culture bloom. From a business perspective, the Kista Science Tower, Sweden's tallest building, will be ready for occupancy within two years. It will house 2500 new offices. Kista's IT University welcomed its first class of engineers in 2000 and it is anticipated that it will soon have 10,000 students.

Links: www.kista.com (mostly in Swedish); www.kistasciencepark.org (information on companies in English).

Essential Links

www.wajb.freeserve.co.uk/UK.HTM
for links to all major airports worldwide.

Oulu, Finland

In 1998, Nokia passed Motorola to become the world's number one mobile phone manufacturer. The company has done much to establish Finland as the mobile laboratory of the world. The Finns also have more internet hosts per capita than any other country. Yet until the 1980s, Finland's main export was timber.

(Nokia took its name from a timber mill on the Nokia River in southern Finland.)

Although there is a growing technology cluster in Helsinki, the town of Oulu on the edge of the Arctic and 370 miles north of the Finnish capital, is widely recognized as the country's high-tech hub. In 1959, a technology university was established in the town, and by the 1970s, Nokia had begun to develop radiotelephones in the region for the Finnish army. Oulu Technopolis, a purpose-built technology park founded by 18 companies, followed in 1992, and is now home to 150 companies, employing 3500 people.

Finland is now recognized as being at the cutting edge of mobile telecommunications and wireless technology. Its small domestic market and traditional strengths in engineering make it an ideal test market for mobile technology, and it has attracted the likes of HP and others to set up research facilities.

Links: www.oulu.fi (in English and Finnish);
www.suomi.net/business/index-E.HTML (for information on companies in Oulu, in Finnish); www.pohjois-pohjanmaa.fi/uudet/me/esp16.htm (for virtual tour, in English);

Oulu may or may not become the next Silicon Valley. Whatever happens, a number of cities remain hardy perennials for business travellers. We have identified twenty-five which have legs.

Amsterdam

With just 730,000 inhabitants, Amsterdam is one of the smaller key European cities and the only one to have museums devoted specifically to sex and marijuana, which says a lot about the Dutch and their culture. The Dutch are the traditional free-thinkers of the continent and Amsterdam has a reputation for being a city of fun and sin – the two not being mutually exclusive. But it's also a key business centre and a European leader in e-business.

The city isn't as romantic as some of the travel guides with their talk of tree-lined canals might suggest. It can be crowded and a little scruffy and somewhat tired, especially after a long tourist-packed summer. Most of the city-centre buildings are old but some new architecture is going up along the canals, though nothing as yet to match arch-rival Rotterdam.

Coming and going

Amsterdam is one of the best-connected cities in the world. It is at the centre of the Netherlands' excellent rail network, which links seamlessly into the rest of Europe. The only airport is **Schiphol** (one of the best in the world) about 15 km south-west of the city. (**www.schipol.nl**) Trains run to the centre every 15 minutes (hourly through the night). A one-way ticket costs fl7.00. Taxis take around 30 minutes to the centre, depending on traffic, and cost around fl65. (**www.ns.nl/reisplanz.ASP**)

Out and about

Travel around the city is easy, with the same tickets valid on trams, buses and the metro. You can even hire a bicycle if you're brave or simply walk: the city is very compact. Traffic jams on the narrow streets and canal bridges are frequent and heavy. Taxis can be hailed but are more usually picked up at ranks. The Circle Tram (line 20) leaves from Centraal Station every 20 minutes and stops at virtually every tourist trap and major hotel.

Networking

As a small country with an impenetrable language and a history of global trading, the Dutch are the world's great cosmopolitans. Amsterdammers have neither the aloofness of Parisians nor the reserve of Londoners. In general the city is relaxed, friendly and international. Network away.

Behaving yourself

Even so, in business the Dutch are somewhat formal. Do not let appearances deceive you. Shake hands on meeting and leaving. Business dress is usually conservative. Use last names and business titles unless you are invited to do otherwise. Be punctual. Almost everyone speaks English (and often German and French as well). The Dutch don't expect you to learn their difficult language so English is fine. Trying halting French, or especially German, would probably be a mistake.

The business tourist

What people think of as 'traditional' Amsterdam – gabled canal-side housing with the signature joist for hauling up supplies – is being increasingly taken over by small, start-up dotcoms or similar. A lot of business goes on outside the tourist centre, in the 1.4 million population Greater Amsterdam, which is home to nearly 1400 foreign companies. The new media, transport and distribution, and banking are particularly strong sectors.

Zaanstad, with a direct link to the Port of Amsterdam, has become a centre of the food industry. Haarlemmermeer, west of Schiphol around Hoofddorp, has become the hub of transport and logistics firms. With burgeoning demand the business parks of Haarlemmermeer are growing rapidly, as is associated housing. Unisource has its European HQ in Hoofddorp; Microsoft is in the

Breukenhorst business centre. Probably most popular is **Amstelveen**, a few minutes from the centre of Amsterdam, and host to many major corporations, including KLM Royal Dutch Airlines, Canon, HP, Yakult, Xerox, and KPMG. Amstelveen is also home to publishing houses, advertising agencies, graphic designers and insurance companies.

The three-hour tourist

Must-sees include the **Rijksmuseum** (Dutch National Museum – **www.rijksmuseum.nl**), which houses the largest collection of Dutch art in the world including fabulous paintings by Rembrandt; the nearby **Vincent Van Gogh Museum**, and a boat trip on the canals. If you've already done that try **Anne Frankhuis**, where Anne Frank spent two years in hiding during World War II and wrote her diary (on view in the museum).

The **Leidseplein Square**, near the Rijksmuseum, is full of cafés, theatres, nightclubs, restaurants and bars. A lot of the infamous 'smoking cafés', where marijuana and hashish are sold and smoked, are here. For those interested, the **Erotic Museum** (collections of erotic art) and the **Marijuana Museum** (how to recognize and grow the stuff) are both in the red light district.

Amsterdam is also a centre of the diamond trade, and for something a bit unusual try a free conducted tour of a workshop to see diamonds being cut and polished. There are also tours of the old **Heineken brewery** in the centre of town.

Amsterdam is pretty safe by international standards but the usual rules apply. Especially in the red light district, keep to the crowded main thoroughfares and watch out for pickpockets. Outside of the smoking cafés drug taking is frowned on (it's also illegal).

Gift buying

Amsterdam is packed with shops, from designer boutiques to big-name outlets and speciality shops, especially in the **Negen Straatjes** (Nine Alleys) that criss-cross the main canals. Designer wear is concentrated on **PC Hooftstraat**, antiques in the **Spiegelkwartier**. There is a famous flea market on **Waterlooplein**.

Leidsestraat, Kalverstraat, Nieuwendijk, Damrak and Rokin are the main shopping streets, with department stores, boutiques and souvenirs. The more exclusive shops are mainly along **Beethovenstraat**, Van

Baerlestraat, PC **Hooftstraat**, and **Rokin**. The **Jordaan** district is quaint, with narrow streets and trendy shops.

Try the Amsterdam Diamond Centre (Rokin) for stones; Wegewijs Kaas (Rozengracht) for cheeses; and Focke & Meltzer (PC Hooftstraat) for porcelain.

Bare facts

Weather

OK-ish. Reasonable summers of up to 25°C, mildish winters (snow is rare), and wet springs and autumns. Since most of the country is below sea level, the Dutch are hoping that climate change is minimal.

Hours

Shops: 11.00–18.00 Monday; 09.00–18.00 Tuesday, Wednesday, Friday; 09.00–21.00 Thursday; 09.00–17.00 Saturday. Many large downtown stores also open 12.00–17.00 Sunday. **Banks:** 09.00–16.00/17.00.

Public holidays

1 January; Easter Friday; Easter Sunday; Easter Monday; 29 April (Queen's Birthday); 5 May (Liberation Day); Ascension Day; Whit Sunday; Whit Monday; 25 December; 26 December.

The boring stuff

No vaccinations are required to enter the Netherlands. The water is safe. There are very few restrictions on what the average business traveller can bring in. There is no duty-free allowance for travellers from other EU countries. No visas required for visits under three months.

The country code for the Netherlands is 31, followed by the city code, 20, and Amsterdam is one hour ahead of GMT.

Amsterdam online

www.amsterdam.nl – masses of information on this official site – or try www.cwi.nl/~steven/amsterdam.html for a great basic guide written by two Amsterdammers.

Amsterdam's café culture now includes cyber cafés – such as Café Internet, five minutes' walk from the Centraal Station (**www.care.euronet.nl**) and the Cyber Café (**www.cybercafe.euronet.nl**).

PS

Amsterdam is home to the world's first memorial to persecuted lesbians and gays, the Homomonument (on Westermarkt). The three, pink granite triangles are said to reflect the pink triangles homosexuals were forced to wear in concentration camps during the second world war.

Beijing

A little over ten years since those infamous pictures of students battling with tanks in Tiananmen Square, there is talk of a beach volleyball competition taking place in the shadow of Mao's Mausoleum. Add to that Western concessions, a neon skyline and adverts for loft accommodation, and it's easy to forget that Beijing is still the capital city of a single party state, dominated by the Communist Party of China (CCP).

Coming and going

The torturous 30 km journey into the city centre from Beijing's **Capital Airport** can last anything up to one and a half hours depending on how clogged the roads are with other red taxis swerving from lane to lane. The journey will cost about Rmb150 but remember this is China, and English really is a foreign language, so a card with the address of your hotel is helpful.

For Rmb300–800 round trip, you can arrange to be picked up at Capital Airport through the China Council for the Promotion of International Trade.

Some hotels offer airport pickups for between Rmb100 and 450 and buses are available but after a long flight are not really to be recommended.

On leaving Beijing, there's a departure tax of between Rmb90 and 120.

Out and about

Given the congestion on the roads, the easiest way to navigate the city is the subway, which has recently been extended, and has place names in English, as well as Mandarin.

Beijing has 75,000 taxis, in various states of repair, and all display their rates on a sticker in the window, with the higher the rate, the higher the 'comfort' factor. And like taxi drivers the world over, Chinese cabbies don't miss a trick, and you'll pay for time stuck in traffic, too.

Buses are confusing and a favoured haunt of pickpockets, while rickshaw pullers charge high prices to drag Westerners around. As for car rental, forget it. Apart from anything else you'll need a special licence, some under-standing of Mandarin, and the reactions of Michael Schumacher.

Networking

Dubbed Wine Bar Street, **Sanlitun Lu** is the heart of the city's ex-pat district. So if you need to escape Chinese Beijing for a few hours, and simply want to mix in a more Western environment, this is the place, with its roadside bars, Mediterranean restaurants and recognizable brands of booze.

Behaving yourself

Before you call for the manager, most hotels add a service fee of 15 per cent to their advertised room rates. As for tipping, don't – it can cause offence. Most restaurants will add a service charge of between 10 and 15 per cent anyway.

In terms of social etiquette, punctuality is a must, and on arrival, or departure, a slight bow or handshake is *de rigueur*. Next, remember not to consign that business card – usually offered with both hands – straight into your pocket. Read it first, and yours should have a Chinese translation on the reverse.

Despite a propensity to stand close together during conversations, the Chinese don't believe in whispering; they're loud. Refusing hospitality is a no-no and don't, whatever you do, offer to pay part of a restaurant bill. Either claim 'the honour' of paying for the whole thing, or keep quiet.

The business tourist

Beijing's banking and legal concerns flourish in the Chaoyang and Xicheng districts of the city, while several state-backed technological parks have appeared over recent years, helping to establish Beijing's own Silicon Valley. Foremost among these is Zhongguancun high-tech park, in the Haidan District, which is home to the nation's best universities, a fledgling internet industry and well-known Chinese computer and telecommunications companies.

The three-hour tourist

Beijing's list of must-see attractions has changed little over the years.

Tiananmen Square is perfect for people watching, whether it's kite fliers, huddles of taxi drivers engrossed in a game of cards, or goose-stepping guards around the entrance to **Mao's Mausoleum**.

At one end of the square is the Forbidden City, a sprawling collection of buildings and courtyards that makes up the 600-year-old Imperial Palace, once the sole domain of the emperor and a few chosen courtesans, concubines and eunuchs. Make sure you hire the audio tour, as the plummy voice of Roger Moore's narration strangely adds to the whole experience.

It's rather depressing to hear that the **Great Wall** wasn't actually all that great and invading hordes often just bribed the guards to let them through. But it's still a magnificent sight as it winds its way over the hills. **Badaling** is closest to Beijing, and the most touristy stretch, while Mutianyu or Simatai, about two hours' drive away, are a lot more secluded.

Gift buying

If you see shopping as a treat not a chore, **Hong Qiao**, or Pearl Market, offers the ultimate experience with two floors devoted to antiques, luggage, watches and electrical items, some, admittedly, of dubious origin. The top floor houses a pearl market.

Antique markets are big in China, with Mao memorabilia topping the list. **Panjiayuan** on Hua Wei Lu Beili is said to be one of the best. Only open at weekends, it's nicknamed 'ghost market' as serious dealers arrive before dawn to examine goods under torchlight.

Bargaining is the key when visiting the **Quianmen Carpet Factory**, 44 Xingfu Dajie, while **Dreamweavers**, 51 Taiyuancun Lu, is the favoured tailor of Beijing's embassy crowd.

Bare facts

Weather

Beijing is a city of extremes: from December to March things rarely rise above freezing, yet during June and August, the wettest months, the heat can be stifling.

Hours

Banks: 09.00–12.00 and 14.00–17.00 weekdays. Outside these hours look out for ATMs, particularly those of Citibank and the Bank of China, which accept most Western bank cards. **Offices:** 08.00–11.30 and 13.00–17.00. Some governmental offices are more flexible. **Shops:** 09.00–19.00 every day.

Public holidays

New Year's Day (1 January); Chinese New Year (late January/early February – the exact dates change each year); Women's Day (8 March); Labour Day (1 May); Youth Day (4 May); Children's Day (1 June); Chinese Communist Party Day (1 July); Army Day (1 August); National Day (1 October). Despite the plethora of holidays businesses only shut down for the Chinese New Year and National Day.

The boring stuff

EU citizens require a visa to enter China. They cost about £50 and are valid for three months. It usually takes three days to process a request, but express visas are available.

The country code for China is 86, followed by the city code, 1, and Beijing is eight hours ahead of GMT.

In terms of jabs, Hepatitis A is recommended while you may wish to consider Hepatitis B and typhoid. The Chinese boil all tap water so stick to bottles, even for cleaning your teeth, and forget about ice in your drinks. If the worst comes to the worst, seek out an English-speaking doctor at somewhere such as the International Medical Centre.

The China Daily is the main English language paper but is not exactly riveting. For details about what's on, check out some of the city's ex-pat titles such as *Beijing Journal* and *City Weekend*.

Beijing online

China in general, and Beijing in particular, is in the grips of an e-commerce revolution. Both Bill Clinton and Madeleine Albright have popped into **Sparkice** to check their e-mail address. There are new branches all over the city. E-mail info@sparkice.co.cn for details.

Many hotels have rooms that have all the necessary portals and points to log on and as for websites on Beijing, www.Chinanow.com is hard to beat.

The China Council for the promotion of International Trade offers a helpful website with essential business and travel information, **www.hytour.com/index.html**. For discounts on 3 to 5 star hotels throughout China, check **www.chinattic.com**. The site also has lots of links on business, government, culture etc. throughout China. The China Internet Network Information Center provides statistics on internal development in China as well as domain name registrations, **www.cnnic.net.cn/develst/e-index.shtml**

PS

For an eating experience with a difference head for the **Donghuamen Night Market**, near Wangfujing. There are over 60 stalls, each selling their own line in skewered treats, from traditional chicken and pork to more unusual deep-fried scorpions and lamb entrails.

Berlin

While the bohemian glitz of Isherwood's Berlin may have long since faded, the city, so recently the epitome of a grey Cold War, is shining again. First came the reunification, then the decision to move the government back to Berlin's Reichstag, and now, if all goes to plan, the city's economic recuperation will follow.

Already the huge amounts spent on building a new infrastructure are paying dividends. Berlin has always had a strong research and development sector, with the presence of companies like Siemens and Sony, and now other companies are relocating to the capital in their droves, with the eastern part of the city proving a lure for dot-com ventures.

Berlin now covers an area nine times the size of Paris, and once again it finds itself at the centre of Europe, and the capital of a reunited Germany.

Coming and going

Berlin has three airports:

- **Tegel**, the city's main airport, is 8 km from the city centre and serves destinations across Europe. Various buses offer an express service into town, while a taxi costs DM60.
- **Schönefeld**, 25 km from the centre, used to serve East Berlin, and there are plans to turn it into the city's main airport. A free shuttle bus

will take you to the S-Bahn where an express train, costing DM4, takes about 30 minutes to reach the city centre. A cab costs about DM70.

- **Tempelhof**, 6 km from the centre, is a gigantic 1930s structure only used by smaller planes arriving from nearby European cities.

Further information is available at www.berlin-airport.de (in German).

Out and about

Berlin's new commercial hub is **Potsdamer Platz**, a former no-man's land created by the Berlin Wall. Some business is also concentrated around **Bahnhof Zoo**, the **Europa-Center** and Kurfürstendamm, while **Mitte** and **Prenzlauer Berg** are littered with galleries, cafés, bars and cabarets.

A new wave of five star hotels has sprung up around **Potsdamer Platz**, while **Kurfürstendamm** offers more traditional retreats.

Berlin has a highly efficient, highly integrated public transport system which includes the **U-Bahn** (underground), **S-Bahn** (commuter rail see www.metropla.net/eu/bln/berlin.htm for maps and information), buses, trams and a ferry service. However, because of the monumental changes over recent years, don't rely too heavily on any maps.

Taxis tend to be Mercedes Benz in a far-from-fetching beige colour. The initial charge is DM4, and then it's down to distance and the time of day. The standard tip, if you feel so inclined, is 5–10 per cent.

You'll find all the major car-hire firms in Berlin, although the one-way system can be tricky.

Bicycles are also available for hire, with the flat terrain and network of cycle paths making it the healthy way to see the city.

Networking

Kaffee und kuchen (coffee and cake) is something of an afternoon ritual in Berlin and cafés can be a great place to enjoy an informal chat with associates. They're great for breakfast, too.

Behaving yourself

As in all aspects of life, the Germans conduct business with a high degree of efficiency. They are punctual and formal, and love detail. Waffle is un-necessary but case studies and supporting documents, which should be translated into German, can help sway things in your favour. But Germans won't be rushed into decisions.

As well as a firm, brief handshake, a slight nod of the head is expected when making introductions. When introduced to a woman, let her make the first move in the handshaking department. Business cards are big business.

In hotels and restaurants it's common to give a 10–15 per cent tip and round the bill up to the nearest DM5 or DM10.

The business tourist

The capitalist heart of the city is **Potsdamer Platz**, full of glimmering corporate HQs, including that of Daimler-Chrysler. The **Berlin Stock Exchange** can be found on Fasanenstrause (www.berlinerboerse.de) There is also a lot to see business-wise in the **Berlin-Brandenburg region**, home to six universities, over 300 research institutes, six biotechnology parks, as well as over 200 trade fairs and conferences. Berlin is a biotech centre and the centre for German genome research – this has spun off varioius companies and initiatives.

The three-hour tourist

Formerly little more than a vantage point from which to peer over at the East, **Potsdamer Platz** is now home to hotels, restaurants, shops and attractions such as the IMAX theatre, a casino and the Filmhaus, a film museum featuring the Marlene Dietrich collection.

When Parliament returned in 1999, it came to Sir Norman Foster's new, renovated glass-domed **Reichstag**, designed to symbolize the transparency of democratic government. Both have since received something of a mixed reception.

A short walk away is the **Brandenburg Gate** and the historical boulevard **Unter den Linden**, where you'll find some of Berlin's richest cultural treasures and architectural relics.

Berlin has over 150 museums (see www.berlin.de/home/english/visitors/guide/museums/index.htm) for a directory although renovation after the end of the Cold War means many are still closed. The cluster of museums dubbed Museum Island, at the eastern end of Unter den Linden, is now a world heritage site and includes the **Pergamonmuseum**, with its enormous Pergamon Altar dating from the second century BC.

The museums and galleries in and around **Schloss Charlottenburg** include the **Egyptian Museum**, with its bust of Queen Nefertiti, and over 50 works by Picasso in the **Berggruen Collection**. The **Kulturforum** offers another selection of galleries, including Old Masters in the **Gemaldega-lerie** and something a little more modern in the **Neue Nationalgalerie.**

Also worth a look is the **Bauhaus Archiv**, Klingelhoferstrasse 14, with its architectural plans and models, industrial designs and furniture.

State museums are closed on Monday.

The **Haus am Checkpoint Charlie**, offers a history of some of the most daring escapes over the Wall to the West, while a lone, disintegrating segment still stands in nearby Niederkirchner Strasse.

Tiergarten is Berlin's large central park, stretching from the Brandenburg Gate to the zoo. It was once a royal hunting reserve, but nowadays wildlife comes in the form of nude sunbathers who are allowed in certain areas.

For alternative suggestions go to <u>www.lonelyplanet.lycos.com/europe/berlin/OBT.html</u>.

Gift buying

Kurfurstendamm and **Tauentzienstrasse**, with their elegant department stores and designer boutiques, are worth exploring, as are the shops on **Savigny Platz**.

Kaufhaus des Westens, opposite U-Bahn Wittenbergplatz, is a department store from the old school with eight floors of everything from designer clothes to cooking utensils. Pride of place goes to the food hall, with an estimated 33,000 items on sale, including 1300 different cheeses.

Some interesting antique shops can be found in the arches near **Bahnhof Friedrichstrasse**, while **Meissen** has a showroom for its famous porcelain at Unter den Linden 39b.

Bare facts

Weather

With a continental climate, Berlin can get nippy in the winter, while summers are warm with the odd heatwave thrown in for good measure.

Hours

Banks: 09.00–13.00 Monday, Wednesday, Friday; 09.00–18.00 Tuesday, Thursday. **Offices:** 09.00–17.00 weekdays. **Shops:** 09.30–20.00 Monday–Friday; 09.30–16.00 Saturday. For the time being at least, all shops are closed on Sundays. Many restaurants are closed on Sundays and Mondays.

Public holidays

1 January (New Year's Day); Good Friday; Easter Monday; 1 May (Labour Day); Ascension; Whit Monday; 3 October (Day of German Unity); 25–26 December (Christmas); 31 December (New Year's Eve).

The boring stuff

No vaccinations or health certificates are required except for visitors from certain developing countries. The water is safe. Very few restrictions on what the average business traveller can bring in. There is no duty-free allowance for travellers from other EU countries. For EU citizens no visa is required for a stay of up to three months.

The country code for Germany is 49, followed by the city code, 30. Berlin is one hour ahead of GMT from October to March, and two hours between April and September.

There are no English language newspapers printed in Berlin but editions of some British papers may be available at international newsstands.

Berlin online

Internet cafés are dotted all over the city. www.berlin.de is one of the best online guides with a special section on business interests, www.brandenburg.de/wfb is the home of Brandenburg Economic Development.

PS

One thing worth remembering – some streets are numbered up one side, and back down the other.

Boston

Americans tend to think of anything over 50 years old as an antiquity. Boston is over 50 years old and is, as a result, venerated as the historical pulse of America. Founded in 1630, Boston is one of America's oldest cities. Unlike many cities it is easily walkable and navigable (except in winter, when the only walkable distance is from a taxi to a door). At the same time as being of interest for its historical links, Boston is the most European of American cities – though it comes replete with the usual skyscrapers.

Boston is undergoing a striking business renaissance. The city may be old but it has embraced the new economy with something approaching abandon.

One of its prime advantages is the presence of centres of intellectual excellence close by. Two of the world's leading business schools – Harvard and MIT's Sloan School – are based in the city. This adds student gusto and intellectual brilliance to an already potent commercial mix.

Coming and going

Boston **Logan International Airport** (www.massport.com/logan) is 6 km from downtown Boston. It's the largest airport in New England and serves as the region's international gateway. Logan has five passenger terminals, each of which has its own ticketing, baggage claim and ground transportation facilities.

There are plenty of options for ground transport into Boston from Logan. A free shuttle bus (marked MASSPORT) stops at each airline terminal and the MBTA subway station where trains depart every 8–12 minutes for a 15–minute trip to the city centre. For a scenic approach, try the MASSPORT Water Shuttle (reached by a separate bus) for a 17-minute, $10 boat ride from the airport to Rowes Wharf and Long Wharf in downtown Boston. For the more conventional, a taxi will take 20–30 minutes and cost $18–24. Hotel shuttle buses, unless complimentary, cost $7.50 and take 20–30 minutes. Public buses and limousine service are also available.

Out and about

Don't even think about driving into Boston, or worse, parking. Beantown is in the midst of the 'Big Dig,' 'the largest, most complex, and technologically challenging highway project in American history' (**www.bigdig.com**). Boston's central artery is an elevated highway that carries more than twice its originally capacity, and traffic is jammed for eight to ten hours a day. A new underground highway is being built to replace it. Big Dig equals Big Mess. Fortunately downtown Boston is wonderfully walkable – most of the central city is within a half-hour's walk, and the 'T' subway system is user-friendly and relatively safe and clean.

The T consists of four lines: red, orange, blue and green. You may view a map online (**www.mbta.com/schedmaps/subway/index.cfm**), or inside each train car and station. It runs from about 5.30 to 00.30, with an average wait time of five–ten minutes on weekdays, and 12–15 minutes on weekends. A ride on the T's just a buck ($1) a trip, including transfers; bus fare is $0.75 – with all the traffic you can tolerate. Or you can buy a visitor pass that is valid for unlimited travel on the subway, local bus and inner harbour ferry. A one-day pass is $6, 3-day $11, and 7-day $22. A real bargain.

Networking

For high-tech connections, check out the Boston Globe's Digital Mass.com website at **http://digitalmass.boston.com/networking**. The site provides a searchable list of cyberbrews, seminars, career expos, and other events in the region, as well as job and company searches (the latter via the Massachusetts Software Council's database of nearly 3000 companies). Exemplary site.

For networking opportunities in a wider diversity of industries, the *Boston Business Journal* (published every Friday) offers lists of daily business events and networking opportunities throughout the Boston area. For current information go to: **http://boston.bcentral.com/boston**, scroll down the page and click on 'Calendar of Business Events'.

The **Greater Boston Chamber of Commerce www.gbcc.org** also provides a full calendar of networking and informational programmes 'that give members the opportunity to broaden their contacts, gain valuable information, and meet the area's foremost leaders from business and government'. They also 'offer a broad range of sponsorship, advertising, and leads referral programs that provide high-profile marketing opportunities for member businesses'.

Behaving yourself

First off, don't go dumping any tea into the harbour (stop by the Boston Tea Party Ship and Museum if you need to refresh your American Revolutionary history – **www.bostonteapartyshbip.com**).

Otherwise, if you're feeling insecure about your grasp of American business etiquette (yes, there is such a thing – at least in Boston), you came to the right place. The Etiquette School of Boston offers corporate etiquette and international protocol training for all ages. Programmes include: Business Etiquette, Dining Skills, How To Succeed in the International Arena, and Dine Like a Diplomat, which includes a tutorial luncheon or dinner (**www.bostonetiquette.com/corporate.html**).

The business tourist

To get the lay of the land in 'Beantown' before your arrival, spend a few minutes perusing the *Boston Globe*'s 'Globe 100' companies of 2000 (www.boston.com/globe/business/packages/globe_100/2000). You'll get a quick overview of the major players in Massachusetts' thriving new/old hybrid economy.

With many fine academic institutions, Boston is a prime generator of business brainpower. Three of *Business Week*'s top-30-ranked b-schools are in the Boston area: Harvard (number 3), MIT (number 4), and Northeastern (number 13). There's also Babson, Bentley and Boston Colleges, Boston U., and University of Massachusetts at Amherst.

The three-hour tourist

If you haven't already, explore one of America's first historic walking tours, Boston's 2.5-mile **Freedom Trail**. The full tour covers 16 colonial revolutionary historic sites spanning two and a half centuries, and you can cover the whole trail in three or four hours. Just follow the red brick or painted line that connects the sites on the Trail. The National Park Service offers guided tours that begin every half hour at 15 State Street, across from the Old State House, or you can pick up a guide and set off on your own. Trolley tours are also available that allow unlimited reboarding for around $22.

Faneuil Hall is one of the 16 stops on the tour. For some it's also one of the top five sites to see in Boston. If you're looking for somewhat touristy shops and restaurants, you may want to spend your full three hours here, where you can also step into America's oldest restaurant – **The Union Oyster House**. The other four top sites are the **John F. Kennedy Presidential Library** ($8); the North End, which is Boston's **Little Italy** – a neighbourhood of narrow streets with brick buildings and wonderful restaurants (the Freedom Trail also winds through North End); **Fenway Park** for a Red Sox game – especially on a warm summer night; and **Hatch Shell** on the Charles River where summer concerts are held.

If, on the other hand, you've done the Freedom Trail, are beyond sated with American colonial history, and need to get off the beaten track, you might try a walk on the Boston **'Bizzaro Trail'** (www.boston-online.com/bizarro.html). See the place where people drowned in molasses in 1919, the book bound in human skin, and the site where a local man caught a grape with his mouth that was dropped from 60 storeys, among other captivatingly bizarre local highlights.

Gift buying

You can find various traditional souvenirs like pewter ware, old street signs, and used furniture at **Faneuil Hall Marketplace** along the Freedom Trail. As you walk through Boston you can take in an eclectic mix of shopping experiences, but don't miss **Filene's Basement** (426 Washington St). Filene's is a Boston landmark and legendary paradise for clothing bargain-hunters. Or hop the Red Line on the T to Harvard Square in Cambridge for great bookstores like **Harvard Book Store** (1256 Massachusetts Ave. – no relation to Harvard U.) for its huge scholarly collection, and **Schoenhof's Foreign Books** (76A Mount Auburn St), with adults' and children's books in more than 24 languages. Of course Boston also has plenty of fancy shopping centres, including the **Prudential Center** and **Copley Place**, for high-end national and international brands like Gucci, Godiva chocolates and Sonoma wines.

Bare facts

Weather

Fall in New England is spectacularly beautiful. Expanses of brilliant colour give way to blankets of snow and cold winters. Spring is generally pleasant and summers warm and sunny. Bring an umbrella.

Hours

Banks: 09.00–16.00 Monday–Friday. **Offices:** 09.00–17.00 Monday–Friday; **Shops:** 10.00–21.30 Monday–Saturday, and 12.00–18.00 Sunday.

Public holidays

There are five fixed-date federal holidays: New Year's Day (1 January); Flag Day (14 June); Independence Day (4 July); Veterans Day (11 November) and Christmas (25 December). Floating federal holidays include the birthday of Dr Martin Luther King (third Monday in January); Inauguration Day (20 January every four years); President's Day (third Monday in February); Memorial Day (last Monday in May); Labor Day (first Monday in September); Columbus Day (second Monday in October); and Thanksgiving Day (fourth Thursday in November). Businesses may or may not be closed on these days, but most typically close on the major holidays. When a fixed-date holiday falls on a Saturday, the holiday is taken on the Friday before it. When it falls on a Sunday, the holiday is taken on Monday. August is the most popular month for family vacations, and although businesses typically remain open, key contacts may be on leave.

The boring stuff

No vaccinations are required to enter the USA and the water is safe. No visa is required for visits under three months for visitors from countries covered by the US Visa Waiver Program. Comprehensive health insurance is an absolute must.

Boston online

The *Boston Globe*'s (**www.boston.com/business**) has extensive business coverage, including an entire section dedicated to the high-tech sector in Massachusetts. The *Globe* is also a terrific site for information on dining, arts and entertainment throughout the region: **http://ae.boston.com**. Restaurants are catalogued by cuisine, city or neighbourhood, and price range. You can search for specific cultural events, or click on a particular day on the convenient calendar to see what's happening that day.

The *Boston Business Journal* online (**http://boston.bcentral.com/boston**) features local and national business news, legal and insurance resource centers, leads on new businesses in the area, an archive search, a business-to-business marketplace, and the *Business Times Book of Lists* (available by subscription) – a business reference guide which compiles this paper's weekly Top 25 lists. Business newspapers for 39 other US cities may also be accessed from this site.

The Boston Chamber of Commerce site (**www.gbcc.org/html/links.html**) offers an extensive list of useful links to business news, resources and information, education, employment, healthcare, museums, art, music, newspapers, restaurants, sports, and travel and transportation.

PS

Last but certainly not least, there's the local dialect. According to Adam Gaffin at Boston-Online.com, 'It'll take a lot moah than dropping yoah ahs to talk like a native. We have our own way of pronouncing other words, our own vocabulary, even a unique grammatical construct. Journey outside the usual tourist haunts, and you just might need a guide to understand the locals.' Fortunately for you, Mr Gaffin provides just such a guide online (www.boston-online.com/glossary.html).

Brussels

Sooner or later everyone has to go to Brussels. This small-scale city makes the most of the fact that most of the offices of the European Union are there plus a handful of international corporate headquarters. Brussels is also home to Management Centre Europe, the European outpost of the American Management Association – and host of regular conferences in the city (www.mce.be).

Most famous (and the butt of some cruel jokes from other Europeans) for their love of french fries, Brussels inhabitants are becoming increasingly sophisticated and the city has some great places to eat out. Indeed the city boasts more Michelin-starred restaurants per square kilometre than Paris. But it's still a magnet for anyone with a love of fries and/or beer. The city offers literally hundreds of types of beers. This may make it a better place to do business. (Beer lovers in search of the genuine article should visit **La Fleur en Papier Doré** where René Magritte once surreally propped up the bar.)

Brussels is largely francophone though it is within the Flemish (Dutch)-speaking sector of bilingual Belgium. English is rapidly approaching fourth-language status (German is also an official language).

Coming and going

Brussels' airport is the unexceptional **Zaventem,** about 14 km north of the city (www.brusselsairport.be). Trains run into the centre about every 20 minutes for the 20-minute ride and stop at the three main stations, Gare du Nord, Gare Central and Gare du Midi. Tickets cost around BF100. A taxi to the city centre takes as long as the traffic will allow and costs around BF1000.

The rail system is good and Brussels is plugged into the European network, including a direct link to London.

Out and about

The good metro system **www.metropla.net/eu/bru/brussels.htm**), the trams and taxis (pick them up at ranks) are probably the best way to get around. Don't attempt to drive. Defying stereotype, Brussels drivers can be worse than any in Europe. The city is pretty safe but is gaining a reputation (deserved) for pickpocket activity on the metro and around railway stations.

Networking

Belgium is really carved-up bits of the Netherlands and France plus Brussels. The city prides itself on being 'the capital of Europe' (it isn't, except in the sense that Canberra is the capital of Australia while everyone knows it's really Sydney – or possibly Melbourne). In other words, this is where the Euro bureaucrats live and have their offices. Because of that, Brussels is highly cosmopolitan in the true sense.

Behaving yourself

Business is relatively formal. Shake hands on meeting and leaving. The Belgians may be a little unpunctual. But visitors shouldn't be.

The business tourist

The main European Union office district is about 2 km east of the city centre near the **Schuman** subway station. The European Commission will move back to the renovated **Berlaymont** building on Rond-Point Schuman in 2001–2. The European Parliament meets in a modern complex near Gare Léopold. Most international banks and embassies are based in this district.

International companies are largely based around **Avenue Louise** with a subway stop at Place Louise, at the city end of the avenue. Several business hotels are in this district.

Gare du Nord is the centre of a growing business area that includes the World Trade Centre and the headquarters of the Belgian telecommunications company Belgacom. The Place Rogier subway stop is close by.

A number of international companies are located outside the centre (about 6 km) on the airport road near to NATO headquarters.

The three-hour tourist

Do the **Grand Place** if you haven't already – it's one of the most beautiful and best preserved squares in Europe. Get one up on the irritating Manneken-Pis (a statue of a little boy urinating) by ignoring him in favor of the much less-well-known female equivalent Jeanneke-Pis.

Outside of the Grand Place you can visit the ludicrous **Atomium**, a 140 m steel representation of an iron crystalline molecule, built for the 1958 World Fair. You can go inside to get a fine view but the exhibition is weak.

Better bets are **Autoworld** (Parc du Cinquantenaire) if you like cars; **Belgian Comic Strip Centre** (Rue des Sables) if you like Tintin and other cartoon characters; **Museum of Modern Art** (Rue de la Regence) if you like Magritte; and a tour of the **Gueuze Museum** (Rue Gheude) if you like beer – and you'll have a hard time in Brussels if you don't.

Gift buying

Brussels isn't really well known for its shopping and there are few areas that cater exclusively for the shopaholic. Most of the big shops are around the **Gare Centrale** or **Avenue Louise** though there are shops all over the city. Nor is Brussels particularly famous for any type of souvenir. A few years back Belgian chocolates might have been gratefully received back home, but these are now so widely available that they have lost their cachet to some extent.

Bare facts

Weather

Typical northern Europe. Reasonable summers of up to 25°C, mildish winters (snow is rare), and wet springs and autumns. It rains a lot. Reckon on it being exactly like London but 24 hours later.

Hours

Shopping: 09.00–18.00 Monday–Saturday. **Banks:** 09.00–12.00; 14.00–16.00 Monday–Friday.

Public holidays

1 January; Easter Friday; Easter Sunday; Easter Monday; 1 May; 21 July (Independence Day); Assumption Day; 11 November (Veteran's Day); 25 December; 26 December.

The boring stuff

No vaccinations are required. The water is safe. Very few restrictions on what the average business traveller can bring in. There is no duty-free allowance for travellers from other EU countries. No visas required for visits under three months.

The country code for Belgium is 32, followed by the city code, 2, and Brussels is one hour ahead of GMT.

Brussels online

www.webguidebrussels.com is the unofficial starting point to most of the websites about Brussels. A very useful set of links to Belgian trade associations and similar bodies can be found at www.obcebdbh.be/en/services/adresses.html. The federation of Belgian companies' website is also quite useful, www.vbo-feb.be/ukindexol.htm. Beer lovers should visit www.beertemple.com to order online.

PS

Brussels is divided into the Lower Town and the Upper Town, which were occupied by the poorer, Flemish-speaking workers and the French-speaking aristocrats. No need to ask which was which.

Chicago

Chicago is 'capital' of the Midwest but its location on the southern shore of Lake Michigan often makes it feel like a coastal town. It is a strange combination of out-of-season seaside town and soaring metropolis, a kind of cross between Atlantic City and New York. The full flavour is best appreciated by Chicago's greatest laureate, Saul Bellow, whose work celebrates the city's complex cornucopia of people and experiences.

The city has a colourful history of jazz, blues and crime, but today feels a lot more conservative (though there are some great jazz and blues clubs). To some extent the city has missed out on the e-business revolution in the USA (Marc Andreeson, founder of Netscape, was a student at the University of Illinois but left for California; likewise, Chicagoan Lawrence Ellison went west to build Oracle.)

But that may have its advantages: Chicago's economy is increasingly becoming more diversified even as its signature exchanges feel the weight of competition.

Coming and going

Chicago has two airports, **O'Hare International Airport**, about 30 km from the city, and **Midway**, about 16 km out (www.chicagoairports.com). All foreign and most domestic flights land at O'Hare, which is big and busy. It's also a key US hub so if the weather's bad at O'Hare the whole of the US network can start to snarl up. An airport bus service to the centre takes 40 minutes and costs $14.75. The subway takes 45 minutes and costs $1.50. A taxi into the city centre should take 40 minutes and cost about $35.

Midway is on Chicago's South Side. The 30-minute subway ride to the centre costs $1.50. Taxi fare should be around $25.

Out and about

Getting around Chicago is fairly easy. The subway (known as the 'L', short for elevated railway) is one of the sites of the city (at least the elevated sections are) and must be tried at least once. Buses are also OK. Use Chicago Transit Authority's online trip planner (www.transitchicago.com). Chicago is also famous in the USA for the quality of its taxi cabs and their friendly drivers. But then if you've been to New York …

Chicago is like any US city, with good and bad parts. Be sensible and keep to the well-trodden areas.

Networking

Chicago doesn't have the brashness of New York or Los Angeles, but it is one of the great US cities and a great place to do business and some tourism. Crime is falling and some inner-city areas, notably Lincoln Park, are booming. It is also home to an international business school with notably stellar Nobel-winning faculty (www.gsb.uchicago.edu). Outside of the city there is Northwestern University whose equally famed b-school numbers marketing guru Philip Kotler among its faculty (www.northwestern.edu).

The Chicagoland Chamber of Commerce (www.chicagoland chamber.org) provides a full calender of networking events.

Behaving yourself

Chicago is friendly and businesslike. Outside of the dot-com sector (and Chicago isn't an e-business hotspot), business dress is formal. As with the rest of the USA, first names are used readily and business negotiations are open and direct.

The business tourist

Chicago's key companies are in manufacturing, retail, finance, insurance, real estate, business services and healthcare. Top businesses headquartered in the city include Abbott Laboratories, Baxter International, Caterpillar, Sara Lee, MacDonald's, Motorola, Quaker Oats, Archer Daniels Midland and Sears Roebuck.

Most businesses are located downtown inside the area known as 'the **Loop**,' because the elevated railway circles it.

Chicago is also, of course, a major trading centre, home to the **Chicago Board of Trade** (CBOT – www.cbot.com), the **Chicago Board Options Exchange** (CBOE – www.cboe.com/exchange) and the **Chicago Mercantile Exchange** (the 'Merc' – www.cme.com), though these have lost some influence in recent years to electronic trading exchanges elsewhere in the country and also in Europe. The exchanges have public galleries for spectators.

The three-hour tourist

Not easy to do in three hours, since there's so much to see and do. A ride on the Brown Line of the L provides a picturesque view of the Loop and the Chicago River. The 103rd-floor **Skydeck** of the **Sears Tower** (South Wacker Drive) provides great views over downtown and Lake Michigan. The 90-minute **Chicago Architecture Foundation (www.architecture.org)** river cruise is the best way to take in the city's famed skyscraper backdrop.

The **Art Institute of Chicago** (Madison Avenue – www.artic-edu) has excellent art exhibits.

Alternatively, read Saul Bellow and wander around – Bellow's *The Adventures of Augie March* is the definitive Chicago novel.

Gift buying

Downtown shopping is concentrated around **Michigan Avenue** and **State Street**, with Cartier, Bloomingdale's, Saks Fifth Avenue and Neiman Marcus concentrated on Michigan Avenue north of the Chicago River. **Marshall Fields** on State Street is worth visiting for the architecture alone and its Frango mints.

Slightly odd shops to visit include the somewhat bizarre **Nike Town** (Michigan Avenue), **Savvy Traveler** (Michigan Avenue) for every conceivable travel-related artifact, and **FAO Schwarz** (Michigan Avenue) for toys.

The refurbished **Navy Pier** area is also a centre of shops, theatres and museums.

Bare facts

Weather

Extreme. Summer can be very hot with high humidity. Winters are cold and wet or very snowy. Locals reckon September is the best month.

Hours

Shops: 09.30–18.00 Monday–Saturday; some shopping centres and malls stay open till 21.00. **Banks:** 09.00–15.00 Monday–Friday.

Public holidays

There are five fixed-date federal holidays: New Year's Day (1 January); Flag Day (14 June); Independence Day (4 July); Veterans Day (11 November) and Christmas (25 December). Floating federal holidays include the birthday of Dr Martin Luther King (third Monday in January); Inauguration Day (20 January every four years); President's Day (third Monday in February); Memorial Day (last Monday in May); Labor Day (first Monday in September); Columbus Day (second Monday in October) and Thanksgiving Day (fourth Thursday in November). Businesses may or may not be closed on these days, but most typically close on the major holidays. When a fixed-date holiday falls on a Saturday, the holiday is taken on the Friday before it. When it falls on a Sunday, the holiday is taken on Monday. August is the most popular month for family vacations, and although businesses typically remain open, key contacts may be on leave.

The boring stuff

No vaccinations are required to enter the USA and the water is safe. No visa is required for visits under three months for visitors from countries covered by the US Visa Waiver Program. Comprehensive health insurance is an absolute must.

Chicago online

The city's home page is www.ci.chi.il.us.. A useful source is the *Chicago Tribune* – www.chicagotribune.com – and the *Chicago Sun-Times* (www.suntimes.com)

The Chicago Board of Trade website is at www.cbot.com and there is always the home of the Chicago Bulls: www.nba.com/bulls/.

PS

Reputedly Chicago earned its sobriquet 'the windy city' from loquacious local politicians. We prefer to think it's something to do with the bitingly cold draughts of air that come in off Lake Michigan in winter.

Frankfurt

Anyone going to Frankfurt is almost certainly in finance of some sort. The city is host to the Bundesbank, Germany's central bank, and now the European Central Bank (www.ecb.iht), guardian of the euro. It also has a powerful stock exchange, including the high-tech Neuer Markt, the fourth largest in the world with ambitions to challenge London, and strong insurance and stockbroking sectors. International trade fairs are also a key Frankfurt industry.

You might not want to go otherwise. Frankfurt lacks the beauty, romance and sheer enjoyment of a lot of other European cities though its ambitious building programme (see 'the business tourist' below) could catapult it into the 21st century ahead of the field.

Coming and going

Flughafen Frankfurt Main (www.frankfurt-airport.de) is Europe's biggest and busiest airport after London Heathrow. There are two terminals connected by the Sky Line rail link. The airport is nine km south-west of the city. Cabs take 20 minutes to the city centre, twice that in rush hour. Hotel shuttles and car rentals are also available but much easier to jump on a train, which stops near the Terminal 1 arrival area.

Out and about

Germanic and efficient public transport (www.metropla.net/eu/ffm/frankfurt.htm)

Networking

Frankfurt is an increasingly cosmopolitan city, driven by its financial power. Over 160 nationalities live in the city and more than 3000 foreign companies are based here, with nearly 200 foreign business and leisure clubs.

Behaving yourself

Business meetings are regarded as formal and both men and women should wear suits. Outside of that, dress generally is fairly casual. But nights out at the opera or theatre may require more formal wear. Shake hands on meeting and departing. Despite service being included on most bills, it's customary to add a small tip of about 5 per cent. Note that shops and restaurants prefer cash to cards.

The business tourist

In 1998, Frankfurt produced a high-rise development plan, 'Frankfurt 2000', designed to meet growing demands for residential and office space. Three areas were designated for development: the traditional banking district and the **Trade Fair (Messe) District** will come first, followed by further building in the Messe and the Park District, near the main railway station.

These developments include the **Europaviertel** (European Quarter), west of the city. Developers are working on 90 hectares of property that used to be Frankfurt's freight train depot to create a new inner-city district. Plans include the expansion of Frankfurt's trade fair operations to create a new Messe Hall 3, a proposed multifunctional building holding 20,000 to 30,000 visitors for concerts and sports events as well as fairs.

Redevelopment of Frankfurt's former **West Port** directly on the banks of the River Main will combine buildings for working and living to create a regenerated waterfront district. Plans for building around the port will create an estimated 3200 jobs as well as space for 1000 apartments.

The three-hour tourist

The tour probably won't take the nominal three hours since the city was flattened by the Allies during the war and Frankfurters haven't bothered to restore it, even though the city was once a power centre of the Holy Roman Empire. Best you can do is a scale model of the old city at the **Historisches Museum** (Historical Museum) on Saalgasse 19 (see **www.frankfurter-museen.de** for a directory of all Frankfurt museums, in German). Best other things are **Romerberg**, a square that is the historical centre of the city. The **Kaisersaal** was used for feasting after crowning the Holy Roman emperors and portraits of all 52 German emperors and kings are still there. The square is bordered by a row of reproduction 15th-century buildings. You can also visit **Goethehaus**, where Johann Wolfgang von Goethe – Germany's top thinker and writer – was born in 1749 (Grosser Hirschgraben 23–5). A better bet might be the city's numerous parks, botanical gardens and the famous zoo, one of the best in Europe.

Gift buying

The **Zeil** pedestrian zone, going east from the Hauptwache to the Konstablerwache, is the main shopping drag. Upmarket shops are in the side streets leading away from the Zeil, Hauptwache and Fressgass. East of the Konstablerwache, shops are more downmarket.

Designer clothes and luxury shops such as Cartier and Luis Vuitton are on **Goethestrasse**. **Schillerstrasse**, near the Zeil, is also good. **Nordwest Zentrum** and **Zeilgalerie** are shopping malls. There's a Saturday flea market on the banks of the Main.

For out-of-the-ordinary gifts you might try wooden toys at **Hannah Kley** near the Hauptwache at Rossmarkt or local wine at **Weingut der Stadt Frankfurt am Main** at Limpurger Gasse 2 on the Romerberg. Porcelain is also big in Frankfurt, with two 18th-century factories, **Meissen** (John Montag Meissen Porzellan, which also sells silverware, crystal, jewelry, and ivory) at Kaiserstrasse 41 and **Hochster Porzellan** with a shop on Berliner Strasse.

Bare facts

Weather

Hot and sticky in summer; freezing in winter, with some snow. Spring definitely best.

Hours

Banks: 09.00–13.00 Monday, Wednesday, Friday; 09.00–18.00 Tuesday, Thursday. **Offices:** 09.00–17.00 weekdays. **Shops:** 09.30–20.00 Monday–Friday; 09.30–16.00 Saturday. For the time being at least, all shops are closed on Sundays. Many restaurants are closed on Sundays and Mondays.

Public holidays

1 January (New Year's Day); Good Friday; Easter Monday; 1 May (Labour Day); Ascension; Whit Monday; 3 October (Day of German Unity); 25–26 December (Christmas); 31 December (New Year's Eve).

The boring stuff

No vaccinations or health certificates are required except for visitors from certain developing countries. The water is safe. Very few restrictions on what the average business traveller can bring in. There is no duty-free allowance for travellers from other EU countries. No visas required for visits under three months.

The country code for Germany is 49, followed by the city code, 69. Frankfurt is one hour ahead of GMT from October to March, and two hours between April and September.

Frankfurt online

www.deutschland-tourismus.de/e/dest_cities_frankfurt_e.html   will give you everything you might ever need to know in terms of general tourist information. Frankfurt Economic Development's 'Digital marketplace' website provides economic data and helpful links and information (www.frankfurt-business.de in English and German).

PS

Beware: building work. A project known as **'Frankfurt 21'** entails constructing a seven-kilometre tunnel under the city to replace rail lines running to the main station. The tunnel would reroute inbound and outbound trains underground, thus freeing up the aboveground land for new development. Construction of the tunnel is expected to begin in 2004, with the project completed in 2012. Of the 62 hectares of land available, 33 should be used for building, 19 for traffic, and 10 as green-field sites. Apartments for roughly 7300 people, as well as office buildings with space for up to 17,800 jobs are also in the plans.

Hong Kong

Once a British colony, now part of China, Hong Kong is a bustling city where some 7 million live cheek by jowl, crammed into an area of just over 1000 square kilometres.

Political power may have passed from the British to the Chinese in the autumn of 1997, but business travellers will be hard pressed to notice. There is still a large ex-pat presence along with all the major corporations you might expect in one of the principal commercial gateways to Asia.

Coming and going

Arriving at Hong Kong by air used to entail a white-knuckle descent into Kaitak airport through a valley of high-rise buildings lining the approach to the airstrip. Those of a nervous disposition will be glad to learn that landing at the new airport on Lantau Island is considerably more sedate.

Although the new **Chek Lap Kok Airport** is 20 miles from town, getting to the main city is simple: take a taxi or try the new express train service.

The Airport Express train is quick – it should take a little over 20 minutes; it is also cheap – about HK$90 to Hong Kong Island and HK$80 to Kowloon. The round trip is about HK$160 for a ticket that is valid for one month. If you're leaving the city via the Airport Express you can check in for your flight at both the Kowloon and Hong Kong Island stations. The train also connects with Hong Kong's MTR (Mass Transit Railway). Or, for a scenic approach, take the ferry from Chep Lap Kok ferry pier for $HK15.

Take a taxi and it may well take you over an hour to make your way through Hong Kong's congested traffic. And it won't be cheap – the journey is likely to cost some HK$300-plus.

Out and about

Most business travellers will probably choose to use Hong Kong's plentiful supply of red-liveried taxis to get about the city. The meter starts at HK$15.

A word of warning: if you take a taxi it's best to have your destination written down in Chinese as few taxi drivers speak English.

The taxi averse should try the underground, trams or buses.

The underground is extensive, has several lines, and is signposted in English as well as Cantonese and Mandarin. It's clean, fast, safe and should suit travellers with a little more time on their hands.

Trams are to be found on the Hong Kong side of the bay. They are cheap – about HK$2. Get on at the back of the tram and pay when you get off at the front. The trams run through Causeway Bay, Central and beyond.

Buses come in the single- and double-decker varieties. Their routes criss-cross Hong Kong Island and through the tunnel to the mainland. Don't get one if you're in a hurry though – like buses in most cities they can be frustratingly slow.

If you are staying in TST (Tsim Sha Tsui) on the Kowloon side or simply want to cross the water from Kowloon to Hong Kong Island, then you will want to use the Star Ferry. The ferry runs from TST to two piers on the island – one in Central and one next to the Hong Kong Convention and Exhibition Centre – and costs around HK$3.

Networking

A favourite of business travellers, situated on the 'Golden Mile' in the TST district of Kowloon is the Hyatt Regency (**www.hyattregency.com.hk**). It has all the usual business facilities, boasts a highly regarded Chinese restaurant, and has its own Feng Shui master. It is also particularly well positioned from a transport point of view.

Check out *The South China Morning Post* for the local news in English as well as *imail* and the *Asian Wall Street Journal*.

Behaving yourself

Greet people either in the Chinese fashion with a bow, or in the Western fashion by shaking hands; either will do usually. The indecisive can even give a small nod of the head and shake hands as well. Always greet the most senior person in a group first and when bowing to someone of seniority bow lower than they do and let them rise first. Chinese surnames precede personal names – Chan Jiang would be Mr Chan. Address business acquaintances as Mr etc. unless they tell you otherwise.

As in many other Asian countries they are big on business cards in Hong Kong. When offering the business card, hold it with both hands with the Chinese translation face up. When receiving a business card, use both hands. This is important business etiquette. What you do with the card is equally important. Don't put it away immediately, make sure you study it first: this demonstrates respect for the person's status.

Punctuality is important in Hong Kong; something to be borne in mind when travelling across the congested city to a meeting. If late, apologize profusely.

Finally be prepared to do some serious eating. Business dinners may span in excess of ten courses.

The business tourist

The business centre of the city is the **Central District**, home to the city's stock exchange (deceptively quiet because it is all computerized), and whose architectural landmarks include the 180-metre-high **Hong Kong Bank** (just walk in to have a look). Another skyscraping giant worth looking out for is the **Bank of China Building**, which is in the middle of the Central District and is one of the world's ten highest structures.

The three-hour tourist

Standard tourist fare would include, some or all of the following:

- Take the peak tram to Victoria Peak for the spectacular view over the harbour, Hong Kong Island and Kowloon.
- The bustle of Stanley Market, 10.00–19.00 (take Citybus 6 or 6A from Exchange Square), and shopping along the 'Golden Mile' in Kowloon.
- A trip to Lantau Island to see the largest outdoor statue of a Buddha. Take a ferry from Central Pier to Mui Woi. It's a longish trip – six-plus hours there and back and only suitable for those with a lot of spare time.

Gift buying

Tales of the shopping bargains to be had in Hong Kong are legendary. The legends are true to an extent, but maybe not as true as they once were. Yes you can get a suit made up in 24 hours but there's a strong possibility it will look just that. The more time the tailor has and the better fitting he conducts, the better suit you are likely to get. The most famous of the speed merchants is probably **Sam's Tailors** off Nathan Road. It numbers Margaret Thatcher and George Bush among its clients. Draw your own conclusions.

Antiques can be found along **Hollywood Road**. Be careful to check there aren't restrictions that prevent you exporting your treasured purchase. **Temple Street Market**, Kowloon, is Hong Kong's most popular market, nightly 20.00–22.30. Keep your valuables safe.

Bare facts

Weather

Hong Kong is in a typhoon region and typhoons can batter the territory any time from May until September, especially September. Watch out for signal warnings 8 and 10 – sustained high winds. Humidity can be a problem too. In spring and summer it can reach a sticky 85 per cent.

As a general rule, expect the following seasonal weather: spring and summer (humid, hot, wet), autumn (warm and sunny), winter (humid, cool). Temperatures fluctuate widely from a summer average of 28°C to 15°C in winter.

Hours

Banks: 09.00–16.30 Monday–Friday; 09.00–12.30 Saturday. **Offices:** 09.00–17.00 Monday–Friday; 09.00–13.00 Saturday. **Shops:** 10.00–21.30.

Holidays

There are numerous festivals that take place in Hong Kong throughout the year. Many of these bring commerce to a halt as well as making an already crowded city more crowded. The biggest festival celebrated by the Chinese is the Chinese Lunar New Year some time in January/February. Other festivals include: the Spring Lantern Festival on the 15th day of the lunar year (lots of colourful lanterns); Ching Ming, the 'Remembrance of Ancestors' Day', in early April (visiting of family graves to show respect); the Tuen Ng Festival, the internationally renowned Dragon Boat Festival on the fifth day of the fifth lunar month (boat racing); the Mid Autumn – moon – Festival, mid-September (coloured lanterns and moon cake); and the Cheun Yeung Festival in October (visiting of family graves to show respect again).

The boring stuff

Travellers are advised to vaccinate against polio and tetanus. Hong Kong is a Special Administrative Region of China: travellers entering Hong Kong without a visa but intending to travel to mainland China will need a visa before arriving at the Chinese border.

The international dialling code for Hong Kong is 852, and it is eight hours ahead of GMT.

Hong Kong online

Helpful websites about Hong Kong include the Hong Kong Tourism Board (www.webservl.discoverhongkong.com/flash.html; the world executive site (www.worldexecutive.com/cityguides/hongkong); and www.info.gov.hk/eindex.htm for links to governments departments and services.

The *South China Morning Post* (www.scmp.com) has extensive business coverage in English, including a special technology section. It also provides information on special technology section. It also provides information on restaurants, arts and entertainment. Also check out IMAIL (www.hk-imail.com/relisme) and the *Asian Wall Street Journal* (www.dowjones.com/awstjweekly/sub.html) which requires a paid subscription.

PS

As you would expect, Hong Kong is a paradise for fans of Chinese food. There are over 8000 restaurants on Hong Kong Island and Kowloon. The cuisine that dominates is Cantonese, but the gamut of Chinese cooking is available from Yunann to Sichuan, as well as most other Asian culinary styles. Visitors should at least try some dim sum or yum cha. Served from morning to mid-afternoon, dim sum are dishes steamed in small bamboo baskets trolleyed around the dining room (in less traditional restaurants you may have to choose from a menu). Just point at a dish that looks appealing.

Johannesburg

Alternatively known in Nguni as 'Egoli', the city of gold, Johannesburg is South Africa's largest city. It may lack the eye-catching beauty of Cape Town, but what it lacks in beauty it makes up for in hard-headed commercialism. Jo'burg generates more than 35 per cent of South Africa's GDP and is now the biggest city in Africa.

Jo'burg has always been a commercial city. It was named after Johan Rissik who was the surveyor general sent to select a site for the original village and Johannes Joubert, the mining commissioner sent to investigate claims that gold had been found. It has been coining it in ever since.

Coming and going

Most international flights land at **Johannesburg International Airport** (formerly Jan Smuts Airport – **www.airports.co.za**), which handles around 10 million passengers a year and is one of the African continent's key transport hubs. It's about 19 km from the city centre. Taxis are safe so long as you take a metered Johannesburg airport taxi. Fare is around R180 and the journey should take around 35 minutes. Many hotels provide pick-up from the airport for guests. If you're going to the northern suburbs it may be easier to catch the Sandton Shuttle – tickets are available near the international arrivals exit. Other bus services include Magic Bus, which stops at different hotels and shopping areas, and Impala Tours, which runs to Johannesburg's train station in Braamfontein, close to the central business district.

Out and about

Johannesburg isn't that safe – muggings, even in daylight, happen often – and driving is the best way to get about (though most Rosebank and Sandton hotels offer shuttle services to shopping malls and the downtown area, about ten minutes away). Keep the car doors locked, especially at traffic lights ('robots' in South Africa speak). It is said that women driving alone are allowed to shoot red lights at robots in Johannesburg – but you wouldn't be driving alone anyway, would you? If you don't fancy driving, take a taxi and in any case always take a taxi at night. Don't walk around the central district alone during the day unless you are in a large group and avoid it at night.

The city centre is laid out in a grid, with Jan Smuts Avenue running north from the centre through suburban Parktown, Rosebank, Dunkeld, Hyde Park, Craighall and Randburg. The William Nicol Highway comes off this avenue and runs toward Sandton, rapidly developing as the new city centre.

Though you can usually find taxis easily at the airport, rail station and other major landmarks, generally you have to phone to book one. The meter starts at R2 and charges around R3 per kilometre.

Behaving yourself

Though polite and friendly, the atmosphere can be formal. Sport is always a good conversational gambit, especially cricket and rugby. Be on time for appointments.

Though general South African dress is casual, businessmen and women are expected to wear suits for business meetings and conferences. Wear a jacket and tie when dining out.

Tipping is customary and expected in South Africa, a bit like the USA. Add around 10 per cent to a waiter or bartender. A service charge added to the bill means you don't have to tip but it is still appreciated. Note that, by law, hotels do not include a service charge in their bills. Even so, hotel porters should be tipped a couple of rands per luggage. Hairdressers and taxi drivers expect tips of around 10 per cent.

If you're driving, there are no self-service stations – an attendant will fill your tank and usually check oil and water as well. Give a couple of rands as a tip.

Remember that the city is 2000 ft above sea level and this can effect what alcohol does to you.

The business tourist

Johannesburg is a mining town – gold mining at that – as the mine dumps and mine shafts that surround the town attest. The city grew up almost overnight as a gold rush shanty town on the open veldt after gold was discovered there in the late 1860s. Now it's South Africa's, and probably the continent's, commercial hub. Most of the country's industrial and commercial concerns are centred here, though undermining means the city is short on those familiar high-rise tower blocks. Johannesburg is also center to the thriving **Witwatersrand** metropolitan district of around five million people.

The three-hour tourist

The **Johannesburg Art Gallery**, though not in the safest area, is worth a visit, as is **MuseumAfrica** and **Nelson Mandela's home**, one of the most visited sites in South Africa. The four-roomed house, where Mandela lived with his wife and children during the 1950s, offers a running commentary on the anti-apartheid struggle.

More unusual are Chamber of Mines tours of a working goldmine, though they take all day, and three-hour tours of **Soweto**, which can also be taken at night to include a traditional meal and township jazz.

And if you want to see the Johannesburg skyline, try the observation deck of the downtown 50-storey **Carlton Centre** (Main Street).

Gift buying

Not a great place for shopping, though the **Rosebank** African craft market is probably the best place to buy local crafts and curios cheaply. **Sandton City** shopping is a massive underground sprawl of shops, restaurants and bars.

Bare facts

Weather

Johannesburg has hot, pleasant summers (the winter months in the northern hemisphere) though with afternoon thunderstorms. In winter, days are chilly and nights frosty. Peak tourist season is from October to March, especially during December and January.

Hours

Offices: 8.30–16.30 weekdays. **Banks:** 8.30–15.30 weekdays; on Saturdays, some banks open 08.00–11.30. **Shopping:** 09.00–18.00 Mondays–Friday 09.00–13.00 Saturdays.

Public holidays

New Year's Day; 21 March (Human Rights Day); 5 April (Family Day); Good Friday; 27 April (Freedom Day); 1 May (Workers' Day); 16 June (Youth Day); 9 August (National Woman's Day); 24 September (Heritage Day); 16 December (Day of Reconciliation); Christmas Day; Boxing Day (also known as Day of Goodwill).

The boring stuff

Visas are required by all except citizens of Australia, Canada, the European Union, Iceland, Japan, Liechtenstein, New Zealand, Norway, Singapore,

Switzerland, and the USA for up to 90 days' stay. Citizens from most South American and African countries can stay for up to 30 days.

There are restrictions on how much cash you can take out of South Africa so keep receipts of any currency exchanges.

Tap water in Johannesburg is safe for drinking, but outside the city stick to bottled water. There's little risk of malaria in the city but it can be a risk outside. The standard of medical care is generally good.

The country code for South Africa is 27, followed by the city code, 11, and Johannesburg is two hours ahead of GMT.

Jo'burg online

The city's website is **www.joburg.org.za** which gives details about tourist venues and contact details for business organizations. *The Daily Mail and Guardian*, South Africa's national newspaper, can be found at **www.mg.co.za/mg**. Also useful are the city's Chamber of Commerce site – **www.jcci.co.za** – and the Securities Exchange site – **www.jse.co.za**.

The *Time Out* city guide for the city (**www.timeout.com/johannesburg/links/index.html**) is rich with useful information and terrific links, including a restaurant research engine for all of South Africa, a web portal for the region, big game reserves and local enterprises.

PS

If you're up to it, a must is the **KwaZulu Muti Shop**, a little downtown shop complete with traditional herbal cures, baboon skulls, ostrich feet, and animal skins, (corner of Diagonal and President Streets).

London

'When you are tired of London you are tired of life, for there is in London all that life can afford.' So said Dr Samuel Johnson, the famous lexicographer. Of course Johnson never spent 40 minutes in a taxi stuck in traffic on the Fulham Road, yet his sentiments still ring true for many of the 12 million souls who inhabit this bustling cosmopolitan metropolis. After years spent nursing an inferiority complex the biggest city in Europe has enjoyed a renaissance of late, restoring it to its rightful position as one of the great cities of the world.

London may look a little down at heel, a bit tatty around the edges. It may be choking on its own traffic fumes. It may buckle under the weight of incessant grey skies. But walk along Fleet Street, up High Holborn towards St Paul's Cathedral on a bright summer's day, watch the theatre crowds disgorged on to the pavements of Drury Lane or sit by the fire in a mews pub with a pint of beer and you too might see London through the eyes of the venerable Dr Johnson.

Coming and going

Five airports serve London: **Heathrow**, **Gatwick**, **Stansted**, **City** and **Luton**. The majority of business travellers to London will arrive at Heathrow or Gatwick.

Heathrow (www.heathrow.co.uk) is 15 miles west of London. The best way of getting into the city is to use the Heathrow Express (05.00–23.50). It takes 15 minutes, costs less than £15 and takes you to Paddington Station. A London underground or 'tube' train (Piccadilly Line) will cost less than £5 but take much longer – almost an hour – and is a struggle with a lot of luggage. A black taxi cab will cost about £50 and times into central London will depend on how desperate the traffic situation is. The airport limousine service is cheaper and more stylish (you travel in a Bentley or Rolls), but no faster.

Gatwick (www.baa.co.uk/main/airports/gatwick) airport is almost 30 miles south of London. By far the best way to get from Gatwick to London is via the Gatwick Express. Leaving every 15 minutes, it costs about £10 and arrives in Victoria Station in 30 minutes. Non-Gatwick Express services to London Bridge, Blackfriars and Kings Cross run nearer to London's financial district but take longer, 40 minutes to an hour.

Thirty miles north-east of London, the city's third airport **Stansted** (www.baa.co.uk/main/airports/stansted) is a 41-minute train ride away on the Stansted Skytrain. It costs under £15 and arrives at Liverpool Street station. A taxi will take 80 minutes and will cost some £60.

If you are arriving at London **City** (www.londoncityairport.com) airport you will be only six miles from London's financial district. A taxi will take less than 20 minutes to central London on a good run (about £30). Shuttle buses run to Canary Wharf from where you can pick up the Docklands Light Railway to Bank tube station.

From **Luton** airport (www.london-luton.com) 30 miles north-west of

London a Thameslink train to Kings Cross station departs every 15 minutes and takes half an hour. A taxi will take 90 minutes plus and cost approximately £40.

Out and about

For travelling short distances in London, hail a black cab. Taxis indicate their availability for hire with a shining yellow light on the front of the cab. Generally easy to come by during the day, they become harder to find as the evening progresses. Stick to licensed cabs – the traditional black sedan cab (they do come in other colours) as they are generally more reliable and the drivers a lot more knowledgeable about London's addresses than those of unlicensed taxis.

For trips over a slightly greater distance, for example one side of London to the other – Knightsbridge to the City, say – taxis are still an option. The vagaries of London's traffic may leave you a nervous wreck however as you sit in the back of the cab in traffic, late and watching the meter tick over. For this type of journey the tube is often a better choice.

Tube stations are clearly marked on a colour-coded map, a design classic in its own right, making navigation fairly simple. Train destinations are on the front of the trains. The London Underground (**www.thetube.com**; **www.londontransport.co.uk**) can become extremely crowded during the rush hour and during the summer months tempers get frayed as the crowds jostle for position. Before you travel you must purchase a ticket or travelcard (valid for seven days, requires passport-size photo). Make sure you retain the ticket until your journey's end, as you need to run it through the automatic ticket barriers to escape. The tube closes before midnight.

Buses are an alternative to taxis and the tube. In parts of the West End it is easy and convenient to hop on a red bus, travel the length of a long street and jump off at the other end. Cross-London journeys, while cheap and scenic, can be a slow.

If it's only a short distance and you're not in a rush, then buy an A–Z map of London and walk: it's often the easiest way getting from A to B and very pleasant in the summer.

Networking

Network away in the legion of London pubs. Alternatively, there are the traditional big-name hotels – famous names include the Dorchester, Claridge's, the Ritz and the Savoy, as well as a number of 'boutique'-style hotels opening their doors across the city, such as the Covent Garden Hotel, the urban chic of the St Martin's Lane Hotel; the Westbourne Hotel in trendy Notting Hill is another wired hotel with DVDs, flat-screen televisions and other digital comforts.

Behaving yourself

The English tend to be fairly formal in their approach to business. Despite the US influence from both dot-com culture and dress-down Fridays, suits are still very much *de rigueur* in much of the city, certainly in the financial institutions. Shake hands on meeting and leaving. Do not stray into personal conversation when conducting business over dinner unless you know your host well, and even then it is better to be reserved.

Long lunches coupled with alcohol used to be the norm in the City. In the health- and time-conscious new millennium, however the boozy lunch is increasingly making way for the power breakfast.

The business tourist

As well as the art galleries, theatres, museums, opera and other entertainment to be found in the UK's capital city, London has a thriving commercial district – the **City of London** is Europe's leading financial centre. One-third of the world's foreign exchange trading is done from the City and it's the world's largest centre for international bank lending and marine and aviation insurance. Among the world-famous institutions packed into 'the square mile', are the **Bank of England** (www.bankofengland.co.uk), **London Stock Exchange** (www.londonstockexchange.com) and the **Lloyds** insurance market. Take the tube to Bank and you're there.

Alternatively, there is a media cluster around **Charlotte Street**, a profusion of film makers (and more) in **Soho**, hip new economy companies in funky **Hoxton** and a cluster of newspapers in the somewhat isolated **Canary Wharf**, part of Docklands.

The three-hour tourist

London is a great place for sightseeing as all the major tourist attractions are close together. **Buckingham Palace**, the **Tower of London**, the new **Tate Modern** gallery, the **British Museum**, the **National Portrait Gallery** are all a short taxi ride away from each other.

For a stunning view of the city, visitors who do not suffer from vertigo can take a ride on the **London Eye**, a huge modern take on the Ferris wheel towering above London on the bank of the River Thames.

Gift buying

If you have not been before then no shopping spree in London is complete without a trip to **Harrods**, **Liberty**, **Fortnum & Masons** or **Harvey Nichols**.

At the other end of the scale, pay a visit on a Sunday to **Brick Lane** market in London's East End. Once the home of the Truman beer brewery, Brick Lane is now at the heart of London's growing dot-com culture. The market, however, pre-dates the internet revolution and is a fascinating collection of market stalls offering consumer goods, antiques, bric-a-brac and junk. Other markets worth a visit are **Portobello Road** in Notting Hill and **Camden Lock** in Camden.

Bare facts

Weather

Never terribly cold or roasting hot, London has a fairly even temperature throughout the year. One thing visitors should come prepared for is rain. Sometimes it appears that London is permanently beneath dark clouds. Drizzle, torrential downpours, hail, London excels in varieties of rain. Bring a coat and bring an umbrella.

Hours

Banks: 09.30–16.30 Monday to Friday (some open Saturday morning). **Offices:** 09.00–17.00 Monday–Friday. **Shops:** 09.00–17.30 (19.00 in central London) Monday–Saturday; many open 11.00–16.00 Sunday.

Holidays

The City winds down over the Christmas holidays (with the exception of the retail industry) which extend from as early as the second week in December to the end of the first week in January. The other main holiday of the year is Easter at the beginning of April. Most people take personal holidays during July and August, so while London is crowded with tourists during the summer months businesses are often missing key personnel. In addition the first and last Mondays of May and the last Monday of August are holidays.

The boring stuff

Visas are not required by nationals of EU countries, the USA and Canada for tourist visits not exceeding six months. The UK has no major health threats and the tap water is safe to drink, if not always pleasant.

London online

Useful tourist sites include www.london-pages.co.uk, www.london town.com and www.thisislondon.com.

The growing number of internet cafés include the UK's first – Cyberia in Whitfield Street (www.cyberiacafe.net); Webshack (www.webshack-café.com); Internet Exchange (at various locations and at www.internet-exchange.co.uk) and the Portobello Gold, a combination of bar, restaurant and hotel (www.portobellogold.com).

PS

British cuisine? It does exist. For a British flavour of food, however, try some pub grub and real ale at one of the city's many public houses. The **Scarsdale** (Edwardes Square), although not in the financial district, is a charming example of a London pub and a good place to start. Other traditional food options include fish and chips at Terence Conran's restaurant in Fulham, **Bibendum**. Good but pricey. Or for the atmosphere of the gentleman's club there is **Simpsons** on the Strand.

Mexico City

Mexico City: a teeming megalopolis of over 20 million people, the second most populous city in the world after Tokyo; a sprawling city both ancient and modern, rich and poor. Mexico City has art museums, symphony orchestras, ballet companies, opera, Aztec ruins, and mariachi music. Unfortunately for business travellers it also has crime – a lot of it.

Any visitor to Mexico should consider their personal security very carefully. Mexico City can be a very rewarding place to visit, but it can also be an extremely dangerous one: up there in the top ten dangerous cities according to security experts Kroll; second after South Africa for countries with the worst public safety, according to the World Economic Forum in Geneva poll 'Crime in Mexico'.

Don't be too discouraged. Thousands travel to Mexico on business every year and return unscathed. As Mexico is the US's second largest trading partner they will continue to do so. Just remember to be on your guard.

Coming and going

Eight miles east of the city Mexico City's **Benito Juarez International** airport is a 30-minute taxi drive from the city. Take one of the airport taxis, yellow with an airport symbol on the door. You can prepay at one of the special booths in the airport. Expect to pay a couple of pesos.

Out and about

Taxis on the streets are plentiful but should be avoided (green VW Beetles and newer Japanese vehicles) in favour of the hotel-owned sedans, which can be pre-ordered. It's far safer to use the hotel car or a radio cab (*sitios*). If you use a radio cab, get the concierge to call one for you and take a note of the firm and cab number.

Mexico City has an extensive subway system that covers most of the city. It's clean and efficient and relatively safe during daylight hours. The metro has its share of pickpockets and thieves so take sensible precautions (www.metropla.net/am/mexico.htm, in English). Also avoid the rush hour – 8–10 am and 6–8 pm – if possible when the subway becomes a heaving mass of humanity. If you are planning to use the subway frequently, buy a book of tickets for convenience.

Networking

Mexicans eat their main meal between 2 and 4 pm, occasionally combining a long leisurely lunch with business. Restaurants are of course open in the evening when the local populace will dine late – after 9 pm.

Favoured meeting places include the **Zona Rosa** (Pink Zone) where the best hotels are located overlooking Chapultepec Park. In the city the **Melia Mexico Reforma** bristles with hi-tech equipment. It has a corporate center complete with computers, stock-market indicator, messenger and secretarial services and each room has a PC port, fax modem outlet and three phones. The **Sheraton Maria Isabel Hotel & Towers**, located next to the US embassy and near the Zona Rosa, is another favourite meeting place for business travellers.

Behaving yourself

Mexicans frequently use three names: first name, paternal family name and maternal family name. So Sr Juan Hierro Batistuta would be addressed as Sr Hierro. You may also see the full name written as Sr Juan Hierro B or with the maternal family name excluded entirely. Wait to be asked before addressing someone by their first name.

The pace of business can be leisurely in Mexico. Try not to cram too much into the day or to rush meetings. Kick back and show some interest in your host. Lunches in particular can be very long and extend throughout the afternoon. While business may be discussed at lunch, business breakfasts are increasingly popular. Although many Mexicans, particularly in northern Mexico, are bilingual, they often prefer to conduct business in Spanish. If you are not a Spanish speaker, it might be well worth hiring an interpreter.

The business tourist

The city's business hub is in the Centro Historico, recently enhanced by a $300 million facelift. Banks and offices and much more line the Champs-Elysées-style **Paseo Reforma** in the city's Zona Rosa.

The three-hour tourist

Built on the remains of an ancient Aztec civilization, Mexico City is packed with museums and palaces and other sites of architectural and historical interest. The **Centro Historico** (Historical Centre) is a 500-block area built on the ruins of the Aztec capital Tenochtitlan. Ancient artifacts found locally are on display at the **Museo del Templo Mayor.**

Other sites worth visiting include **Casa de Azulejos** (the House of Tiles), the **Museo Nacional de Arte**, and the art deco **Palacio de Bellas Artes**, constructed entirely from marble. One of the world's greatest museums, the **Museo Nacional de Antropologia** (Museum of Anthropology), can be found in the city's largest park, Chapultepec Park. (See **www.cnn.com/travel/city.guides/wtr/north.america.profiles/nap.mexicao.html** for a directory of museums, historic sites, malls and markets, and some restaurants, in English.)

Outside the city the **Pyramids of Teotihuacan** to the north can be visited in a day, as can the floating gardens at **Xochimilco.**

For authentic Mexican food coupled with Mexican music check out **Café de Tacuba**. You can also have a Mexican breakfast here or you could try the famous Casa del Azulejos in the Historic Centre.

Gift buying

Designer labels and exquisite jewelry can be found along **Presidente Masaryk**. For pottery, a craft for which Mexico is renowned, try the **Uriarte** (Pabellon Altavista).

Another good place to find gifts is the **Bazar Sabado** (Plaza San Jacinto, in San Angel). Visitors can purchase goods displayed there made by local craftsmen. There is also a government-funded store, **Fonart** in Ave. Juarez, which sells local craftwork.

Bare facts

Weather

Mexico City's high altitude means the days are often chilly in the morning, gradually warming up through the afternoon. May to September the skies tend to be cloudy with rainfall in the evening. October to March is the dry season: very little rain, plenty of sunshine.

Hours

Banks: 09.00–17.00 Monday–Friday. **Offices:** 09.00–14.00 and 15.00–18.00 Monday–Friday. **Shops:** 09.00–14.00 and 16.00–20.00 Monday–Friday.

Holidays

6 January (Epiphany); March/April (Easter); 2 May (Day of the Holy Cross); 13 August (Commemoration of the Invasion of Tenochtitlan); 15 August (Assumption Day); 1 September (Presidential State of the Union address to Congress); 29 September (Feast of the parish of San Miguel – downtown); 1–2 November (erection of altars in honour of All Souls and All Saints, visits to cemeteries); 16–24 December (Jesus birth processions – 'Posadas') 24 December (Christmas Eve); 31 December (New Year's Eve).

The boring stuff

For anyone lacking a tourist card a visa is necessary. Health risks include Hepatitis A, polio, tetanus and typhoid. Since the city is situated over 7000 feet above sea level, visitors may be affected by altitude sickness and should take time to acclimatize. For the same reason sunblock is a good idea.

The country code for Mexico is 52, followed by the city code, 5, and Mexico City is six hours behind GMT.

Mexico City online

General information can be found at **www.mexicocity.com** and hotel websites include **www.hilton.com/hotels/MEXAHHF**.

PS

With low humidity and light winds, Mexico City suffers from appalling pollution that may cause problems for visitors, particularly if they suffer from asthma.

Milan

Milan is Italy's business and economic locomotive and, with its strong work ethic, much more like northern European cities than other parts of the country. But though business rules, it's also a historic city with plenty of churches and museums.

Coming and going

Milan has two airports, both of which are used by domestic and international flights.

Linate (**www.sea-aeroportimilano.it/eng/linate**, in English) is the older and more convenient, about seven km from the city centre. A 15-minute taxi journey to the centre should cost around L1,500. There are also regular bus services to the centre, costing L1,500. Tickets may be purchased at newsstands. Buses depart every 10 minutes for the 25 minute trip; #73 has special luggage racks. There is also a coach service between the air terminal at the Central Station and Linate Airport which departs every 20 minutes. The 20 minute ride costs L1,500.

Malpensa airport (**www.sea-aeroportimilano.it/eng/malpensa**, in English) is new and a good 50 km out of town. This is where most international travellers will arrive. A 60-minute taxi ride into the centre costs around L100,000. There are bus services, including the Air Pullman Malpensa

Shuttle, which goes to the Central Railway Station. Fare is L13,000. The new Malpensa Express train service offers a quick (40 minutes) and comfortable route to the city for L15,000.

Out and about

Milan radiates out from the Piazza Duomo and the city centre is fairly compact. The underground metro is safe and easy, though it doesn't go everywhere (www.metropla.net/eu/mil/milano.htm). Taxis, too, are easy to find in main squares. Buses and trams are convenient, but tickets need to be bought from bars or newspaper kiosks before boarding.

It's easy to rent a car, but driving may be best left to the locals unless you drive like an Italian.

Networking

Networking Milanese-style is a part of life, as automatic as breathing or checking the soccer scores. All cafés, bars and restaurants are networking centres. MBA students can be found hanging out at Capo Horn, Lighthouse and Shu, while the model and fashion set can be found at Hollywood, Propaganda and Shocking.

Behaving yourself

Business in Milan is relatively formal and polite. Dress conservatively (and smartly if you can – this is Europe's fashion capital after all). Shake hands on meeting and leaving. More and more Italians speak English but you may need a translator. Most also speak at least some French and Spanish. Milan is a business city so punctuality is expected.

A service charge is usually added in restaurants, but it is customary to leave a 10 per cent tip.

Crime is not a real problem but as in any big city beware of pickpockets.

The business tourist

As an economic powerhouse, Milan majors on finance (it is said that there are as many banks as churches in the city) and fashion, though telecoms-focused high tech is also getting big. Milan hosts lots of trade fairs and conferences so accommodation can be difficult at times. Most businesses are concentrated in the compact city centre, so getting around isn't difficult.

The three-hour tourist

Milan is more about business and eating and drinking than sightseeing (it isn't really a tourist town). But must-sees include **Piazza del Duomo** for the cathedral, Italy's largest Gothic building and the third-largest church in Europe. The view from the top is excellent on a clear day. You can walk through the nearby modern **Galleria Vittorio Emanuele** mall, **La Scala**, Milan's famous opera house, and the attached museum, which contains among other things Verdi's top hat and Toscanini's baton. Another must is the **Santa Maria delle Grazie** church (Corso Magenta) which houses the restored *The Last Supper* by Leonardo Da Vinci. The **Museo Poldi Pezzoli** (Via Manzoni) has works by Raphael, Bottocelli and Piero della Francesca. The **Accademia Brera** (Via Brera 28) was started by Napoleon, who filled it with looted works of art.

Gift buying

Lots of people think Milan is the shopping capital of the world. But as home to Armani and Versace and others it can melt your plastic.

The poshest shops are in the **Quadrilatero** (Via Monte Napoleone and Via Saint Andrea) and include Valentino, Gianni Versace, Giorgio Armani, Gucci, and so on. The **Duomo**, the **Brera** area, and **Via Vittorio Emanuele** are also pricey but good. The **Corso Buenos Aires** is good middle-range value as is **La Rinascente** (Piazza del Duomo), Milan's largest and oldest department store. **Galleria Vittorio Emanuele** is also interesting and great for coffee shops and people watching.

There are also some lively markets, notably the **Papiniano** market on Tuesdays and Saturdays.

Bare facts

Weather

Hot and sticky in July and August, relatively mild in the winter, though prone to both rain and fog. Best months are April, May, June, September and October. Many locals leave the city during August.

Hours

Banks: 08.30–13.30 and 15.00–16.00 Monday–Friday. **Offices:** 09.00–17.00. **Shops:** 08.30–12.30 and 15.30–19.30 Monday–Saturday.

Public holidays

1 January; 6 January; Easter Sunday; Easter Monday; 25 April (Liberation Day); May 1, 15 August (Assumption, normally referred to as Ferragosto); 1 November (All Saints' Day); 8 December (Immaculate Conception); Christmas Day; Boxing Day. Many businesses and shops may be closed in Milan on 7 December in honour of patron saint St Ambrose.

The boring stuff

Food and water are safe, though most locals drink bottled water. No visas needed by visitors from the EU, USA and Canada for a stay of up to 90 days.

The country code for Italy is 39, followed by the city code, 02, and Milan is one hour ahead of GMT.

Milan online

The local government site can be found at www.provincia.milano.it (Italian only). More specifically the Italian Stock Exchange site is www.borsaitalia.it. The Milanese Chamber of Commerce can be found at www.mi.camcom.it/ milano.htm (Italian only). The British Chamber of Commerce for Italy (www.britchamitaly.com, in English) facilitates business contacts between Italy, the UK and beyond.

When in Milan and in need of an online fix, try the Hard Disk Café – www.hdc.it (Italian only).

PS

It is said to be good luck to step on the testicles of the mosaic Taurus on the Zodiac-design floor of Galleria Vittorio Emanuele (Piazza Duomo).

Moscow

Read any travel guide to Moscow and it won't be long before you stumble across the word bureaucracy. It's legendary, and although many of the vestiges of Cold War Moscow have gone, many legacies also remain. There is a sense of new-found wealth throughout the city – mobile phones that play the Hymn of the Soviet Union are just as annoying as those that warble William Tell – and the city has escaped the worst excesses of Russia's recent industrial decline, but at the same time it has proved to be a magnet for criminals and racketeers. This said, General Electric, Procter and Gamble, Peugeot and Hewlett Packard are just some of the household names who have set up shop in the city.

Coming and going

The chances are arrival in Moscow means Terminal 2 at the **Sheremetyevo** airport (**www.sheremetyevo-airport.ru/rus.(englishversion/index 3e.htm**, in English and Russian). Built for the 1980 Olympics, the building is showing its age and, along with the traditional slog through customs, is not a pleasant introduction to Moscow. You'll be expected to fill in a detailed customs declaration, indicating everything from foreign currency to valuables such as laptops. And keep it safe as it could speed things up when it comes to leaving.

The traditional gaggle of taxi drivers greets you in the arrivals hall. You can either haggle or take an official cab. Non-Russian speakers should expect to pay £20 and upwards for the 45-minute journey to the city centre.

There's no metro at the airport, but there is a regular **marshrutnoye taksi**, a minibus that runs along a fixed route for a fixed fare and allows passengers to alight wherever they want.

Most flights to destinations within Russia and the former Soviet Union are served by Moscow's four other airports, Sheremetyevo Terminal 1, Bykovo, Domodedevo and Vnukovo, and bear in mind that the two terminals at Sheremetyevo are about six miles apart.

Out and about

Anyone and everyone is a cabbie in Moscow and it's quite common for cars to be flagged down in the street and take on passengers. For foreigners, however, this isn't always a good idea. Instead look for the registered yellow taxis which are marked with a 'T'. They are more expensive than the 'gypsy cabs' and meters are rarely used, so you'll need to start negotiations before you set off.

Despite the fact it is hidden beneath the streets, one of the best ways to see Moscow is to use its world famous underground (**www.metropla.net./en/mos/moskva.htm**, in English). It is busier than New York's subway and the London Underground combined, and 8 million Muscovites travel the system every day, many now oblivious to the mosaics, sculptures and stunning vaulted ceilings that have made stations such as **Mayakovskaya Ploshchad Revolyutsii**, and **Komsomolskaya** such marvels. In the centre you're never more than a ten-minute walk from one of the 'M's that mark each station entrance, although confusingly, some stations have multiple names – one for each line that intersects them.

There is also a network of buses, trolleybuses and trams that zig-zag across the city.

Car hire can be expensive, and there's also Cyrillic road signs to cope with, so it is often easier and safer, and sometimes cheaper, to hire a car with a driver.

Networking

The Russians take socializing seriously and it often involves drinking serious amounts of vodka. As the very minimum you can get away with is the equivalent of two Western shots, keeping a clear head while networking may be dificult.

In the olden days networking was done at the party cafeteria, Spetsbufet No. 7. Now you might prefer the Grand Imperial or the host of restaurants now on offer. Business travellers can be found *en masse* in the city's only airport hotel – Aerostar Hotel Moscow, across from the Kremlin at the Hotel Kempinski Baltschug Moskau, and at a handful of top hotels including the Sheraton Palace, National Hotel (which includes Maxim's restaurant) and Marriott Tverskaya.

Safety

Although most Russian crime remains an internal affair, it pays to be vigilant. In recent years Moscow has been the target of terrorists from several disaffected groups, and if bombs weren't enough, it wasn't that long ago that a team of karate experts from Britain were robbed on the Metro by a gang of gypsy women and their children. Increasingly attacks are becoming racially motivated, with gangs of skinheads targeting foreigners of Asian and African descent.

Behaving yourself

There's a male chauvinist attitude to business dealings in Moscow. The finer points of a deal are often thrashed out late into the evening over a meal and drinks, and don't forget that tradition stipulates once a bottle has been opened it should be finished. Perhaps as a result, many Russian business deals are based on strong personal relationships, with legally binding contracts considered a mere formality.

A whole culture has grown up around *krutoi*, although you're unlikely to find it in any management guides. In Moscow anyone exuding *krutoi* is someone who is considered cool, confident and capable of drinking copious amounts of vodka.

Russians are not always punctual but you should be and, as ever, your business cards should have a translation on the back. If you are invited back to a Russian's home, a gift is obligatory, and for any children too.

The business tourist

The Moscow business telephone guide (www.mbtg.net/index.html, in English) is an essential resource for locating businesses in Moscow. Conveniently available in online, mobile, and printed editions, the guide provides a directory of companies by business type, the capacity to search for specific companies, a Moscow city map, an e-business guide, an internet commerce directory, and more.

The three-hour tourist

Red Square is a fine starting point. Along one side is the **Kremlin**, a seat of power for the past 800 years. Behind the redbrick walls are churches and palaces as well as the **Armoury Museum**, with its Fabergé eggs, and the 180-carat diamond given to Catherine the Great. (A 'welcome to Moscow' website – www.dimkin.df.ru/moscow/index.html – offers a fascinating overview of these major cultural sites, including half a dozen live webcams.)

Back outside, the famous multicoloured domes of **St Basil's Cathedral** loom up, but gone are the queues that once snaked round the square en route to see the mummified body of Lenin in his **Mausoleum**. And surrounding everything are the eerie yet beautiful monolithic skyscrapers of the Soviet era.

Near the Kremlin is the **Pushkin Museum of Fine Arts** and its fine collection of impressionism, while the **Tretyakov Gallery** houses traditional Russian paintings as well as an extensive collection of icons. You'll find details of most museums at www.museum.ru.

One of the most spectacular sights in the city is the 16th-century

Novodevichy Monastery, with its stunning frescoes and graves of Muscovite luminaries such as Gogol, Prokofiev and Chekhov.

And then there's **Gorky Park** with its miles of paths and a wild, unkempt feel unheard of in Hyde or even Central Park, but perfect in Moscow.

Gift buying

The **GUM** department store was once the retail jewel in the Soviet crown. It's now little more than three floors of shops at one end of Red Square, but worth a look for the architecture if nothing else. Nearby **Tverskaya Street** and **Pushkin Square** have more to offer, and although a tourist trap, the pedestrian mall on **Arbat Street** has an atmosphere all of its own.

The **Izmailovsky Flea Market** is great for nests of **matrioshka** dolls which are as ubiquitous as fur hats, as well as lacquered boxes, and painted wooden cups, saucers and spoons. Regulation mementos from the Red Army abound. As for antiques, the hassle of the paperwork needed to get you through customs makes them a gift too far.

Bare facts

Weather

In winter, long-johns and a hat are a must with temperatures dipping to an average −13 °C in January. However, summer temperatures of over 30 °C are not unusual.

Business hours

Offices: 09.00–18.00 Monday–Friday; ever civilized, Russians won't welcome the suggestion of a breakfast meeting. **Shops and banks:** 09.00–18.00 or later Monday–Saturday. **Restaurants:** 12.00–15.00 and 19.00–23.00.

Public holidays

1–2 January (New Year); 7 January (Russian Orthodox Christmas); 23 February (Motherland Defenders' Day); 8 March (International Women's Day); 30 April (Russian Orthodox Easter); 1–2 May (May Day); 9 May (Victory in Europe Day); 12 June (Victory in Russia Day); 7 November (Agreement and Reconciliation Day); 12 December (Constitution Day).

The boring stuff

No vaccinations are required to enter Russia. All foreign visitors need a visa to enter Russia. Tourist visas are valid for up to 30 days and business visas for 60, and both are available from Russian embassies or consulates, as well as specially authorized travel agents.

The country code for Russia is 7, followed by the city code, 095. Moscow is three hours ahead of GMT from October to March and four hours from April to September.

The rouble is in a constant state of flux against foreign currencies. What doesn't alter is the fact that it doesn't pay to change money on the black market. Stick to ATMs and credit cards.

Moscow online

Babouchka (www.babouchka.org, in English), designed for the expat community, is packed with useful information and links on business associations and services, emergency information, arts and culture.

An online version of *Pravda* (**www.english.pravda.ru**) provides the latest news from the Russian capital. Russia Today (**www.european internet.com/russia**, in English) is a daily internet newspaper that provides extensive links to business directories and businesses throughout Russia.

Among numerous Internet cafés dotted across the city are **Image.ru**, 16 Novoslobodskaya Ul, and **Newmail.ru**, Novaya Potshta, 3/1 Ul. Zabelina. Many hotels also offer internet provision.

PS

Useful info can be found in English-language publications, including the *Moscow News*, the *Moscow Tribune* and the *Moscow Times*, which has excellent listings on a Friday.

New York

New York is the most populous and diverse city in the USA. Just spending a few days there is enough to inject most people with a go-getting spirit of adventure that usually lasts for a few months. The city oozes adrenaline.

It is difficult to avoid superlatives. New York has the best business, the best shops, the best galleries, the best restaurants and bars, the best sights

– just about the best everything. Of course, there is a downside. Some people hate the eclectic freneticism of New York life. But, love it or hate it, all life is there.

Coming and going

As befits its size, New York has three airports, **John F. Kennedy International**, **Newark International**, and **La Guardia**.

JFK (www.panynj-gov/aviation/jfkframe.htm) is by far the biggest and where most international flights arrive. The airport, about 25 km south of the city, is being refurbished, which should improve it a lot. A taxi to the city centre costs $30 plus tolls and takes about 40 minutes. There are also a number of bus companies operating to Manhattan. The subway takes about 70 minutes and costs $1.50.

Newark (www.panynj.gov/aviation/ewrframe.htm), the city's second-largest airport, is about 26 km south-west of the city centre and an increasing international entry point. Taxis into Manhattan take up to an hour and cost around $35 plus tolls and tip. There are frequent bus services to Manhattan.

La Guardia (www.panynj.gar/aviation/lgaframe.htm), about 13 km east of Manhattan in Queens, is mainly used for domestic flights.

Out and about

New York's 714-mile subway system is a lot more convenient, cleaner and safer than it used to be. The flat fare for a journey is $1.50. MetroCards, which can also be used on New York's excellent bus service, can be bought at ticket machines and booths. The Metropolitan Transport Authority site provides maps, schedules and information on public transit throughout New York City and Long Island.

Taxis are good value and easy to find. The toll is $2 plus $0.30 per fifth of a mile, with an extra $0.50 charge after 8.00 pm. Drivers are often recent arrivals to the city and may not know every destination. Give the address, avenue and cross street, rather than just a name.

Because of its grid pattern, Manhattan is so easy to find your way around that walking is often a sensible option.

Networking

What to say? If you can't network in New York you can't do it any-where. The city is built on the concept. Go forth and multiply your connections.

Behaving yourself

New Yorkers (and the US as a whole, come to that) love to tip and to be seen to be tipped. Expect around 15 per cent in bars and restaurants, 10–15 per cent for cabs, and $1 per item to airport and hotel porters and cloakroom attendants. New York is a lot safer than it used to be but still be aware. Use cabs rather than the subway late at night and don't go into Central Park after dark.

The business tourist

New York is a huge place, but most travellers will find themselves in **Manhattan**, which is really one giant business district. The financial district, **Wall Street**, occupies the tiny tip of Manhattan around Wall Street and Broad Street. The city also hosts the headquarters of lots of global businesses and banks, many in the mid-town section.

The three-hour tourist

We are going to assume you've done the Statue of Liberty, the Empire State Building, the World Trade Center, Central Park and the great museums and galleries that grace New York.

For something a bit out of the ordinary, try the public gallery of the **New York Stock Exchange**, which is above the trading floor. You can get free tickets starting from 20 Broad Street (between Wall Street and Exchange Street).

The **United Nations** has guided tours every 30 minutes (1st Avenue at 46th Street). You can walk around **Grand Central Terminal** (42nd and Lexington Avenue) for nothing and have a great experience (**www.grand-centralterminal.com**). Grand Central is a peaceful cathedral in the midst of traveller chaos. The largest train station in the world reopened after renovation in 1999. The major constellations on the ceiling (strangely reversed) are outlined in gold and tiny lights.

If you like jazz, check out **The Blue Note** (131 W. 3rd St at 6th Avenue), especially the Sunday jazz brunch.

Gift buying

New York is shopper's paradise. The department stores like Macy's and Bloomingdale's are obvious. For something a bit out of the ordinary, try **J. N. Bartfield Galleries and Books** (30 W. 57th St), **Tiffany's** for jewelry, and the arty shops of the **SoHo** and **Tribeca** areas.

Bare facts

Weather

Like everything else, the weather in NYC is extreme: very cold winters with not infrequent heavy snow (though often rain) and hot sticky summers that can be unbearable. It does, though, have seasons, again extreme; wet springs and autumn (fall) that is clear and crisp. It doesn't really matter. New Yorkers like to get out whatever the weather, just dress appropriately. And then be prepared to redress once you get inside – the heating will be too hot in winter and the air conditioning freezing in the summer.

Hours

Shops: 09.30–18.00 Monday–Saturday, but, hey, this is New York, the city that never sleeps. If you want it you can find it. **Offices:** 09.00–17.30 Monday–Friday (again something of a joke, business goes on 24/7). **Banks:** 09.00–15.00 Monday–Friday (but the cash machines never sleep).

Public holidays

There are five fixed-date federal holidays: New Year's Day (1 January); Flag Day (14 June); Independence Day (4 July), Veterans Day (11 November) and Christmas (25 December). Floating federal holidays include the birthday of Dr Martin Luther King (third Monday in January); Inauguration Day (20 January every four years); President's Day (third Monday in February); Memorial Day (last Monday in May); Labor Day (first Monday in September); Columbus Day (second Monday in October) and Thanksgiving Day (fourth Thursday in November). Businesses may or may not be closed on these days, but most typically close on the major holidays. When a fixed-date holiday falls on a Saturday, the holiday is taken on the Friday before it. When it falls on a Sunday, the holiday is taken on Monday. August is the most popular month for family vacations, and although businesses typically remain open, key contacts may be on leave.

The boring stuff

No vaccinations are required to enter the USA. The water is safe. Very few restrictions on what the average business traveller can bring in. No visas required for visits less than three months for visitors from countries covered by the Visa Waiver Program. Comprehensive health insurance is an absolute must.

New York online

There are – as you would expect – a profusion of New-York-related sites. The official voice can be found at **www.nyc.gov** and at **www.ci.nyc.ny.us**. Details of hotels and useful maps are at **www.nycmap.com** while other tourist sites include **www.nycmap.com**, **www.nyctourist.com** and **http://go-newyorkcity.com**. The city's Convention and Visitor site is **www.nycvisit.com**. The mysteries of the subway are explained at **www.nycsubway.org**. For those in need of specialist knowledge and refreshment there is also **www.nycbeer.org**.

PS

New York introduced a scheme some years ago for retiring police officers to become cab drivers. The idea was that they would be an ideal source of criminal intelligence. Great fun if you can get them talking about their experiences while you're trapped in the traffic.

Paris

Stereotypically, Parisians – all 9 million of them — are rude and arrogant *bon viveurs* who don't take kindly to foreigners and dedicate their lives to lunching and spending the entirety of August sunning themselves on the Côte d'Azur. Back in reality, it is true that Paris is awfully quiet in August. The rest of the time it is a commercial cornucopia, a sophisticated commercial smorgasbord. Munching a Pain Poilâne sandwich at La Tartine on the rue de Rivoli, you may ponder the wisdom of doing business anywhere else in the world.

Coming and going

Paris is well connected. Its two main airports are **Charles de Gaulle** (also known as **Roissy** from the local area), where most international flights arrive, and **Orly**, some international but mainly internal and charter flights. Roissy is about 30km north of the city, Orly about 15km south of Paris.

Roissy is a decaying testament to 1960s architecture. Central Paris is accessible by taxi, bus, train. A taxi costs around FF200 and take 45–60 minutes for a not very scenic journey. Air France coaches take about the same time to Porte Maillot and Charles de Gaulle Etoile in the centre and cost around about FF60. RER trains run directly from the airport to Chatelet, St Michel and other main stations, and take about 40 minutes, for FF50 one way.

The modern airport is a shopping mall. **Orly**, however, is not a modern airport. But it is as well served with transport connections as Roissy. A taxi to the city centre costs about FF150 and takes just under an hour. The frequent Orlyval train serves the main Paris stations, taking about 45 minutes for around FF50. Air France has a coach service from Orlysud (the south terminal) to Montparnasse and Invalides.

The French rail system is excellent. **Eurostar** offers a three-hour direct connection to central London – this gives you the opportunity to compare the speedy French system (maximum public investment) with the lamentably decrepid British system (privatized).

Out and about

You may decide to hire a car. Unless you are from Milan, this is not the best idea. Parisian driving is at best frenetic, at worst, dangerous.

Best bet for business travellers is the metro – clean, safe and efficient (www.metropla.net/eu/par/paris.htm, in English). Some of the stations are works of art in their own right (notably Louvre, Varenne and Franklin-Roosevelt). The metro system, and the linked RER or suburban rail system, are relatively straightforward to use.

Buses are a good way to see the city, but require some time to get to know and are subject to Paris's appalling traffic jams. They use the same tickets as the metro. The River Seine offers a more serene mode of transport.

Taxis are most readily available at ranks: it is difficult to hail one in the street. They are usually easy to come by, however, and relatively cheap. Beware of drivers who hold a city map in one hand while driving and talking on a mobile phone.

Networking

Parisians are protective of their culture and language – witness the furore surrounding the Anglicization of French. While most business professionals speak English well, try to learn (and use) at least a few simple phrases.

The business culture tends to be formal compared to the USA and UK and the country as a whole is rather bureaucratic and centralized.

Parisians place a high value on education, intellectualism and sophistication. Many senior managers will have a background in mathematics or engineering from one of the grande écoles that produce most of the French elite. Business entertaining is almost always done in restaurants. Business lunches/dinners are semi-social events, indeed, almost religious. Don't come on heavy. Wait till dessert before talking business. It is very rare to be invited into the home of a Parisian business acquaintance.

Behaving yourself

Shake hands on meeting and leaving. Don't kiss men. 'Air kissing' (between men and women) is for friends only; the French do it twice – once on each cheek. Be formal. Dress in a business suit, unless you know the company's culture is relaxed. Use last names and business titles. At the very least address everyone, including waiters/waitresses and shop assistants as *monsieur/madame/mademoiselle*. Women may be less conservative in their dress than in the USA or UK but don't be tempted to try to emulate Parisienne *chic*.

Be on time for meetings: lateness is not fashionable. Speak French if you can, but if you are not confident don't use it for serious negotiations. Parisians are better English speakers than they let on.

The business tourist

The new area of **La Défense**, a couple of kilometres west of the Arc de Triomphe, is emerging as the key business district, with many leading French and international companies having offices there. It already has 2.5 million square metres of office space and 140,000 jobs. An extension of 300,000 square metres, more housing and a rail station is now underway. Central Paris is also a key business area, as is the area Val-de-Seine.

The three-hour tourist

We're assuming that you've done tourist-style Paris. You've witnessed the metallic beauty of le Tour Eiffel (274m of French bombast), l'Arc de Triomphe, Notre Dame, the Louvre, Musée d'Orsay (works of art from the period 1850 to 1914), the Orangerie, Jardins des Tuilleries (contemporary art), and the wonderful testament to plumbing that is the Centre Georges Pompidou. If you haven't, do it. If you have, try: **Musée du Vin** (5, Square Charles Dickens) – glass of wine included in the price of entry and also a museum restaurant; and **Musée du Parfum** (39 Bd des Capucines).

Gift buying

Opera and **Chaussée d'Antin** for department stores Galeries Lafayette and Printemps. **Rue du Faubourg**, **Saint-Honoré** and **Avenue Montaigne** for haute couture and designer shops. **St Germain des Prés** has a range of smaller, moderately priced clothes stores. **Rue Royale** and **Rue de Paradis** for glassware and porcelain.

Bare facts

Weather

Not the Côte d'Azur. Winters are cold, though rarely snow-bound, and summers can be temperamental. Rain is frequent.

Hours

Shops: 10.00–18.00 Monday–Saturday. **Banks:** 09.30–12,00, 14,00–16,00 Monday–Friday (some banks, particularly outside Paris, may be closed on Mondays).

Public holidays

1 January (New Year's Day); Easter Monday; 1 May (Labour Day); 8 May (Victory Day); Ascension; Whitsun; 14 July (Bastille Day); 15 August (Assumption); 1 November (All Saint's Day); 11 November (Armistice Day); 25 December (Christmas Day).

The boring stuff

No vaccinations are required to enter France. The water is safe and in any case is generally bottled. For the average business traveller there are very few restrictions on what you can take into the country. There is no duty-free allowance for travellers from other EU countries. No visas required for visits under three months. Always carry your passport: it's French law that you must have some form of ID on you at all times.

The country code for France is 33, followed by the city code, 1, and Paris is one hour ahead of GMT.

Paris online

The best tourist sites include **www.paris.org**, **www.paris-touristoffice.com** and **www.smartweb.fr/paris**. Perhaps the best for English speakers is the excellent **www.paris-anglo.com** and **www.timeout.hom/paris/index. html**. The Parisian Stock Exchange can be found at **www.bourse-de-paris.fr**.

The biggest cybercafé in Paris is the new Easy Everything café with 375 computers. Others include Espace Vivendi (cheap) and Le Sputnik (fashionable).

PS

Most people know not to try doing business in France during August, but many Parisians only take two weeks' holiday then so you might be lucky. But the city is hot and full of tourists. Many Parisians also take longish breaks at Christmas and Easter.

San Francisco

If great cities are those that inspire song, then San Francisco is among the greatest: 'If you're going to San Francisco, be sure to wear some flowers in your hair' (Scott Mackenzie), 'To be where little cable cars, climb halfway to the stars' (Cory/Cross), 'San Francisco, I'm comin' home again, never to roam again' (Walter Jurmann), 'When I come home to you, San Francisco, your golden sun will smile on me' (Cory/Cross).

Like so many others, you may well leave your heart and even your soul in

San Francisco, high on a hill. Ironically, however, you cannot leave your body. At least not in the final sense. Burials were outlawed in San Francisco in 1902. Since that time the final resting place for most San Franciscans has been one of the 17 cemeteries of nearby Colma, CA, perhaps the world's only incorporated city in which the living are far outnumbered by the dead. Tidy, and innovative – like so much about San Francisco.

So assuming that you intend to remain firmly embodied during your stay, do bring your heart – and a rather full wallet. San Francisco easily rivals New York as America's most expensive city. But it's worth it. According to one survey, the city is one of the four most desirable US cities to live in, based on arts and culture, air pollution, crime, unemployment, commute times and climate.

Coming and going

You may enter the golden gates via **San Francisco International Airport** (SFIA) (**www.sfoairport.com**) or **Oakland International Airport**, just across the bay (**www.flyoakland.com**). Ground transport options abound. The SFO Airporter bus is a simple, efficient and inexpensive option from SFIA. It runs every 15 minutes, and the half-hour trip to downtown is just $10. Or take a taxi for about $30. If you find yourself tempted by the van service 'barkers' who solicit weary foreign travellers fresh off the plane, be sure to ask two key questions: When are you leaving, and how many stops will you make before you drop me off? Otherwise you may find yourself sitting at the curb waiting for the van to fill with passengers, and/or making numerous stops in far-flung areas before reaching your final destination.

Oakland's airport is a mere 22 minutes and $2.75 away from downtown San Francisco by the clean and easy-to-use BART trains. If you'd like a bit of fresh air and prefer seagulls to subways, you might set sail on the Alameda/Oakland Ferry. It provides service to Alameda, San Francisco's ferry terminal and Pier 39/Fisherman's Wharf. Oakland AC Transit Line 58 will take you from the airport to the ferry. One-way fares are $3.75. Or taxi into the city for $40–50 in 20–60 minutes, depending upon traffic.

Out and about

San Francisco's city centre is wonderfully walkable, but climbing its famed hills may literally take your breath away. So when you hear a metallic 'clang, clang, clang', be sure to hop a ride on San Francisco's only *moving* historic landmark – its cable cars (www.sfcablecar.com). You can embark at any cable car turntable (the beginning/end of each route) or anywhere you see a brown and white 'Cable Car Stop' sign in between.

The cable cars are part of the city's excellent public transit system, which also includes buses, trolleybuses, and BART trains. A one-day transit 'Passport' costs $6 ($10 for three days, $15 for seven days).

Although the most frequented areas in San Francisco are relatively safe, some adjacent areas are not, for example the Tenderloin District near Union Square, and the Western Addition near Japantown. Be cautious and respectful when approached by aggressive panhandlers (beggars) anywhere in the city, and take extra care when exploring off the beaten path South of Market (SoMa), in Haight-Ashbury, the Mission District, or Golden Gate Park, especially at night.

Networking

Every month the San Francisco Chamber of Commerce hosts a low-cost after-hours (17.30–19.30) networking event for members – and prospective members. It's a great way to get a feel for the business pulse of the city, and to meet businesspeople from small to large companies in a variety of Bay Area industries. Three times each year, Chamber members get a chance to showcase their products and services at a Tabletop Forum. Go to www.sfchamber.com/business_after_hours.htm for information on upcoming events.

Or if you happen to be in town at the time, don't miss the 'CityBeat Insiders Breakfast', also produced by the Chamber three times each year.

The *San Francisco Business Times* (published every Friday) offers lists of daily business events including a cornucopia of diverse networking opportunities throughout the Bay Area. For current information go to: http://sanfrancisco.bcentral.com/sanfrancisco.

Behaving yourself

San Franciscans are a stylish breed – wear your best suit for business. But to look like a true, independent Californian, add an eccentric flair or two – perhaps a flower in your hair?

The business tourist

The San Francisco Bay Area's nine counties and 6.6 million residents comprise the fifth largest metropolitan area in the USA, boasting a thriving annual economy of $200 billion. Key industries include banking and finance, venture capital, international business and trade, air transportation, telecommunications, professional business services, internet industries, creative services, film, video and television production, construction, engineering and design, petroleum, health care and bioscience, hospitality and tourism (the city's number one industry), convention, meeting and conference services, retail and shopping, and fashion and apparel manufacturing.

The Bay Area is home to two of *Business Week*'s top-30 ranked b-schools: Stanford of course (number 11) – the fertile womb of Silicon Valley – and Haas School of Business at Berkeley (number 18).

The three-hour tourist

If you haven't covered the basics, from the financial district hop on a cable car on the California line. Head through **Chinatown**, then change at Powell to the Powell–Mason line for a jaunt over **Nob Hill** to **Fisherman's Wharf**, or to the Powell–Hyde line excursion over Nob and Russion Hills to Aquatic Park near Ghiradelli Square. Both are great trips with famed – and touristy – shopping and dining destinations on the waterfront.

With a bit more time, walk the three-mile-long Golden Gate Bridge for an unforgettable experience. Avoid jumping, even with your portable bunjee cord. Or for something different, try a walking tour. Possibilities include:

- Historical and culinary walking tours of Chinatown. Includes lunch. $25–$55, 415-355-9657
- All About Chinatown! Walking Tours. $25
- Haight-Ashbury – hippie tours Tuesday and Saturday mornings.

Gift buying

San Francisco is the gateway to the golden east and west, and a paradise for dedicated, gold-laden shoppers. **Union Square** is the heart of shopping heaven, home to San-Francisco-based **Gumps** (don't miss it), Macy's, Nieman Marcus, Saks, and a rich cornucopia of upmarket shops. Hunt and bargain for quality jade, silk and porcelain goods in Chinatown and

Japantown. Or hop the cable car's California line to its end at Market to explore the **Embarcadero Center** with eight buildings of restaurants, speciality food and gift shops. Factory outlets are clustered around the garment district on or near 3rd St, south of Market. Some of them offer great deals.

Bare facts

Weather

While San Francisco's weather often changes by the hour, and even from one area of the city to another, overall San Franciscans enjoy a perpetual spring. Cool fog caresses summer mornings and evenings, with bright sun emerging in the middle of the day. Autumn is the warmest season, late autumn and early winter are the rainiest. But temperatures hover between a pleasantly cool 48 and 65 °Fahrenheit (8–14 °C) year round. Wear light wools and knits; dress in thin layers.

Hours

Banks: 09.00–15.00 Monday–Friday. **Offices:** 09.00–17.00 Monday–Friday. **Shops:** 09.30–18.00 Monday–Saturday. **Shopping Centers:** 09.30–21.00 Monday–Sunday.

Public holidays

There are five fixed-date federal holidays: New Year's Day (1 January); Flag Day (14 June); Independence Day (4 July); Veterans Day (11 November); and Christmas (25 December). Floating federal holidays include the birthday of Dr Martin Luther King (third Monday in January); Inauguration Day (January 20th every four years); President's Day (third Monday in February); Memorial Day (last Monday in May); Labor Day (first Monday in September); Columbus Day (second Monday in October) and Thanksgiving Day (fourth Thursday in November). Businesses may or may not be closed on these days, but most typically close on the major holidays. When a fixed-date holiday falls on a Saturday, the holiday is taken on the Friday before it. When it falls on a Sunday, the holiday is taken on Monday. August is the most popular month for family vacations, and although businesses typically remain open, key contacts may be on leave.

The boring stuff

No vaccinations are required to enter the USA and the water is safe. No visa is required for visits under three months for countries covered by the US Visa Waiver Program. Comprehensive health insurance is an absolute must.

San Francisco online

San Francisco Chamber of Commerce (**www.sfchamber.com/index.htm**) offers a quick overview of business in the Bay Area, with valuable links and resources. For online business news from the Bay Area, check out the *San Francisco Business Times* at **http://sanfrancisco.bcentral.com/sanfrancisco**. Features include online legal and insurance resource centres, leads on new businesses in the area, archive search, and the *Business Times Book of Lists* (available by subscription) – a business reference guide which compiles this paper's weekly Top 25 lists (e.g. Bay Area management consulting firms). Business newspapers for 39 other US cities may also be accessed from this site. The City of San Francisco's official website (**www.ci.sf.ca.us**) also provides useful information on business opportunities, employment, community resources, legislation and regulations.

If you visit only one website for San Francisco dining, lodging and leisure information, make it **http://bayarea.citysearch.com**. This excellent site arranges hotels by price and neighbourhood, and restaurants by cuisine and neighbourhood. It lists major and minor arts, attractions, movies, music, shopping and sporting events, and bars and nightlife. A very helpful resource.

PS

Mind your 'cable car etiquette' when boarding a cable car en route: wait on the sidewalk and wave to the gripman to stop; once the car has stopped, you can enter the car from either side (if there is sufficient space). It's OK – and fun – to hang on to the special poles on the outside of the car, but if you do, watch the gripman carefully as he will alert you to any potential hazards en route that might cause you to lose your head, so to speak.

São Paulo

Forget the beaches, if you're going to Brazil on business you'll probably be headed for São Paulo, the commercial and manufacturing centre of the country (though surprisingly many business travellers manage a side trip to Rio). Sorry – São Paulo is a bit grim in appearance, with sclerotic traffic and smog problems. It can also be dangerous.

São Paulo is Brazil's richest city and the world's third most populous metropolitan area, with nearly 17 million people. Residents of the city and its suburbs, in south-eastern Brazil, make up half the population of São Paulo state and 10 per cent of the country's 170 million people. The city mixes wealth with poverty, deluxe hotels with shanty towns, world-class restaurants with water shortages and no sewage systems for 40 per cent of its inhabitants.

Coming and going

São Paulo's international two-terminal airport, **Guarulhos**, is where most international travellers arrive. It is about 30 km north-east of São Paulo, and a taxi journey from the airport to the city centre can take anything from 45 minutes to two hours, depending on São Paulo's appalling traffic.

There are numerous bus companies, including the EMTU executive buses that run between the airport and the downtown Praca da Republica; fare is around the equivalent of $6. There is a special EMTU service connecting Guarulhos to Congonhas airport and other city destinations.

This is important since business travellers tend to rotate between Brazil's three main cities – São Paulo, Rio de Janeiro and Brasilia. A shuttle system or air bridge (*ponte aerea*) connects them. Flights between Rio de Janeiro and São Paulo leave every 15 minutes from downtown airports – Santos Dumont Airport in Rio and Congonhas in downtown São Paulo.

Out and about

Taxis are safe and relatively good value. They can be hailed or booked by phone. But São Paulo traffic is terrible and a good alternative is the underground metro system (www.metropla.net/am/sao-paulo.htm, in English). The trains are frequent and clean. Buses are cheap but complicated. Rental cars are costly. In any case, you'd be crazy to drive. Quite apart from the traffic, Brazil's roads are poorly maintained and hazardous.

Networking

The social centre of the city is the **Jardins** district. Be prepared to start and finish late. Restaurants typically do not begin serving until after nine o'clock and often remain open until the early morning.

Safety

São Paulo is dangerous, especially at night. The city's central commercial district is OK for pedestrians during the day. Rua Nestor Pastana is the red light district. Avoid.

Behaving yourself

For a first business meeting you will need an introduction, from either a mutual friend, a trade association or a professional go-between. Many Brazilians speak English but may prefer to do business in Portuguese. English is preferred to Spanish as an alternative to Portuguese.

Don't expect Brazilians to be punctual – arrive on time and expect to wait. Because traffic tends to make everyone late anyway, carry a local cell phone. Shake hands on greeting and leaving and avoid excessive eye contact, which is considered aggressive.

Business is conducted on personal terms so most first visits to São Paulo will tend to be social with little business conducted.

In hotels and restaurants, tips are usually 10 per cent.

The business tourist

São Paulo is Brazil's most important industrial and business centre. Most of Brazil's major industries are based there. These include telecoms, automotive, banking, pharmaceuticals, electronic appliances and computers, consulting and construction. The city hosts a lot of conferences and trade fairs, the bigger ones at the **Anhembi** conference centre. The centre of the city's skyscrapers is the **Avenida Paulista**.

The three-hour tourist

São Paulo isn't that great as a tourist city, to add to which it can be murderously hot in summer. If you are walking the street, dress down. You can get a view of the city from the 30-storey observation deck of the **Banespa building** (24 Rua Joao Bricola)

São Paulo has lots of museums, but not all are good. Best is the **Museu de Arte de São Paulo** (Av. Paulista 1578), which is the most important museum of Western art in South America and one of the few that regularly hosts important visiting exhibitions.

The **Trianon Park** (949 Rua Peixoto Gomide) is also worth a visit.

Paulistanos are a surprisingly diverse ethnic mix. Some are based on geographical areas. For example, the **Bexiga** (the area around Avenida Brig. Luis Antonio and Rua Santo Antonio) is mainly Italian with lots of restaurants and coffee shops. The **Liberdade** (around Rua Galvão Bueno) is primarily Japanese.

Gift buying

The best shops are concentrated around **Avenida Giovanni Granchi.** It's also one of the nicer parts of the city, with good bars and restaurants.

Bare facts

Weather

Can be summed up in one word: tropical.

Hours

Offices: 8.30–17.30. **Banks:** 10.00–16.30 Monday–Friday. **Shops:** 09.00–19.00 Monday–Friday, 09.00–13.00 Saturday. **Shopping centres:** 10.00–22.00 Monday–Saturday, 15.00–22.00 Sunday.

Public holidays

New Year's Day (1 January); Carnival (four nights and three days preceeding Ash Wednesday); Good Friday; Easter Sunday; Tivadendes Day (21 April); Labour Day (1 May); Corpus Christi; Independence Day (7 September); Nossa Senhora Aparecida (12 October); All Souls (2 November); Proclamation of the Republic (15 November); Christmas Day. São Paulo has a special holiday on 25 January to mark its foundation.

The boring stuff

Citizens of most EU countries do not need a tourist visa for entry into Brazil. Americans and Canadians do require visas. A temporary business visa is necessary if you are going to transact 'business' – e.g. signing legal documents, engaging in financial or commercial transactions, or working or engaging in research.

Tourist visas are generally valid for a stay of 90 days. A temporary business visa is also valid for 90 days. Transit visas are valid for ten days and require travellers to enter and exit through the same port.

Mosquito-borne diseases can be a risk in some areas. There have been some cases of cholera in the north east, and a recent surge in reported cases of yellow fever. Visitors should take sensible precautions, including vaccination. It is recommended that visitors drink bottled water.

The country code for Brazil is 55, followed by the city code, 11, and São Paulo is three hours behind GMT.

São Paulo online

The Exploring São Paulo site at **www.interknowledge.com/brazil/saopaulo/index.htm** gives as much info on the city as any other.

PS

An unusual venue is the **Butantã Snake Institute** (Avenida Dr Vital Brasil 1500, in Butantã near São Paulo University Campus). If you're that way inclined you can watch the huge collection of snakes catch live prey at feeding time. Or enjoy the exhibits of live and stuffed venomous reptiles, spiders and tarantulas. The tropical gardens in the grounds are nice, though.

Seoul

Seoul, capital of South Korea and the site of so much conflict during the latter half of the 20th century, has firmly established itself as one of the principal commercial cities of Asia. Bisected by the River Han, this city of 10 million people is situated in the centre of the Korean peninsula linking the Pacific region to Eurasia, and at the centre of the strategic BESETO (Beijing–Seoul–Tokyo) economic belt.

As well as having traditional manufacturing industry and financial markets, Seoul is determined not to be left behind by the internet revolution. The Seoul High-tech Industries Centre is under construction in Gaepo-dong, in the southern district of Gangnam-gu, and is due for completion by the end of 2001.

Coming and going

Ten and a half miles west of Seoul lies **Seoul Kimpo International Airport** (**www.kimpo-airport.co.kr**). To get to the city take a subway train – line 5; they leave every 10 minutes or so. The journey will take 50 minutes and cost about W600.

A taxi will take a similar length of time but cost substantially more, some W7500. Alternatively there are a variety of bus services, including the airport bus.

Out and about

Seoul's subway (**www.metropla.net/as/seol.htm**, in English) seems to be in a permanent state of flux. Long-term construction continues to make steady progress towards a total of eight subway lines. The lines open at present are modern and efficient with some signs in both Korean and English. Beware of strikes, an irritating and unpredictable hazard on the subway system.

Above ground a choice of taxis offers a standard (grey cars) or deluxe (black cars, more expensive, more room) ride. If you take a taxi, hold tight and cover your ears. Taxi drivers appear happy to ignore the various speed restrictions in force, and aren't averse to giving other drivers/cyclists/pedestrians a piece of their mind.

Visitors on a short stay might do well to avoid the buses. Destination signs and timetables are in Korean and the buses often lack air conditioning, an essential comfort in the summer.

Networking

If you feel in need of Western voices you are likely to encounter a lot of Americans in the Itaewon because of its proximity to the US army base. With their local knowledge, services personnel can be an excellent source of information, so don't be afraid to ask them for advice or information.

The cluster of high-quality hotels around City Hall Square provides many networking opportunities. The new deluxe 33-storey JW Marriott Hotel comes complete with a business centre equipped with high-speed internet access plus, for the sports minded, an impressive array of facilities including an indoor golf range, 50 ft climbing wall and scuba-diving pool.

If you are out and about and interested in an authentic Korean dining experience, you could try *Sollongtang*. A beef soup with rice and noodles, *Sollongtang* is served in a black stone pot and seasoned with onions and salt. Cold noodles or *naengmyon* is another traditional dish. It was brought to the south from North Korea during the Korean War. The noodle shops are dotted about the city. They will usually be called 'Hamhung Naengmyon' or 'Pyongyang Naengmyon' after two North Korean cities. Each serves its own particular brand of *naengmyon*.

Behaving yourself

Personal introductions are a must: cold calling will generally be a waste of time in a country where business and personal relationships are closely intertwined.

Make sure you take an adequate supply of business cards. A translation of your details in Korean should be on one side. Use both hands to receive/give business cards. Do not use the left hand. When addressing people remember that Koreans commonly have three names, a surname and two given names. The correct way to address someone is to use the prefix (Mr, Ms, etc.) plus the name mentioned first, inevitably single syllable and frequently one of three most popular Korean surnames – Lee, Kim or Park. Bowing used to be normal practice; however handshaking is increasingly popular and this applies equally to women.

Be prepared to remove shoes before entering homes or certain areas of restaurants. When passing objects or receiving them, use both hands. Try not to blow your nose at the table, refuse an invitation, make too much eye contact, say no without explanation, or compare the Koreans unfavourably with the Japanese.

Koreans have a definite style of negotiation and will expect you to have the same. Flexibility is essential. This flexibility is even reflected in written contracts, which in Korea serve to outline the points of an agreement rather than cover every eventuality.

Finally it might be worth practising your singing in the shower before travelling to Korea. The *no-ray-bang* is the Korean take on a karaoke bar and singing along with your hosts may go a long way to building that all important *entente cordiale* – or not, depending on how well you hold a tune.

The business tourist

The **Kangam** area south of the Han-gang River and east of the Seoul Express Bus Terminal is Seoul's newest and fastest-growing business district. The Korean World Trade Centre complex is located here and contains the Korea Exhibition Centre (KOEX), the Trade Tower, the City Air Terminal, the Intercontinental Hotel and Hyundai Department Store. See www.orientmag.com for information in English on the trade centre, foreign trade association and other business organizations.

The Korean Chamber of Commerce (www.g77tin.org/kccisvs.html) publishes the Korean business directory, business journal and the *Doing with Korea* manual, all in English, annually.

The three-hour tourist

There is no escaping the fact that much of South Korea's recent history has been inextricably linked to that of North Korea. Although the military solution has largely given way to a political one, for a poignant reminder of the anguish suffered by Korea and the surrounding region during the Korean and Vietnam wars pay a visit to the **War Memorial** near Yongsan Army Post.

For a view over Seoul, ride the lift to the top of the **Seoul tower**, a tall (237 m) pointy structure that overlooks the city. It is situated on a small mountain, and access to the tower is by cable car.

You can take a trip back through Seoul's history by visiting the **Gyeong-bokgung Palace**. Surrounded by the Naksan, Inwangsan and Bugaksan mountains, the palace was built at the end of the 14th century and for 500 years during the Joseon dynasty kings lived and conducted their affairs of state there.

Gift buying

The five or so blocks of the **Itaewon** contain Seoul's main tourist shopping area with some 2000 stores packed into the streets and back alleys. Don't overpay for goods – haggling is an accepted practice. The area is famous for its cut-price tailors where you can pick up a suit for around W200,000 (less than £150).

Another area that is worth investigating is the traditional **Namdaemun** market. It is the largest general wholesale market in Korea and dates back to 1414.

Bare facts

Weather

Situated in the temperate zone, Seoul has four distinct seasons. Temperature fluctuates considerably from a sweltering 35°C in the summer down to a chilly −10 °C in the winter. Summers tend to be hot and humid, winters dry and cold. The monsoon season runs from June to September and accounts for 70 per cent of the annual rainfall.

Hours

Banks: 09.30–16.30 Monday–Friday, 09.30–13.30 Saturday. **Offices:** 09.00–18.00 Monday–Friday, 09.00–13.00 Saturday. **Shops:** 10.30–19.30 Monday–Saturday.

Holidays

Holidays and festivals in Seoul include: New Year's Day (1 January, not as important as the lunar New Year's Day); Lunar New Year's Day (lunar 1 January: for three days long locals pay respects to their ancestors, eat rice cake soup for breakfast and wear traditional dress); Independence Movement Day (1 March, celebrates independence from Japanese colonial rule in 1919); Arbor Day (5 April, a day for planting trees); Buddha's Birthday (lunar 8 April, multicoloured lanterns lit in temples); Children's Day (5 May, children get gifts); Memorial Day (6 June, remembrance day); Constitution Day (17 July); Liberation Day (15 August, from Japanese rule – fireworks); Ch'usok – Thanksgiving Day (lunar 15 August, three days: Seoul empties as Seoulites go to their home towns and extended family); National Foundation Day (3 October: Tangun founded this country in 2333 BC); Christmas (25 December).

The boring stuff

No visa is required for stays of up to three months by nationals of EU countries (except Italy and Portugal for stays of longer than two months) and Canada. Nationals of the USA can stay for up to 30 days for touristic purposes without a visa. Vaccinations are recommended against Hepatitis A, polio and tetanus.

The country code for South Korea is 82, followed by the city code, 2, and Seoul is nine hours ahead of GMT.

Seoul online

The world executive guide to Seoul (**www.worldexecutive.com/cityguides/seoul/index.html**) provides tourist-style information. **www.hotelskorea.com** also gives information on hotels in the city.

PS

A word of warning. Pay attention when walking around the city. Traffic in Seoul frequently displays a cavalier approach to the rules of the road, including the one about driving on the highway, as opposed to the pavement.

Shanghai

Shanghai is a city in a hurry: it's in a rush to grow, a rush to forget its colonial past and a rush to, quite literally, cement its place as the fastest-growing metropolis in the world. In fact, as you are jostled along the commercial thoroughfare that is Nanjing Dong, or glance across the Huangpu River towards the Pudong district and its ever-growing skyline, it's easy to forget you're in China at all.

Given the size and the sprawl of Beijing, it's incredible to think that Shanghai is actually bigger and home to 14 million people. It's also the Chinese hub of industry, commerce, science and technology, and of course, Shanghai is a port, and a vital centre for foreign trade.

Coming and going

Shanghai has two airports – the ageing **Hongqiao International Airport**, about 15 km from the city centre, which now handles most domestic flights, and the gleaming new **Pudong International Airport** (PIA), which is gradually stealing most of the international business.

PIA has helped put some pleasure back into business travel and is one of the most modern airports in the world. It's about 45 km east of the city and a cab will cost around Rmb80. As with anywhere in China, it helps to be able to show your taxi driver the name of your hotel or destination in writing. Airport shuttles to your hotel may also available from 6 am to midnight.

Departure taxes are Rmb50 for domestic flights, and Rmb90 for international.

Out and about

Apparently there are so many taxis in Shanghai that the government once cut the fares to encourage people to use them. This, of course, has led to congestion, despite the appearance of new expressways across the city. An alternative way of getting around is the Shanghai metro (www.metropla.net/as/shanghai.htm, in English), which also offers some air-conditioned relief during the sweltering summers, something not offered by the city's crowded buses and trams.

It's worth taking a map to show cabbies where you want to go, but don't totally rely on it as Shanghai is changing so quickly it will probably be out of date before the ink is dry.

And naturally enough, driving in Shanghai is not for the faint of heart.

Networking

Old Shanghai, around Renmin Square, is the city's entertainment zone while the restaurants along Nanjing Road open late and attract Shanghai's glitterati.

For some, the best business is done on the golf course, and Shanghai has a number of courses. The best way to see them is to contact **Malone's Bar and Grill**, where you can join one of the regular Sunday trips.

Behaving yourself

As well as the etiquette detailed in the Beijing section, bear in mind that business visitors are usually entertained in restaurants. If you can, hire an interpreter, who may be able to give you some advice on your body language. For instance, in China it's rude to point your feet at the person you're talking to, and remember to sit up straight with both feet on the floor.

The business tourist

Most business in Shanghai now takes place in the new **Pudong** financial district, where all the foreign banks are required to have their main offices. Yet strangely just 50 years ago this area was known as the 'Wrong side of the Huangpu', an area frequented by prostitutes, murderers and destitute gamblers.

The three-hour tourist

With all the new hotels springing up on the Pudong side of the Huangpu, catching the ferry back across the river gives you a chance to see the **Bund** as it should be seen, from the water. It's a shoreline that smacks of Liverpool, with its Edwardian and Victorian facades, now framed against a towering backdrop of skyscrapers. From the Custom House to the old Hong Kong and Shanghai Bank and the art deco Peace Hotel, the Bund is one of the last remaining clues to Shanghai's colonial past. Go to **www.sh.com/arch/ archch2.htm** for extensive information on historic buildings on the Bund.

Back on the Pudong side, the sky is the limit. On a misty day you can't actually see the top of the **Oriental Pearl TV tower**, even if it is bright purple, while among the five-star hotels that have arrived on the coat-tails of the city's economic boom is the Grand Hyatt, which occupies the top 35 floors of the **Jin Mao Tower**, itself the tallest building in China.

For a bit of history, a fascinating museum lurks underneath the stone monument to the 'Heroes of the People' in Huangpu Park, at one end of the Bund. It helps fill in some of the gaps about Shanghai's more recent past. The **Shanghai Museum**, at 201 Renmin Da Dao, concentrates on Chinese art.

The **French Concession** offers a unique opportunity to visit the former homes of some of the people who shaped modern China, such as the nationalist leader Sun Yatsen who spent six years living at 39 Sinan Lu. The house is now a museum and its easy to imagine heated debates about the future of the emperor taking place in the small drawing room.

Others attractions include the **Chinese Acrobatic and Magic Show**, at the Shanghai Centre Theatre, which is touristy but fun, and the **Shanghai Grand Theatre** at Renmin Da Dao, which features concerts, operas and ballets.

Gift buying

By far the most exciting shopping to be had in Shanghai is at the outdoor antiques market, at **Dongtai Lu.** It's one vast Aladdin's cave of goodies from Buddhas to vases, reclaimed wooden panels to enough Little Red Books to fill the British Library. But you must be prepared to bargain – there's no sport otherwise.

For shops with price tags, **Nanjing Road** is Shanghai's main shopping district. Here you'll find all the Western brands you could wish for. The **Friendship Store**, close to the Peace Hotel, has three floors of everything from Chinese medicines to arts and crafts. But perhaps the best buy in Shanghai is a tailored suit, although given that few tailors speak English, agreeing on an inside leg measurement poses a whole new set of problems.

Bare facts

Weather

Shanghai summers are hot and humid with temperatures reaching 40 °C. The rainy season begins in June. Autumn is mild but in winter temperatures can reach below freezing.

Hours

Banks: 9.00–12.00 and 14.00–17.00 weekdays. Outside these hours look out for ATMs, particularly those of Citibank and the Bank of China, which accept most Western bank cards. **Offices:** 08.00–11.30 and 13.00–17.00. Some government offices are more flexible. **Shops:** 09.00–19.00 every day.

Public holidays

New Year's Day (1 January); Chinese New Year (late January/early February – the exact dates change each year); Women's Day (8 March); Labour Day (1 May); Youth Day (4 May); Children's Day (1 June); Chinese Communist Party Day (1 July); Army Day (1 August); National Day (1 October). Despite the plethora of holidays businesses only shut down for the Chinese New Year and National Day. Jan. 1, New Year's Day.

The boring stuff

EU citizens require a visa to enter China. They cost about £50 and are valid for three months. It usually takes three days to process a request, but express visas are available.

The country code for China is 86, followed by the city code, 1, and Shanghai is eight hours ahead of GMT.

Shanghai online

Among the internet cafés available are **Infohighway**, 181 Rui Jin Er Lu, and **O'Richard's Bar and Restaurant**, 2/F Pu Jiang Hotel, 15 Huangpu Lu.

PS

Time Out's guide to Shanghai (**www.timeout.com/shanghai/index.html**) provides excellent information. Other interesting links can be found at **www.sh.com/welcome.htm**.

Shanghai will eventually (if it is ever finished) be home to the world's tallest building – the 1509-feet World Financial Centre.

Singapore

Singapore is at the same time a city and an island and a nation. Its small size, a little over 650 square kilometres, belies its commercial importance. It is the world's busiest port as well as an important financial centre and is fast becoming one of the most important technology hubs in Asia.

Home to over 500,000 ex-pats, Singapore is a cultural melting pot and destination for foreign workers across the world. The influence of the substantial ex-pat community, over a quarter of the island's 3.5 million population, merely adds to the East meets West multicultural atmosphere of Singapore.

One thing to remember when walking the astonishingly clean streets and marvelling at the lack of crime is that Singapore is nicknamed the 'fine' city for a reason. Jaywalk across the well-ordered traffic, drop litter on the gleaming sidewalk, spit or smoke in public, or fail to flush a public toilet and you will find out why – and return a little lighter in the wallet than you bargained for.

Coming and going

Singapore's **Changi Airport** (**www.changi.airport.com.sg**, in English), 20 km to the east of the central business district, has consistently been rated the best airport in the world. Clean, spacious and easy to navigate, it has the usual shops, plus an internet centre, and a large duty-free complex.

The journey to the city by taxi takes about 20 minutes and costs around S$15. Alternatively take a flat-rate hire-car, usually a Mercedes, to anywhere in Singapore for $35. The Mass Rapid Transit (MRT) line was heading for the airport but hadn't arrived at the time of writing, although it may do so some time in 2001. Buses from the airport connect with the MRT. The airport shuttle bus runs every 15–30 minutes.

Out and about

Singapore is blessed with over 15,000 air-conditioned taxis just waiting to carry you to your business meeting. Well, that's the theory. Flagging a taxi down, however, can prove as taxing in Singapore as in Paris (where the drivers of empty cabs simply smile and shrug their shoulders as they drive past), especially in the evening. If you are travelling by taxi it pays to a) know the approximate route to your destination, b) scrutinize the list of surcharges printed on a card hanging in the taxi, c) dial a cab.

Buses and the ultra modern and efficient Mass Rapid Transit subway system (www.metropla.net/as/siingapore.htm, in English) are equally good alternatives. Avoid buses without air conditioning in the summer. If you decide to walk, especially at the height of summer, carry some water with you. Singapore is sweltering in the summer with extreme humidity.

Networking

Most of the major hotels, The Sheraton Towers, Grand Hyatt Singapore and Hotel Inter-Continental have excellent facilities including business centres, internet access from hotel rooms, fitness centres and first-class restaurants.

Conducting business in Singapore is a slow process. So don't turn down any social invitations – it's all an essential part of the negotiations. It may take several meetings to clinch the deal with golf, tours and lots of dining along the way.

If you want to eat out alone, then good places to start are the food courts, frequented by the locals in droves. These are areas of individual units that serve a variety of excellent cuisines including Chinese, Indian, Indonesian, Malay and Thai, all at very reasonable prices. The **People's Park Complex Food Center** is one place to try.

Popular restaurants serving local specialities like the spicy sambal chile prawn include the **Blue Ginger** and **Ivins Restaurant**.

Surprisingly, for a country with a strong Western influence and where eating out is so important, it is difficult to find good cafés. Or even somewhere to simply hang out without having to eat. There are some bars, serving the local brewed Tiger Beer and Anchor Beer, as well as a number of 'authentic' Irish pubs. Generally drinks are expensive in Singapore wherever they are consumed.

Behaving yourself

You may consider the lives of the Singaporeans to be over regulated, but expressing your opinion to your hosts is not advised. Better to bone up on Singapore's history and impress with your knowledge of how Singapore became an independent state in 1965.

With significant populations of indigenous Malay, Indians and Chinese, cultural flexibility is a useful attribute. For example the simple act of greeting your hosts can be perplexing. With the Chinese a light handshake plus bow is appropriate. With the Malay your hand should brush theirs and then be placed over your heart. Indians should be greeted with a bow, palms together.

Above all be polite and avoid losing your temper. To lose your temper is to 'lose face'.

The business tourist

Sir Stamford Raffles, the original developer of Singapore, split the city into districts that survive to this day – admin was centered on the **Historic District**, then there was Chinatown, Little India and Kampong Glam, home of royalty. Sir Stamford could not have imagined the development of global business and so would be startled to see the impressive skyscrapers of Singapore's central business district.

Land reclaimed from the sea is home to **Shenton Way**, the Singaporean equivalent of the Square Mile. All modern business life is there. Across the river is Suntec City, where Singapore's largest convention and exhibition centre is located. **Singapore Expo**, opened in 1999, is near to the airport.

The three-hour tourist

Although a small island, Singapore's colourful history means there are still a number of things worth seeing if you have some spare time.

One of the obvious places to visit is the **Raffles Hotel** (**www.raffles.com**). A symbol of Singapore's colonial past the hotel still retains much of the splendour of its halcyon days when the likes of

Somerset Maugham were resident. A reminder of its faded decadence is the Singapore Sling, a cocktail invented in the hotel's Long Bar.

Less splendid if no less remarkable is the **Changi Prison Museum.** Scene of unimaginable deprivations during the Japanese occupation in World War II, the museum houses a collection of items donated by its former prisoners-of-war inmates.

Gift buying

As with cuisine, Singapore offers a staggering amount and variety of goods. The most famous shopping district is the **Orchard Road** area. Look for the red and white Merlion sticker that indicates the store is part of the Singapore Tourist Promotion Board's Good Retailer Scheme. The board also produces a free pamphlet, *Your Guide to Good Bargains in the Suburbs*.

Bare facts

Weather

Situated as it is next to the equator, Singapore enjoys a consistent tropical climate all year round. This means it is warm throughout the year. It also means it rains constantly, although during the monsoon period (November–January), the rain is at its heaviest. The most striking feature of Singapore's climate, however, is the persistently high humidity.

Hours

Banks: 10.00–15.00 Monday–Friday; 09.30–11.30 Saturday (09.00–15.00 selected banks only). **Offices:** 09.00–17.00 Monday–Friday; 09.00–13.00 Saturday **Shops:** 10.00–21.00 Monday–Friday; 10.00–22.00 Weekends.

Holidays

With its mixture of Chinese, Hindus, Christians and Muslims Singapore has more festivals and holidays than can be mentioned here. Check the website mentioned below for up-to-date details.

The boring stuff

There are no special health risks and Singapore is not in a malarial region. It is worth reiterating that behaviour considered commonplace else-where such as chewing gum in public may be a crime in Singapore. Penalties for drug-related offences are especially severe, in some cases the death penalty.

The international dialling code for Singapore is 65, and it is eight hours ahead of GMT.

Singapore online

The Singapore information map (**www.sg**) is remarkable for the breadth and depth of links it provides to directories and search engines. Singapore news can be found at **www.singaporenews.net**. *The Straits Times* is also available online.

- **www.sg**
- **www.singapore-inc.com**.
- **http://straitstimes.asia1.com.sg**.

PS

If you are in for an extended stay, a good place to contact ex-pats is through the local hash-house harriers. Running is optional, networking and enjoying yourself obligatory.

Stockholm

Sweden is one of the great European success stories of recent years. Stockholm, built on a complex collection of small islands, is its capital and the heart of its renaissance. At the beginning of the 1990s, the krona was devalued. Now, according to one survey, Sweden is the leading IT country in the world, growth is healthy (GDP grew 3.8 per cent in 1999), and inflation low (0.5 per cent in 1999). Confidence and designer fashions fill the Stockholm streets as the great and the good of the Swedish netocracy mix with American journalists sent to capture the spirit of the moment.

Some things don't change. Stockholm (accounting for 1.3 million of 9 million Swedes) is relatively small and tight-knit. Movers and shakers tend to know each other. Its people are virtually all fluent in English, highly technologically proficient and entirely global in outlook. They are also big on fashion – though black does still seem to be the national colour. The only downside for the visitor are the prices (high) and the temperature (low).

Coming and going

Arlanda, Stockholm's international airport, is a good 40 minutes, – 42 km — drive from the city centre. Taxis are usually available and taxi drivers virtually always speak English. The trip to the city should cost around 300 SKr.

For speed, take the Arlanda Express train, which takes 20 minutes (120 SKr). There are also regular buses (SKr50) to the city city terminal (Cityterminalen), which is next to Stockholm's railway station.

The airline SAS operates a shared limousine to any point in central Stockholm for SKr274 per person; the counter is in the arrivals hall, just past customs. If two or more people travel to the same address together in a limousine, only one pays the full rate; the others pay SKr130.

Out and about

The most effective way to get around the city is to purchase a Stockholmskortet (Key to Stockholm card). Besides giving unlimited transportation on city subway, bus and rail services (www.metropla.net/en/sto/stockholm.htm), it offers free admission to 60 museums and several sightseeing trips. The card costs SKr175 for 24 hours, SKr350 for two days and SKr525 for three days. It is available from the tourist centre at Sweden House on Hamngatan, from the Hotellcentralen accommodations bureau at Central Station, and from the tourist centre at Kaknäs Tower.

Waxholmsbolaget (Waxholm Ferries) offers the Båtluffarkortet, a discount pass for its extensive commuter network of archipelago boats; the price is SKr250 for 16 days of unlimited travel. Also, at sea the Strömma Canal Company operates a fleet of archipelago boats, some of which provide excellent sightseeing tours and excursions. Meanwhile, the city's subway stations are marked by a blue-on-white 't' (Tunnelbanan, or subway).

Driving in Stockholm has been made more difficult by planners who have worked hard at restricting access. The excellent public transport systems mean that driving and car hire are not that attractive. Taxis are plentiful but pricy.

Networking

Internationalization is in the Swedish genes. Exports account for 40 per cent of Sweden's GDP. Transfers to foreign subsidiaries have long been regarded as important learning opportunities rather than demotions.

One of the networking hubs of Stockholm's renaissance is the **Lydmar Hotel**, across the road from the Humlegarden. The Lydmar is small and apparently inconsequential, but walk through its doors and you find that the hotel's unremarkable downstairs bar, a late-night jazz venue, is crowded with the great and the good of the Stockholm digerati. Dressed in black, they talk intensely and noisily. Cigarette smoke – from their heavily taxed American-branded cigarettes – fills the air.

Behaving yourself

Service is generally included, though extra gratuities do not go amiss.

Business is fairly informal. Verbal agreements are important and regarded as binding. The Swedes are generous hosts.

The business tourist

The centre of Stockholm is a standard business centre. There is nothing particularly eye catching. More interesting in new economy terms is the outlying suburb of Kista. The Swedish Trade Council (www.swedishtrade.com) provides information on trade and business opportunities with Sweden. The Stockholm Chamber of Commerce (www.chamber.se/indexe.htm) is another useful resource. Scandinavia Now (www.scandinavianow.com) is an e-zine in English on Scandinavian business.

The three-hour tourist

Stockholm is comfortably navigable on foot. Worth seeing are the **Royal Palace**, which has four facades, each in a different style. The **Moderna Museet** (Museum of Modern Art – www.modernamuseet.se) is worth a visit – for its own architecture (lots of wood and glass) as well as for its collection. Also interesting are the world's first open-air museum, **Skansen** (www.skansen.se) – created in the 19th century and home to a collection of traditional Swedish architecture – and **Millesgården**, a fantastic collection of sculptures gathered by Carl Milles.

The **Vasa Museet** is a new museum dedicated to exhibiting the wreck of a uniquely preserved 17th-century warship, the *Vasa*. Above a grocery store, you can find a museum, **Strindbergsmuseet Blå Tornet,** dedicated to the writer and dramatist, August Strindberg.

Great views of the city can be found from the top of the **City Hall.**

Gift buying

If you like to shop till you drop, then charge on down to any one of the three main department stores in the central city area. Sweden's top department store is **NK** (Nordiska Kompaniet). For bargains, peruse the boutiques and galleries in **Västerlånggatan**, the main street of **Gamla Stan**, and the crafts and art shops that line the raised sidewalk at the start of Hornsgatan on Södermalm. Drottninggatan, Birger Jarlsgatan, and Hamngatan also offer some of the city's best shopping.

Bare facts

Weather

Stockholm is very cold during the Winter – and that can mean from November to April. January to April are the coldest months. Then follows a wet spring at the end of May and a brief summer during June and July, marked by generally warm temperatures and long evenings.

Hours

Banks: 09.30–15.00 Monday–Thursday; 09.30–17.30 Friday; at Arlanda airport 06.30–22.00 everyday. **Shops:** 09.00–18.00 (larger department stores 08.00–22.00) Monday–Friday; 09.00–14.00/16.00 Saturday; 12.00–16.00 Sunday (some shops only). **Offices:** 08.30–17.00 weekdays; flexible working hours common.

Public holidays

1 January (New Year's Day); 5 January (Eve of Epiphany); 6 January (Epiphany); Good Friday; Easter Monday; 30 April (Valborg's Eve); 1 May (Labour Day); Ascension; 6 June (National Day); Pentecost; 24 June (Midsummer Day); 1 November (All Saints' Day); 25–26 December (Christmas).

The boring stuff

Nationals of other Scandinavian countries (Denmark, Finland, Iceland and Norway) need not bring a passport to enter Sweden. Nationals of European Union countries are permitted to enter Sweden upon presenting valid national identity cards, and can stay for a maximum of 90 days. Canadian and American citizens are likewise allowed up to three months' stay without visas, upon presentation of valid passports. Visas are required from most other nationalities.

The country code for Sweden is 46, followed by the city code, 8, and Stockholm is one hour ahead of GMT.

Stockholm online

Internet cafés include Stockholm's first – Café Access (**www.cafeaccess.se**) – based in the Kulturhuset (Culture House), a modernistic glass and stone cultural centre designed by Peter Celsing. After surfing it's worth finding Café Panorama for the view (**www.kulturhuset.stockholm.se**).

Alternatives include NINE on Odengatan (**www.nine.nu**) and Tilt on Grev Turegatan (**www.tilt.nu**).

Information on the city can be found in English at **www.stockholm.se/english** (which includes some basic business information) and **www.stockholmtown.com**.

PS

In Rosendals Trädgården (Rosendall's Gardens) you can help yourself to the flowers – and then pay according to their weight.

Stockholm is also home to two of the new generation of business gurus, Kjell Nordström and Jonas Ridderstråle – see **www.funkybusiness.com** for their funky take on the world.

Sydney

Forget the stereotypes about a provincial city at the other end of the world populated by unintelligible Aussies with a chip on their shoulder. Sydney has entered the new millennium as one the world's great cities, forward looking with a good infrastructure and set in an impossibly beautiful location and with an increasingly diverse and cosmopolitan culture. It's the Olympics that did it, of course. Well, largely. Sydney took every opportunity offered by its place on the world stage and pulled off the most spectacular and well-organized games of recent years.

Sydney likes to think of itself as an Asian city, and certainly its links with the region are strong and growing. But it also has a European feel. Few travellers won't want to go back.

Coming and going

Air travellers, domestic or international, arrive at **Kingsford Smith**, Sydney's main airport about 10 km from the CBD (www.sydneyairport.com.au). A bus to a central hotel is around A$6. The Airport Express serves major suburbs. A new rail link (opened for the Olympics) to Central Station costs A$9 for a single ticket. A taxi to the city costs about A$20.

Out and about

Sydney is fairly easy to get around by bus, rail, monorail, ferries and water taxis (www.metropla.net/au/sydney.htm). Road taxis can be hailed on the street (if the light on the roof is on they're available) or picked up at ranks.

If you're in Sydney for between three and seven days it's smart to buy a SydneyPass, which gives unlimited access to most city transport. Cost is A$135 for seven days.

Networking

There is a cluster of top restaurants and hotels around **Circular Quay** (All Seasons Premier Menzies, Hotel International Continental) and in **The Rocks** (The Observatory, Quay West). Network at leisure. There is always the opera, and **Bennelong Restaurant** is actually inside Sydney Opera House.

Behaving yourself

Shake hands at the beginning and end of meetings. Use full names, though the move to first-name terms is usually quick. Australians are relaxed but they expect punctuality. Business is often done over lunch, rarely in the evenings. Sport is a universally accepted topic of conversation.

In an Australian pub, each person buys a round of drinks in turn.

The business tourist

The Sydney central business district (CBD) is situated along Pitt and George Streets, north of Martin Place. There are four main business areas within the CBD – The Core, Western Corridor, Midtown, and the Southern precinct. Total office space is around 4 million square metres.

Domestic and overseas banks, financial services, insurance, funds management and stockbroking firms are the predominant occupiers of the CBD.

North Sydney, about two km north of the CBD on the northern bank of Sydney harbour, is a large suburban office area, mainly clustered along Miller and Walker Streets. Three main industry groups dominate: communications, information technology and advertising. Cable & Wireless Optus, Nortel, Nokia, Unisys and Intel all have offices in North Sydney.

Further north, along on the western side of the North Shore railway line, Victoria Avenue, Help Street and the Pacific Highway, is **Chatswood**, developed as a lower-cost competitor to North Sydney. Major industry groups include communications, information technology, manufacturing, food processing, business services, insurance, engineering and publishing. Vodafone, Royal & Sun Alliance, and Reed Publishing have offices here.

Parramatta, about 20 km west of the CBD, is Sydney's second major business area. There are lots of government offices but also insurance, financial and manufacturing companies such as AMP, Telstra, NRMA and AGC.

North Ryde, about 14 km north-west of the centre along Waterloo and Talavera Roads, and Riverside Business Park and Macquarie Technology Park, is a high-tech centre. Major companies based in North Ryde include Microsoft, Canon, Sony, Hewlett Packard and Oracle.

Sydney's industrial areas are concentrated south of the CBD around Alexandria, Zetland, Waterloo, Rosebery, Mascot and Botany, close to the airport and Port Botany. There are also industrial areas well to the west of the city around Huntingwood, Arndell Park and Wetherill Park, and to the south-west in Ingleburn, Smeaton Grange and Moorebank, and closer in around Silverwater, Rydalmere and Chullora.

Sydney has an outstanding website (www.cityofsydney.nsw.gov.au) that includes comprehensive resource links.

The three-hour tourist

The **Opera House** and **Sydney Harbour Bridge,** plus the magnificent harbour itself, are essential must-sees. The latest craze is climbing the arch of the bridge, either at day or night, in organized groups. It takes about three hours. Don't go if heights scare you.

Other things worth seeing are the **Customs House** (Circular Quay), a restored colonial building that is now an art centre; the **Amp Tower** (Centrepoint, corner of Market Street and Pitt Streets), 305 metres tall and offering superb panoramic views; **Bondi Beach**, though there are better beaches at Curl Curl, Freshwater, Whale Beach, Avalon and Palm Beach. The Rocks and Darling Harbour, though attractive, are geared to international tourism. Apart from the beaches, most sights are in easy walking distance of hotels in the CBD.

Sydney is pretty safe, especially during the day. Avoid the Kings Cross area after dark.

Gift buying

We don't expect our readers to be interested in fake boomerangs or didgeridoos, giant koala bears, or fluffy sheepskin slippers, which just about rules out every tourist shop in Sydney.

The one thing that really spells Australia in souvenir terms is opals. These stones, of varying quality and price, are widely available in good jewelry shops. For something a bit different try some of the increasing numbers of shops now selling authentic Aboriginal art. Make sure it is original and make sure the shop can guarantee the artists are well rewarded for their work. A good place to start is the Aboriginal-owned **Gavala Aboriginal Art and Cultural Education Centre** in Darling Harbour.

Bare facts

Weather

Hot in summer; pleasant in winter. The Australian sun is strong in summer and the country has a high incidence of skin cancer. Avoid prolonged exposure and use a blocker.

Hours

Shops: 09.00–17.30 Monday–Wednesday and Friday; 09.00–21.00 Thursday; 09.00–17.00 Saturday, **Banks:** 09.30–16.00 Monday–Thursday; 09.30–17.30 Friday.

Public holidays

1 January; 2 January; 26 January (Australia Day); 13 March; Easter Friday; Easter Saturday; Easter Sunday; Easter Monday; 25 April (ANZAC Day); 25 December; 26 December.

The boring stuff

Citizens of the EU, USA and Canada require visas. Tourist visas are free; a business visa will cost about £30. Visas are valid for three months and are available immediately via the Electronic Travel Authority System (ETA).

The country code for Australia is 61, followed by the city code, 2, and Sydney is eight hours ahead of GMT.

Sydney online

The official tourist site is www.australia.com and there is also www.sydney.visitorsbureau.com.au. *Time Out*'s guide to Sydney (www.timeout.com/sydney/index.html, in English) provides very helpful information and extensive links.

PS

Don't say 'G'day' if you're not Australian.

Tokyo

Japan's economy may be in the doldrums, the Nikkei may be depressed, Japanese banks may be burdened with debt, but Tokyo continues to flourish as a showcase for the products of the future and is arguably the tech capital of the world. The technology in the stores, cars, hotels and streets of Japan's capital city is the technology that's making its way to a store near you soon.

From speedy bullet trains to Pokémon, next-generation mobile phones to robot pets, Tokyo is as close to the city of the future as you can find in the present.

Urban life Tokyo style is not an entirely attractive proposition, however. Behind the shiny neon lights and silver plastic lies the harsh reality of life in one of the world's most populous cities (Tokyo metropolis population – 30 million). Tokyo is overcrowded, high-rise, polluted and, for visitors at least, horrendously expensive.

Coming and going

The majority of travellers arriving in Tokyo by air will do so at **Narita Airport** www.narita-airport.or.jp (if you arrive on a China Airline flight, you might end up at the 'old' Haneda Airport).

There are three main options for getting into Tokyo from the airport: taxi, bus and train.

The easiest way is probably by using the fleet of orange and beige **limousine buses**. These conveniently stop off at the main train stations such as Tokyo and Shinjuku as well as the major hotels. The journey is likely to cost between 2500–3000 yen (¥) and, given the almost permanent traffic jam that clogs Tokyo's arteries, last one and a half hours or so.

The **Narita Express** train is fast and comfortable, taking about an hour to reach the centre of Tokyo (**www.narita-airport.or.jp/airport–e/access/acce-nrt/trnsmp-e.html**). Reserving a seat, however, is essential, both to and from the airport. The airport to Tokyo on the Narita Express will cost some ¥3000.

Other trains that make the journey to the city include the **Skyliner** operated by Keisei Electric Railway, a non-Japanese rail company. Seats on the Skyliner are easier to find but the choice of destinations more restrictive although good if you are staying close to Ueno. The Skyliner costs around ¥2000, and takes about an hour.

There is no shortage of taxis. However, they may charge more than ¥25,000 to take you into Tokyo.

Out and about

The Tokyo subway (**www.metropla.net/as/tokyo.htm**) is a confusing concoction of privately run services. The **Eidan** subway or **Teito Rapid Transit Authority** (TRTA) runs eight lines and is the cheapest of the subway operators. Another operator **Toei,** runs four lines in Tokyo and is the biggest bus operator in central Tokyo.

If you plan to visit several destinations via subway, then a Tokyo combination ticket is a good choice. It allows one day of unlimited travel in Eidan and Toei Subways, Toei buses, and JR trains within Tokyo's 23 *ku* (districts).

Before travelling on the subway, make sure you get a map. Eidan stations will supply a free map in English.

Slow-moving traffic means that taxis, although freely available during the day, can prove expensive.

Networking

Tokyo's service economy is located primarily in the substantial downtown central business district near the Imperial Palace. Outside of the CBD there are a number of important commercial sub-centres the largest of which is Shinjuku. Most of Tokyo's tallest buildings are located here. Convenient hotels for the major businesses include the Royal Park Hotel and the Fairmont Hotel.

If your hosts are entertaining you, it will invariably be after business hours. Dining at one of Tokyo's thousands of restaurants, you may be served anything from *Yakisoba*, cooked noodles, onions and other vegetables 'stir-fried' on a griddle, to *Sukiyaki*, an endless procession of food platters arriving at your table.

Behaving yourself

It's all too easy for a business traveller to make a cultural faux pas in Japan. The following tips should help you avoid common pitfalls.

The traditional greeting is the bow. The depth of the bow reflects the status relationship. The deeper the bow the bigger the difference between greeter and greeted. Bow, lower your eyes, keep your palms against your thighs.

Present your business card after bowing, Japanese side upwards. Business cards are essential – without one you are unimportant in Japanese eyes – carry a plentiful supply, preferably bilingual. Address individuals using their last name plus 'san'.

The gift-giving culture is very strong in Japan. Mid-year and end of year plus first meetings are the time to give gifts. Try to stick to well-known foreign brands.

The business tourist

The city's financial centre is **Nihombashi** (the area east of the central station). Here you can find the Tokyo Stock Exchange and various big-name HQs. The newer business centre is **Shinjuku**, which is also home to the Tokyo Metropolitan Government Office – a skyscraper with an observation floor – and **Hibya**, too, is a business hub. If you're in the electronics business and would like to catch a glimpse of next year's big thing, a visit to **Akihabara**, which has over 600 shops, could provide you with the inspiration you need. And if you want to pay homage to the creators of the Walkman and countless other gadgets, Sony HQ can be found in **Shinagawa**.

The three-hour tourist

The national sport is a peculiar mixture of wrestling and psychological warfare where the protagonists go by colourful names such as 'Dump Truck'. The sport is of course sumo, and if there is a basho taking place while you are in town then it is worth paying a visit to the **National Sumo Hall** (Kokugikan) to watch these highly trained leviathans throw salt and collide with each other.

Not exactly a tourist attraction, but a fascinating taste of Tokyo nonetheless, is **Shinjuku Station**. The busiest train station in the world is at the heart of Tokyo's rail system and also the site of Tokyo City Hall (Tocho).

For a view over the city try the 338-metres high **Tokyo Tower**. The view is best in the winter when the blanket of smog that smothers Tokyo is least obvious.

Gift buying

Despite its deserved reputation as one of the most expensive cities in the world, there are still bargains to be had in Tokyo as well an unrivalled selection of electronic consumer goods.

Check out the electronic gadgets in the **Akihabara** shopping districts. Here you can pick up anything from a humble computer mouse to an exotic robotic dog. Akihabara is also an exception to the general rule in Tokyo that haggling is not an acceptable shopping tactic.

If you are planning on becoming the next Cartier-Bresson, the Shinjuki district is the spot for cameras and associated paraphernalia. The department store **Tokyo Hands** is excellent for futuristic home accessories.

Tokyo's best-known shopping district is the **Ginza**. It has the top fashions and the prices to match.

Bare facts

Weather

The sun may shine during the winter months but the temperatures plummet. Spring and summer tend to be hot, wet and humid with the highest rainfall in September and October.

Hours

Banks: 09.00–15.00 weekdays; closed on Saturdays, Sundays and holidays. **Offices and post offices:** 09.00–17.00 Monday–Friday. **Shops:** 10.00–20.00 every day.

Holidays

1 January (New Year's Day); 15 January (Coming of Age Day); 21 March (Spring Equinox Day); 29 April (Green Day); 3 May (Constitution Memorial Day), 4 May (People's Holiday); 5 May (Children's Day); 20 July (Ocean Day); 15 September (Respect for the Aged Day); 23 September (Autumnal Equinox Day); 10 October (Sports Day); 3 November (Culture Day); 23 November (Labor Thanksgiving Day); 23 December (Emperor's Birthday).

The boring stuff

Nationals of countries with reciprocal visa exemption arrangements with Japan, including the USA and Britain, do not need a visa to stay in Japan for 90 days or less for business purposes. They must, however, present their passport and a return airline ticket to the immigration officer upon arrival.

The country code for Japan is 81, followed by the city code, 3, and Tokyo is nine hours ahead of GMT.

Tokyo online

Tokyo Classified (**www.tokyoclassified.com**) offers lots of links on arts, dining and entertainment. The *Japan Times* is available online in English (**www.japantimes.com**) and includes sections on business and technology.

The Tokyo Chamber of Commerce and Industry (**www.tokyo-cci.or.jp/english/index.htm**, in English) provides excellent databases of Japanese companies seeking foreign partners and vice versa. It also gives links to government agencies and business associations.

PS

While you are eating, remember not to gesture too expansively, as even the tiniest gesture can be loaded with meaning. Do not blow your nose in public. Don't point your chopsticks at other people and, when they are not in use, put them in the chopstick rest.

Toronto

It's an old joke that the only famous Canadians (if there were any) are now dead. And it's true that Canada doesn't rate that high on the global trend scene. But Toronto is a city with a vibrant cosmopolitan feel and a strong financial, commercial and cultural edge. It is one of the top cities in the world for quality of life plus it's got everything the business traveller needs – and it's global in outlook, clean and safe.

Coming and going

Toronto International Airport (www.lbpia.toronto.on.ca/gtaasplash.htm) is located about 27 km from the city. Taxis are easy and all charge a fixed rate of around C$40 for the 40-minute journey downtown.

A regular airport bus takes between 60 and 90 minutes and costs C$6.75–C$8.40.

Out and about

As with everything else, Toronto makes it easy for you to get around. Buses, subway, streetcars and light trams (www.metropla.net/am/toronto.htm) run by the Toronto Transit Commission (TTC) are cheap and efficient. A day pass is around C$6.50, or C$2 a ride. Taxis are easy and reliable.

Networking

If you take the Metro Convention Center as your starting point, networking activities may be concentrated within a few hundred yards, depending on your tastes. The city's top hotels are nearby, including the Crowne Plaza and the Fairmont Royal York. In addition, the financial hub of Bay Street, the Sky Dome, the CNN Tower and over 100 restaurants are within walking distance (if it is walking weather). The **Renaissance Toronto Hotel** is actually at the Sky Dome – the only hotel in the world situated within a domed stadium. This means that 70 of its rooms actually overlook the playing field.

Behaving yourself

Inhabitants of Toronto are proud of being Canadian. It may feel and look like the good old USA but it isn't. It's an obvious cliché, but Canadians of Anglo-Saxon descent really are somewhere between the outgoing Americans and the reserved Brits. That said, of course, there are lots of Canadians not of Anglo-Saxon origin.

Business dress is generally fairly formal for men and women. Shake hands on greeting and on leaving, if your hosts offer. Be punctual. You won't be expected to speak French. This is reserved for doing business in Quebec, where the main business centres are Montreal and Quebec City.

Canadians are not so upfront as Americans, so take business dealings slowly. Canadians are also suspicious of anything that smacks of hype.

The business tourist

Toronto is the second biggest automotive centre in North America – after Detroit. It also boasts the **Toronto Stock Exchange** (**www.tse.com**), the tenth largest in the world.

The Toronto Board of Trade (**www.bot.com**) produces a full schedule of networking events, directories and publications. a potentially helpful site for small businesses and entrepreneurs is **www.enterprisetoronto.com**.

The three-hour tourist

Not everyone goes to Toronto so the sights aren't that well known. In fact, they're great, with lots of museums, galleries and parks. Here's a list that you won't be able to cover in three hours – but do what you can. **CNN Tower** – 553 m tall and one of the tallest buildings in the world. The very fast, glass elevator is not for the faint hearted, nor the glass floor of the observatory platform. But check out the virtual stimulations of the Thrill Zone, the Simulator Theater, and the more solid delights of the 360 Revolving Restaurant; **Royal Ontario Museum** — Canada's largest museum with five floors of collections; **Art Gallery of Ontario AGO** – over 16,000 items in 50 galleries, representing European and North American art; the **Henry Moore Sculpture Center** — the largest collection of Moore's work in the world.

Gift buying

There's a huge underground shopping mall beneath the downtown financial district with more than 1200 stores and restaurants. More upmarket shopping is **Queen Street W** village and **Hazelton Lanes**. Antique shops cluster around the **Harbourfront Antique Market**. **Front Street E** has some small unusual shops.

Bare facts

Weather

Toronto is in the middle of the North American continent and on the shores of a lake. So, as you'd expect, summers are warm and sunny and winters very cold and snowy (though locals claim recent winters have seen less snow and cold than usual – global climate change, perhaps).

Hours

Banks: 10.00–15.00 Monday–Friday (most open 08.00-21.00 Thursday). **Offices:** 09.00–17.00 Monday–Friday; **Shops:** 09.00–18.00 Monday–Friday (most open Saturday, some on Sunday, most main shops open until 21.00 Thursday–Friday).

Public holidays

1 January (New Year's Day); Good Friday; Easter Monday; 22 May; 24 June; 3 July; 7 August; 4 September; 12 October; 13 November; 25–26 December (Christmas).

The boring stuff

There is no visa required for citizens of the EU and USA. The food and water are all quite safe.

The country code for Canada is 1, followed by the city code, 416, and Toronto is five hours behind GMT.

Toronto online

Tourist sites are many and varied. They include www.toronto.com, www.torinfo.com, www.toronto.hm, www. toronto.about.com.

The city's main site is **www.city.toronto.on.ca** which gives a host of information on living in the city and doing business there.

PS

Out-of-the-ordinary tourist sites: Hockey Hall of Fame; Casa Loma, a 1917, baronial-style folly; Sky Dome, home of the Toronto Blue Jays baseball team; Bata Shoe Museum, where you can ogle Ginger Spice's boots.

Washington, DC

Power, money, glamour, scandal, influence peddling, political intrigue … this is not a hyped-up book promotion, this is Washington, DC. Against the backdrop of this dramatic high-stakes political vortex, the American capital boasts the world's largest collection of museums and 8673 acres of parks, and it has emerged as one of the top US high-tech cities. Nevertheless, one cannot escape the all-pervasive influence of government, which ebbs and flows with the political tides.

Coming and going

Three airports serve the greater DC area: **National** (aka Reagan; only domestic flights), **Dulles** and **BWI** (Baltimore-Washington International). To take advantage of inter-airport competition, first check airfares and flights for all three airports, then choose the best deal that will get you closest to your destination.

If you're flying from within the States, **Ronald Reagan Washington National Airport** is *so* convenient to downtown – a quick five miles – and well designed for passengers with most gates close to each other and to ticket counters and baggage claim. A taxi to downtown is your best bet – lots available. The Metro (**www.wmata.com**) stops adjacent to terminals B and C, with a connecting shuttle to terminal A. It's clean, safe and efficient, with one-way fares ranging from $1.10 to $3.25. Don't even think about trying to park at this airport: parking is a scarce, high-priced commodity. **Washington Dulles International Airport (IAD)** (**www.metwashair-ports.com/Dulles/transportation.htnl**) is not terribly convenient or user-friendly. It takes plenty of time from curbside to reach your gate via interminably long corridors, plus a short ride on a rather ridiculous shuttle that you have to take to reach the gates. From IAD a taxi into DC will run $35–50. The Washington Flyer Airport Express Bus offers shuttle service to the nearest metro station ($8 one way, 25 minutes), National Airport ($16 one way, 45 minutes), and downtown D.C. ($16 one way, 45–60 minutes) with stops at major hotels. Thanks to a dedicated access road to the 'beltway' that rings DC, the road trip from IAD to downtown is relatively direct and hassle-free. Plenty of parking available, but parking shuttle buses may keep you waiting for more than a bit.

   Baltimore-Washington International (BWI) (www.bwiairport.com) is 10 miles from Baltimore and 30 from DC. It's about as far from downtown Washington as Dulles is, but traffic on the BW Parkway to DC can be gruelling, especially during rush hours. User-friendly design with gates relatively close to ticketing and baggage claim. During long delays check out the microbrewery near Pier A. Abundant taxis are available for $55 to downtown DC Super Shuttle bus service will take you door to door for $24–$32 one way, but will stop along the way to let off other passengers. Reserve online at www.bwiairport.com/frames/1_washington.html. Or you can take the train to Union Station in DC for about $7, but only try this between 6 am and 6 pm weekdays. Trains are too infrequent at other times. Although BWI has fewer flights to Europe than Dulles, fares are usually cheaper.

Out and about

The award-winning Metro is clean, efficient, and safe. There are five rail lines that connect with a network of bus routes that connect DC with surrounding suburbs in Virginia and Maryland. Taxis are efficient and abundant, with fares determined by zones rather than clocked on a meter.

   The city is divided into four quadrants, Northeast, Northwest, Southeast, Southwest. The design makes navigation relatively easy once you get your bearings. The Potomac runs along the western section, with Georgetown in the northwest, and government buildings straddling the Northwest/Southwest divide. Capitol Street divides the east from west. Each street name is followed by an abbreviation for the quadrant in which it is located, for example Constitution Ave. NW.

Networking

Here's a great way to get inside the DC – and national – business scene fast. The nation's capital is naturally home to the US Chamber of Commerce, located at 1615 H Street, NW. The Chamber sponsors several events each month that provide opportunities to hobnob with high-profile government and industry people. Go to www.uschamber.com for information on upcoming events and the Chamber's many programmes and services.

The *Washington Business Journal* (published every Friday) offers lists of daily business events, including a variety of business informational meetings and networking opportunities throughout the DC metropolitan area. For current information go to **http://washington.bcentral.com/washington**.

Behaving yourself

Washington is more formal than some other US cities, though the general trend is towards more informal wear and behaviour.

Tipping is standard – around 15 per cent is usual; luggage handlers in their various guises should be given around $1 or $2 per bag.

The business tourist

Given Washington's role as the nation's capital, it may be the most important city for business in the States, and most major American corporations have some sort of office close by. The District itself is in the midst of a business and neighbourhood renaissance. For example, MCI opened a major centre that sparked a downtown revival, especially in the East End; a new 2.3 million-sq-ft. convention centre is slated to open at Mount Vernon Square in 2003; business improvement districts were formed in Georgetown, downtown, and the **Golden Triangle** (Central Business District) to provide a cleaner, safer and more attractive business environment. DC also has the third-largest downtown office market in the country, behind only New York and Chicago.

After government, hospitality is the District's strongest industry. The top ten private employers include four universities, three mega hospitals, *The Washington Post*, Potomac Electric and Fannae Mae. And of course legions of lawyers, accountants, lobbyists and other professionals crawl all over Capitol Hill. However, DC also ranks among the top five US high-tech cities, and it tops the list for software services with 70,400 employed.

The region is home to *Business-Week*-top-30-ranked McDonough School of Business at Georgetown (number 26) and Robert H. Smith School of Business at University of Maryland, College Park (number 27), and also to the Kogod School of Business at American University.

The three-hour tourist

Essentials: Walk the Mall, and visit the Washington Monument, Jefferson Memorial, Lincoln Memorial and especially the Vietnam Veterans Memorial. You will also pass the buildings of government, including the White House, and the numerous museums of the Smithsonian, en route.

You can visit the East Room and the State Dining Room of the White House if you have more time (usually involves a lengthy wait). Or visit the Senate and/or House of Representatives, the Library of Congress, or the National Museum of American History Natural History, and/or Art. Check out 'Destination: DC', the *Washington Post*'s tourism website for info on interesting tours and attractions (**www.washingtonpost.com/wp-srv/local/longterm/tours/guide2.htm**).

Gift buying

Georgetown existed before the District of Columbia came into existence. Today it is a shopping hub, including the Georgetown Park Mall. Shoppers may also find what they want at the **Fashion Center** at Pentagon City (across the river in Arlington); **Mazza Gallerie** (near the Friendship Heights Metro station); the **Pavilion** at the Old Post Office; **Union Station** (converted into a mall with over 100 stores); and **National Place** where stores now form part of the National Press Building and the Marriott Hotel.

Bare facts

Weather

June through to August are warm (sometimes in excess of 86 °F, 30 °C) and humid. Winters are cold (24–40 °F, –4–4 °C) and snowy, which leaves spring and fall as the best seasons weather-wise. Be sure to bring an umbrella.

Hours

Banks: 09.00–15.00 Monday–Friday. **Offices:** 09.00–17.30 Monday–Friday. **Shops:** 09.30–18.00 Monday–Saturday; **Shopping centres:** 09.30–21.00.

Public holidays

There are five fixed-date federal holidays: New Year's Day (1 January), Flag Day (14 June), Independence Day (4 July), Veterans Day (11 November), and Christmas (25 December). Floating federal holidays include the birthday of

Dr Martin Luther King (third Monday in January); Inauguration Day (20 January every four years); President's Day (third Monday in February); Memorial Day (last Monday in May); Labor Day (first Monday in September); Columbus Day (second Monday in October) and Thanksgiving Day (fourth Thursday in November). Businesses may or may not be closed on these days, but most typically close on the major holidays. When a fixed-date holiday falls on a Saturday, the holiday is taken on the Friday before it. When it falls on a Sunday, the holiday is taken on Monday. August is the most popular month for family vacations, and although businesses typically remain open, key contacts may be on leave.

The boring stuff

No vaccinations are required to enter the USA and the water is safe. No visa is required for visits under three months for visitors from countries covered by the US Visa Waiver Program. Comprehensive health insurance is an absolute must.

The country code for USA is 1, followed by the city code, and Washington DC is five hours behind GMT.

Washington online

The premier source for inside information is of course *The Washington Post* at **www.washingtonpost.com**. Click on business and scroll down to Industry Watch to search for the latest business news by industry, and for business and technical columnists. The *Post* also offers a terrific site for dining, arts and entertainment information throughout the greater metropolitan area (**www.washingtonpost.com/wp-srv/entertainment**). Restaurants are catalogued by cuisine and city or neighbourhood. Museums and galleries, music, movies, theatre, dance, nightlife and outdoor activities are also arranged by venue, location, and calendar of coming events.

The Washington Business Journal (**http://washington. bcentral.com/washington**) is a helpful source for leads on new businesses in the area, online legal and insurance resource centres, archive search, and the *Business Times Book of Lists* (available by subscription) – a business reference guide which compiles this paper's weekly Top 25 lists. Business newspapers for 39 other US cities may also be accessed from this site.

The DC Chamber of Commerce provides not only District business statistics, resources, and information, but lots of useful stuff for tourists, like pictures and information about DC neighbourhoods, transit links, dining and lodging, schools and religious centres, points of interest, and an online 8-minute video introduction to Washington, DC (**www.dcchamber.org/visiting/default.asp?whatpage=plan**).

PS

Do you properly greet an ambassador as Mr/Ms Ambassador, Excellency, Sir/Madam, or Ambassador Surname? If you're not sure of this or hundreds of other business and government protols, hurry over to the Protocol School of Washington (**www.psow.com/index.html**).

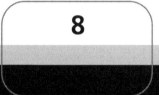

8

Information on the move

The business traveller may be criss-crossing time zones with abandon, but he or she needs to keep in touch and up to date with what's happening in the business world. There are a profusion of business-related websites out in cyberspace. Most fail to deliver, simply adding to the overload of information and factual detritus. A small number cut to the chase.

About.com

About.com is a collection of websites housed under the About.com roof. As the name suggests, it offers information about … well, just about everything. The model is similar to a concept like GeoCities, an online community of home pages organized under broad categories. In About.com's case, however, the focus is much more subject driven.

Everything you would expect to find at a major website of its type is there: news, jobs, shopping, e-mail, etc. But the feature that really differentiates About.com is its site guides – experts who offer advice and support to users. These individuals, selected on the basis of their specialist knowledge, set up their own topic centre within the about.com universe. The guides manage their own specialist area on the site – moderating discussions, providing content and links, giving advice and so on. About.com has a rigorous selection process for its guides. Only one in four of all applicants are accepted onto the company's training programme.

There are currently over 700 guides, which gives you an idea of the scale of the about.com online community. A quick browse of the site reveals just about every subject you can think of and a few that you couldn't or wouldn't want to. And if the subject you need information about isn't covered – then why not apply to be a guide.

Links: www.about.com

Britannica.com

Based on that traditional informational goldmine the *Encyclopaedia Britannica*, this site offers a comprehensive resource – a veritable treasure trove of knowledge. But Britannica.com is more than just an online version of the encyclopaedia.

There is, of course, the complete updated online version of the oldest and largest general reference work in the English language. In addition, there is access to more than 70 of the world's top magazines and the facility to search a listing of the web's best sites selected by Britannica – more than 125,000 in all. News and current event information is supplied to the website courtesy of the editors of washingtonpost.com.

When the Britannica website first went up, a search would often reveal excerpts of information with a charge required to access the entire text. On the present website the service is *free*. And it really is an excellent service. For information junkies, it is a site for sore eyes. Not to be missed.

Links: www.britannica.com

Business2.com

Business 2.0 is an essential read for anyone interested in the new economy. Since its launch in July 1998 by Imagine Media Inc., the US subsidary of the Future Network, the magazine has grown rapidly from a rate base of 125,000 to 210,000. It has firmly established itself as one of the best publications of its kind.

The magazine provides in-depth monthly coverage on the new economy business scene, documenting the ever-changing landscape and providing strategies for living and working in the internet age. It is pitched at 'Transformers', the people, Business 2.0 says, with 'the power, influence, and insight to re-invent their companies for the New Economy'.

Business 2.0 has identified ten driving principles of the new economy: matter, space, time, people, growth, value, efficiency, markets, transactions and impulse. These offer a useful framework for those trying to understand the new world of business and how it is likely to change their industry.

Visitors to the *Business 2.0* website will find sections such as 'Get a Life' – looking at the life–work balance and mental and physical health matters;

'Breakthrough' – an analysis of the technologies driving the change; and 'Vox' – a variation on the vox pop theme where the readers have their say.

Links: www.business2.com

Entrepreneur.com

The fact that entrepreneur.com is one of the largest and most frequently visited sites on the internet is a measure of the entrepreneurial spirit at large in the business world. The company's website has over 500,000 unique users and racks up more than 3 million page views a month.

As you might expect, entrepreneur.com's content is aimed at would-be dot-com millionaires. But it's not simply a site for dot-com start-ups. It offers interesting and practical information for anyone thinking of, or in the process of, starting a business.

In April 2000 entrepreneur.com overhauled, redesigned and relaunched its website. Content on the site is both wide-ranging and deep. Business travellers can check out the 'Quick guide to business travel', for example, and learn how to make their travel budget stretch a little further. Executives in unchallenging, comfortable jobs dithering about joining the free agent society can consult a motivation expert to help them take those first steps to relinquishing the company car.

Elsewhere there are areas where you can chat online to other businessmen and experts. Or you can use the onsite search facility to search through a list of *Entrepreneur Magazine*'s 100 best web sites for small business. And, should you need to buy anything, then head for the marketplace where you can even locate vacant office space to start the next Microsoft or Amazon.

Links: www.entrepreneur.com

Fast Company

Fast Company magazine is widely acknowledged to be the bible of the new economy. Before launching the magazine, in November 1995, Alan Webber and Bill Taylor spent a combined total of 11 years at the *Harvard Business Review,* the bastion of old economy theorizing.

From their vantage point, Webber and Taylor could see the world was changing … quickly. A global revolution, they concluded, was changing business. A new magazine was needed to show how companies were transforming to compete in the new world. The idea clearly struck a chord, and the magazine received the backing of luminaries such as business guru Tom Peters and the esteemed Harvard academic Michael Porter.

Fast Company set out not only to report the business revolution, but play a part in shaping it by creating a vocabulary for the new economy.

Many issues later, the magazine can justifiably claim a spectacular success. A new generation of entrepreneurs has grown up on its diet of cutting-edge informative reporting. Possibly the greatest measure of its success, however, is the place *Fast Company* has found on the shelves of the major players in the new business revolution. Its one great weakness is its US-centric bias, although that may now be changing as the internet revolution rolls across Europe and the rest of the world.

Links: www.fastcompany.com

FT.com

The website of the *Financial Times*, one of the world's most respected business broadsheets, was relaunched in February 2000.

Ambitious from the outset, the FT intends to make ft.com the number one global business portal. And it has the brand, the reputation and the journalists to make it happen.

One of the greatest challenges for any portal site is to organize the mountain of information available into a presentable and navigable format. The ft.com solution is to structure its international business coverage around 14 key industries. Each industry has its own home page, its own editor and senior correspondent.

The business sections are backed up by a massive news-gathering service. A team of over 500 delivers up-to-the-minute information, comment and analysis, on the world's latest business news, from the FT–ft.com integrated newsroom.

Find out about people stoking the fires of the e-commerce furnace in People. It's a who's who of the business world with thousands of dossiers on the movers and shakers of global commerce.

With its mix of highly respected business and financial news, searchable archives of over 3000 business publications and additional work and career services, the ft.com should lead its market. The difficulty will be protecting the visitors from information overload.

Links: www.ft.com.com

Google.com

Most people have heard of Excite, AltaVista, Yahoo and Lycos. All are first-generation search engines that have grown into something much bigger than their original conception – and something much less focused. If Google has its way, then it won't be long before its name is equally well known.

Founded in 1998 by Sergey Brin and Larry Page, Google is a search engine with a difference. For one thing, it has not suddenly erupted on to the scene in a blaze of costly publicity. Instead, momentum has built by word of mouth and strategic deals. For example, in November 1999 it signed its first deal in the UK with Virgin Net – a deal that makes it the main search tool for the ISP's base of over 150,000 users. And, so far, Google remains first and foremost a search engine, a focused website for searching, not an immense and perplexing portal with a search engine.

What makes Google so good? The mathematical analysis behind the engine is dazzling, as you would expect from two US mathematics students. But for the less mathematically inclined, the search engine analyzes each web page for ranking purposes by looking at all the content on the page. This means differentiating between headings and font sizes – which it does. It also takes a peek at the text of nearby pages to get an idea of context, as well as looking at hypertext links.

The upshot is that, because Google is drawing on more information to make a decision, you get good results from a search even when you are searching for something fairly obscure. The search engine covers over 250 million pages, of which 130 million or so are fully text indexed. It allows you to search in different languages. It's fast as well, generating search results in less than 0.25 seconds on most occasions. Expect to see a lot more of Google in the future.

Links: www.google.com

Inc.com

The online extension of *Inc.* magazine, Inc.com proclaims itself as the website for business builders who are 'long on work and short on time'. The site offers advice, information products and online tools aggregated from many different sources. It is a particularly useful website for small to medium- size businesses and entrepreneurs.

One of the best sections on the site is the advice section, divided up into two principal areas: 'Getting Started' and 'Growing Your Business'.

The Getting Started section provides articles, case studies, research reports and tips on the best way to go about starting up your own business. The business plan is a key element in any start-up's strategy to raise finance and yet it is difficult to find good information on the internet about what exactly is required in a business plan – without having to pay for it. Inc.com, however, in the 'Writing a Business Plan' subsection, supplies links to sources on the net where information about business plans is freely available – including comprehensive templates, if required.

Under the Growing Your Business section a comprehensive range of subjects is covered. These include those that you would expect to find, such as marketing, e-commerce, sales, finance and law, plus more surprising, but no less interesting categories, like the section on business ethics.

Links: www.inc.com

Management General

Originally a consulting company owned by Tom and Rita Brown, formerly of the Management Development Center in Honeywell Aerospace. Then began a printed, quarterly newsletter for its clients in the early 1990s. This metamorphosed into an online version, officially launched on 1 January 1997, with a ranking of the top business books and 'ezzays' (the medieval essay, transformed for the 21st century).

One thing led to another. Management General then began to publish e-books – and to get reader response while writing a book – and was reincarnated in early 1999 as the 'New Ideas' website, publishing once a week. Now averages between 35–50,000 hits per week; which translates to 1.5–2-plus million hits per year.

Links: www.mgeneral.com

Match.com

Work long hours? Eat in the office? Get home late? No social life and no time for love? Then maybe it's time to pay a visit to match.com, the premier destination for lovelorn surfers.

Match.com charges a fee for its service. But it does offer a free trial for the merely curious, who don't wish to part with their money without taking a trip around the store.

Newbies fill out a longish form, indicating how they see themselves, how others see them and the characteristics they would want in a partner. There is also the opportunity to leave a brief text message and send photos (up to three).

Once the form filling is done the website's proprietary software conjures up a list of matches ranked according to the personal criteria on the form. The list is ranked by percentage. All that's left is to click on the different profiles to find someone you like the sound of (or look of). If you come across a profile that intrigues you then you can send that person an e-mail via match.com's protected e-mail system, which conceals your true e-mail address.

If surfers tire of clicking though the endless profiles in their match list the site offers other attractions. There's a link through to a singles-type online magazine – 'Mix 'n' match'. Or in the Mingle section there are chat rooms and a message board.

Links: www.match.com

Means Business

Means Business is a one-stop shop for published business content. MB has partnership agreements with many of the leading business book publishers. For those who don't have time to read a whole book to unearth its gems of wisdom, it offers a useful time-saving service. The concept, dreamt up by founder David Wilcox, is based on smart web architecture that allows users to carry out searches on key business concepts and topics. The key excerpts are culled from business books and organized under nine areas on the menu wheel.

Searches allow users to cross-reference topics, for example accessing key excerpts on subjects such as core competencies or market space.

Users get charged in one of three ways:

1 They buy a single excerpt.

2 They order a concept suite – several excerpts about the topic.

3 Or they buy an annual subscription with unlimited access.

MB has already signed up most of the big US publishers and is now busy signing up the rest of the world. It has backing from Knowledge Universe, the online educational company set up by Michael Milken, which recently invested $11 million in MB. Milken is keen to extend the model to other markets such as finance.

Links: www.meansbusiness.com

MP3.com

For those who like a little background music while they work, MP3 technology allows music to be downloaded direct from the internet. MP3.com is one company that has moved to take advantage of the possibilities presented. CEO Michael Robertson set up MP3.com in November 1997 and the site has quickly become one of the leading music destinations on the web with an average of over 500,000 unique daily visitors. 'MP3' has even toppled 'sex' as the most searched for word on the net – if only temporarily.

Using the My.MP3.com flagship service you can add, organize and listen to your MP3 music collection via the web no matter where you are. The site contains over 387,000 songs and audio files from more than 62,000 artists. The site pays featured artists a royalty. MP3.com has its detractors, however. The MP3 file format and its proliferation over the net has raised concerns among music publishers and the writs have been flying. The Recording Industry Association of America, for example, has sued MP3 over copyright issues.

The long-term success of MP3.com is in some measure bound up with the results of the various court actions over music copyright infringement on the net. But one thing is for certain – the MP3 musical genie is out of the bottle.

Links: www.mp3.com

News.bbc.co.uk

The British Broadcasting Company brings its great tradition of news reporting to the internet with the news.bbc website.

Find out about the latest UK and worldwide events through streaming video and audio clips, or read the news in a variety of languages including Russian, Chinese and Welsh.

The site covers the essentials: business, politics, health, education, sport and entertainment. It also covers the most important stories in greater depth and in the Talking point section allows the viewer to have their say. Surfers can post up their thoughts on issues of the moment from children's use of mobile phones to British linguistic isolation.

Links: http://news.bbc.co.uk

Quotez

Writing a speech and can't think of an appropriate quotation? How about strap lines for that report you're preparing?

If you are looking for an apposite quotation or merely need to be reminded of a popular saying that's on the tip of your tongue, then quotez could have the answer.

Quotez is a virtual library of sharp one-liners, pithy retorts and wise words from the great, the good and the infamous. Search from a database of over 5000 quotes; by subject or author. Under 'money' for example you will find the sage advice of Mark Twain: 'There are two times in a man's life when he should not speculate: when he can't afford it and when he can.' Clearly not a day-trader then.

And despite the much-trumpeted revolutionary world of e-commerce, some things never change: 'Here's the rule for bargains – "Do other men, for they would do you." That's the true business precept.' The Machiavellian insights of some master of the universe? No – a passage from *Martin Chuzzlewit*, by Charles Dickens.

Links: www.geocities/Athens/Oracle/6517/intro.html

Redherring.com

Redherring.com is the online version of the magazine that provides leading analysis of the companies and trends shaping the technology business. Many regard *Red Herring* as the new economy investor's bible.

The magazine takes its name from Wall Street parlance. Apparently, in the 1920s, American investment bankers called preliminary investment prospectuses – red herrings. This was to warn investors that the documents were not finalized. The prospectuses were bound in red covers. The magazine aims to provide early information on up-and-coming investment opportunities.

The *Red Herring* website is divided into different channels. These include: Inside Tech, news analysis; Investor News, looking at tech companies from the investor's perspective; IPO News, including information about upcoming IPOs; VC & Startups, who is being funded and why; and Industries, detailing the impact of technology on different industries.

Redherring.com is especially good on the financial aspects of the new economy. It has excellent in-depth coverage on venture capital issues, IPOs and start-ups, for example.

As well as the channels described, there are other areas of interest on the *Red Herring* website. Discussions is one of three special sections (Columns and Special Reports are the other two). Discussions features message boards where users can discuss hot issues covered on the site. Herringtown is an online community of private companies. Redherring.com also offers member services, including an e-mail newsletter, back issues and subscription to the *Red Herring* magazine.

Links: www.redherring.com

Salon.com

Salon is a leading internet media company that produces a network of subject-specific websites – 11 in all. It was founded in 1995 by David Talbot, chairman, director and editor-in-chief, and Andrew Ross, executive VP for business development. Before founding Salon, Talbot wrote for a variety of publications including *The New Yorker*, *Playboy* and *Rolling Stone*.

The network of websites in the Salon stable includes News, Technology, Travel & Food, Mothers Who Think, and Comics. As well as the subject-specific sites Salon offers participation in its web communities. Table Talk is a free interactive community, while The Well is subscription based.

Salon.com pulls in over 3 million unique visitors every month. Visitors lounging in the salon tend to be from a demographic profile particularly attractive to advertisers: 90 per cent are aged between 18 and 49; nearly 20 per cent earn $100 000-plus; over 70 per cent have a college degree; and, probably the best statistic as far as advertisers are concerned, 80 per cent have transacted business electronically over the net. This explains why salon.com has a relationship with over 325 advertisers, including IBM, Microsoft, Intel and Virgin.

Links: www.salon.com

Scoot.co.uk

Scoot describes itself as 'the leading interactive consumer transaction service in the UK, Netherlands and Belgium'. Don't let this put you off, however, as behind the media jargon lies a useful web service.

In its early days, and even into the 1990s, the internet has had a strongly North American bias. UK users were for a long time without even a search and directory facility that concentrated on the UK. Today Yahoo!, Excite and AltaVista all have UK-based websites (at least in the virtual sense). However UK surfers may still feel that these services are merely an afterthought.

Scoot started out as a free paper and then as a web directory, launching its first site in the Netherlands in 1997. Accessing the Scoot.co.uk site brings up a simply laid out directory search form. From this front page searches can be conducted geographically or by business. There are separate guides for finding cinemas, products and hotel rooms.

The Scoot database includes over 27,000 British villages, towns and cities. Although the Scoot directories are the most visible part of their business online, the company also designs websites for companies. Two and a half years from its launch the Scoot web design team had created over 3000 websites for UK businesses.

Links: www.scoot.co.uk

365.com

One for sports fans. 365.com is a useful resource for those who want to follow their sporting passions. A common misconception is that the site is just for soccer fans. This is not true. There are ten different sites available from the front page – what 365 like to call 'passion centres'. Anyone who has attended a major sporting event will understand why.

The passion centres include football, cricket, rugby, formula 1 motor racing, horse racing and a sports overview. Others are on the way.

It's not all sport at 365.com, either. As well as the passion centres, there are others for music and entertainment. And finally for lonely hearts or even bored hearts, there is a personal channel or centre where people can meet with a view to engaging in a sport of a different kind.

Links: www.365.com

Wired Digital

Wired Digital, a wholly owned subsidiary of Lycos Inc., creates a range of online products to help people use the latest technologies at home and in the workplace. The products in the Wired stable include: HotBot, one of the web's top-rated search engines; Wired News, news about the digital world; Web Monkey, a leading resource for web developers; and Suck, an alternative view of pop culture. In 1998, *Wired* magazine, originally part of the empire, was sold to Conde Nast.

Wired Digital's first foray on to the net was in October 1994, with the launch of hotwired.com (the company was trading as HotWired Inc. at the time). This was even before the release of the first Netscape browser. In fact HotWired can justifiably claim to have invented web media, as it was the first website with original content and Fortune 500 advertising.

In many ways Wired Digital has pioneered the business model for the online ventures that have followed. It was one of the first websites to build a business around online advertising and sponsorship revenues – it invented the ad banner. And it was among the first to recognize the value of community building through chat rooms and forums.

Wired Digital remains one of the essential destinations on the internet for anyone with an interest in the digital and technological revolution.

Links: www.wired.com